MORE STEPPING STONES
TO JEWISH-CHRISTIAN RELATIONS

Studies in
Judaism and Christianity

Exploration of Issues in the
Contemporary Dialogue Between
Christians and Jews

Editor in Chief for
Stimulus Books
Helga Croner

Editors
Lawrence Boadt, C.S.P.
Helga Croner
Leon Klenicki
John Koenig
Kevin A. Lynch, C.S.P.

 A STIMULUS BOOK

MORE STEPPING STONES TO JEWISH-CHRISTIAN RELATIONS

*An Unabridged Collection
of Christian Documents
1975–1983*

**compiled and edited by
Helga Croner**

A STIMULUS BOOK

PAULIST PRESS ◆ NEW YORK ◆ MAHWAH

Library of Congress
Catalog Card Number: 85-60289

ISBN: 0-8091-2708-3

Published by Paulist Press
997 Macarthur Boulevard
Mahwah, N.J. 07430

Printed and bound in the United States of America

Contents

B) U.S. STATEMENTS

C) EUROPEAN STATEMENTS

D) LATIN AMERICA

II. PROTESTANT DOCUMENTS

A) WORLD COUNCIL OF CHURCHES

B) U.S. CHURCH GROUPS

C) EUROPEAN CHURCH GROUPS

Foreword

Helga Croner

More Stepping Stones to Jewish-Christian Relations is a supplement to *Stepping Stones to Further Jewish-Christian Relations* and should be perused in conjunction with it. As in the first volume, only official declarations by church bodies and statements at Vatican meetings were included here.

The fact that the present collection of documents became necessary only eight years after publication of the first may be significant in itself. Is it too much to hope that sheer number of written material may bespeak growth in scope and quality of Christian-Jewish relations?

At the beginning of this book stands "The Ten Points of Seelisberg" which originated in 1947. It is considered the starting point of post-World War II relations between Christians and Jews, and its omission from the first volume was pointed out by many reviewers of *Stepping Stones to Further Jewish-Christian Relations*. Also omitted, by inadvertence on my part, was the very important statement by the Belgian Protestant Council of 1967.

Grateful acknowledgment is made to the U.S. Bishops' Secretariat for Catholic-Jewish Relations, the Anti-Defamation League of B'nai B'rith, and the National Council of the Churches of Christ, for making material available to me, and to the various periodicals where the official statements were published.

COMMENTARIES

1
The Catholic Style:
A Reflection on the Documents

Msgr. Jorge Mejia

Msgr. Jorge Mejia is the Executive Secretary to the Vatican Commission for Religious Relations with the Jews.

The Catholic Church has its own style of facing certain challenges and responding to them. This style may change along the years, nay the centuries. It has however a certain continuity of its own, even among changes, which may be worthy of some reflection in the present context.

The way of facing the continuing existence alongside itself of the Jewish people has certainly changed in the Catholic Church. The documents are here to prove it. However, the opposition to a former way, or ways, of dealing with the issue may not always be as clear-cut when all things are considered, as it frequently is held to be.[1] But this is not my point here. I would like to stress instead three aspects of what I have called *the style* of the Catholic Church. These three, I believe, are borne out by the documents hereafter included— and indeed by many others which help in understanding them.

The *first* aspect is this: changes in the Catholic Church are never sudden and not comparable, as the Italian proverb goes, to lightning from a clear sky. They are the ripe fruit of first hidden currents, flowing below the surface, but well nourished by the fertile soil of authentic tradition, which long habit, perhaps even centuries old, has tended to burden and obscure. Those aware of the changing force of the new ideas and insights know well that if they rush they only endanger their intuitions. They wait for the proper time, *kairos,* the time appointed in God's unfathomable design. Sometimes an external fact or facts (external namely to the life of the Catholic Church as such) may serve as a catalytic factor, suddenly precipitating, as in chemistry, the hoped-for reaction, not however as its sole, exclusive cause. If it were not, I believe, for the hidden currents just mentioned, the providential disposition to receive and interiorize such facts would be grievously absent.

When Jules Isaac came to Rome to see Pope John XXIII,[2] and even before, when he met Pope Pius XII, he found a ground already prepared. I can hardly imagine that a corresponding gentleman of Jewish extraction would have been received in the preceding century by Leo XII, Gregory XVII, Pius IX (at least during the second part of his reign), and even Leo XIII. But Pius X had already received Theodor Herzl, and if what happened between them, according to Herzl's diary,[3] was not particularly promising, the very fact that he was received in a private audience is not without significance, especially if one considers the then rather rigid Vatican protocol. Besides this, always according to Herzl's testimony, Cardinal Merry del Val, then Secretary of State, was not at all closed to his ideas,[4] and one may conclude that this could have been a way, even from the Pope itself, to manifest more openness than Herzl got from his actual audience with the Pontiff.

However that may be, the Vatican, or the Holy See, is not the whole Church. At that time biblical studies, notwithstanding the modernist crisis, were reopening Catholic eyes, on the one hand, to the original text and import of the Hebrew and Aramaic Old Testament, and, on the other hand, to the Jewish context and deep roots of the New. It was perhaps not expressed as we do it now after the Council, in terms of the Jewish heritage of the Church, but the substance of the discovery was there. This is why a man like Fr. Augustine Bea, later a cardinal, a close counselor (and confessor) of Pope Pius XII, quite naturally and without a really radical change of mind, entered in 1960 his role of promoter and defender of what one may call the Jewish cause before and during the Council. And, if I may strike here a personal note, it is from no other source than the hidden currents just mentioned (hidden, I mean, in relation to the now public and perhaps fashionable way of thinking) that I absorbed whatever openness and understanding I may now have for questions Jewish. I never felt, neither when I was a student at the Pontifical Biblical Institute in 1948–1950, nor even before when I was writing my theological dissertation at the Angelicum from 1946 on and simultaneously learning Hebrew, Biblical and Mishnaic, with, as a reading text for the latter, Pirke Aboth (of all things), that I needed a radical *metanoia*. And I had come from a country still much in the news because of a not altogether clean record in the field of antisemitism.

Yes, the Catastrophe was behind us. But I confess that I knew next to nothing about it when I left Argentina for Rome in November 1946, and it was only very gradually that I became conscious of the magnitude of the tragedy. Others perhaps knew better, at least from a certain point in time on. But my argument is that this knowledge, upsetting and terribly poignant as it certainly was, would not have had the transforming effect it has had, were it not because of the soil already tilled (at least to a certain extent) that it found.

I have mentioned Bible studies. I should have mentioned too the liturgical movement, which contributed to the same main result, namely the rediscovery of the Jewish foundations of the structure of the main liturgical actions in the Church, the Eucharist in the first place, but also the liturgical feast cycle and its main forms of celebration. It is, I am afraid, easily forgotten that Pope Pius XII introduced the first radical reform of the Holy Week in the now remote year 1951, restoring its central importance to the Pascal Vigil and thereby, by the same stroke, accentuated its intimate connection with the Jewish Pesach. If he received Jules Isaac, he was prepared to *hear* something, however unprepared he may have been at that stage to *do* something. John XXIII, on the other hand, was also prepared to act, not only, I presume, because of the tragedy of the *Endlösung,* by then well affirmed in the consciousness of the Catholic Church, but also because of the slow maturing and final ripening of the hidden currents of which I have spoken, by then, however, hidden no more.

If the Catholic Church is slow and proceeds by careful steps in arriving at any major decision, implying some measure of change of former attitudes, once such decisions are arrived at, it clings to them in a way which can well be qualified as tenacious. This is the *second aspect* I would like to underline in the present context.

Judaism is now seen in a different light, and also practical (in the sense of pastoral) attitudes toward Jews as persons and Judaism as a religious and ethnic community are different from what they used to be, more so in the latter case than in the former. I will not enter now into the detail of such changes, theoretical or practical, theological or pastoral, which will be the subject of a later section of this presentation. But I would like to stress here three brief points, which I hold to be enlightening for a proper understanding of this whole matter.

First, changes in the Church are always intended to express a deeper faithfulness to tradition. "Tradition," it is known, is not in Catholicism a word without real content (nor, for that matter, in Judaism). It means the internal coherence of the Church with its own apostolic origin, all along the ages. Because of the accidents of history and the weakness of human nature, such a fidelity may be obscured in certain times and certain matters. Or rather, as fidelity is to be expressed in thought and action, the actual historical expression of intended fidelity may be less appropriate, or even inappropriate, in terms of what it intends to convey. It is obvious, by the way, that neither thought nor action, especially at a general or common level, is ever able to articulate fully the richness of the apostolic tradition. This is why constant attention and examination is required, and in this process the Church is much helped by the flow of history. But the end result of such soul-searching is, and can only be, a renewed or, as the case may be, a corrected expression of tradition.

Thus, in the question of Judaism the hidden currents and their final public outlet in the Council try to give substance and form to a more, and not less, traditional way of dealing with the continuing existence of the Jewish people and its not less continuous relation with the Church. The new outlook toward Judaism from the point of view of the Church is, one could say, *more apostolic* than the former, in the theological sense of the word.

This is borne out by the remarkable circumstance that such change was ratified by an Ecumenical Council, not by any other Church body. The Ecumenical Council, according to Canon law,[5] is, along with the Pope, the supreme teaching authority of the Catholic Church. If its teaching is not always infallible in the proper sense of the word,[6] there is no doubt that in the doctrinal structure of the Church it has a unique weight. Such weight comes, in the first place, from what is called, in Catholic theology, the special assistance of the Holy Spirit, but also from the position of every Council in the flow of tradition. What a Council intends to do is mainly to find the proper traditional response to a new challenge from inside or outside the Church and give its sanction to such a response. Thus, on the one hand, it is grounded in a deeper understanding of tradition and, on the other hand, it stamps this new (but also traditional) understanding with the seal of conciliar authority. Catholics are supposed to follow suit, not because of the novelty of the teaching, but because of the unique value of this new interpretation of tradition. Now, the Declaration *Nostra Aetate* is the first conciliar document of its kind to be concerned with Judaism.[7] It opens up a new perspective, but, at the same time, marks it with the character of authenticity, of an *authentic interpretation* of tradition. This is then my second point.

My third point in this connection is that a new development, in the light of tradition, regarding matters Jewish, is first and foremost an *internal affair* of the Catholic Church. By this I obviously do not intend to say that the matter in question is anything "internal" to the Church, Judaism being a different religion and a different entity altogether (albeit intimately related). But I mean that the development aiming at and conducive to a new insight toward Judaism flows from a fresh examination and new adaptation of Catholic tradition itself, and is not foreign to it. Again, this is not to deny that "external" factors may have had an influence in determining the fact and orientation of this examination. It is rather to stress the point of the traditional Catholic character of the development. In other words, the new way of looking at Judaism made manifest by the Council and the following documents from Catholic sources here gathered is in no way alien to the great, time-honored and distinctive Catholic tradition coming down from the Apostles (who, one ought not to forget, were themselves Jewish) but, on the contrary, an authentic expression of it. In a comparable way, the post-conciliar liturgical structuring of the Eucharistic celebration and, in due proportion, of the other sacraments of the Church, however new it may seem to unaccustomed eyes, is an appropriate and coherent modern translation of traditional Christian liturgy. And it now has, like the new vision of Judaism, conciliar sanction.

Catholic style is gradual. But when the Church comes to a decision, especially a conciliar decision, it does not go back on it. This however does not at all mean that thereby everything is settled. The Catholic Church is a world in itself, if one may use such an expression, strongly unified but not to the point of uniformity, with many centers of (sacred) authority, but with very little power of coercion, which it uses very seldom. All this amounts to a *third* aspect of Catholic style.

Decisions at the center, even taken with intense participation of all concerned, as in an Ecumenical Council, have still to find their way to all layers and corners of Catholic thinking, teaching and living. To this aim the machinery is in place. Bishops, who voted on the conciliar documents, even if they happened to vote against them,[8] are not only supposed, but formally called, to have them as their fundamental point of reference in all matters dealt with in these documents, whether infallible or not.[9] Parish priests, preachers, theology professors, teachers of religion, catechists and other Church officials are responsible to their bishops for implementing (or not) conciliar decisions, theoretical or practical. Bishops are responsible to the Holy See. And all are responsible to God.

If, therefore, everything is not done immediately and, here and there, examples may be pointed out of preachers, teachers or writers going their own way, outside or against the official teaching of the Church, these instances are to be deplored, the deviations redressed and, if possible, remedies applied. However, these instances in themselves are not very widespread, given the extension and the plurality of the Catholic Church, not to mention human frailty. It is thus an open question whether we who are concerned with the right course of Jewish-Christian relations should expend our energies in chasing out and denouncing to the proper authorities a parish priest here or a pamphlet writer there, or rather concentrate on the foundations and means for sound education in such matters. Those foundations, indeed, and to some extent also the means, are to be found already in the corpus of documents hereafter published. And it is hoped that some kind of framework for the adequate presentation of Jews and Judaism in Catholic education will be published not far from now.

I have just pointed out one possible difference between center and "periphery" (an improper word: not everything which is not "central" is *eo ipso* "peripheral" in the Church)—a kind of measurable difference, or perhaps distance, so to speak.

There is another difference, less conspicuous, I grant, but nonetheless important for the proper reading of the documents here included.

The "center" of the Catholic Church, namely the Holy See (improperly called at times the Vatican), has a perspective of its own: the perspective of the whole Church. It has to take into account needs and sensitivities of peoples and places extremely different among themselves, while at the same time carefully avoiding all appearance of replacing or substituting whatever should be framed and done by the local Churches—all this, while simultaneously proposing in a faithful way what flows, in any given matter, from the apostolic tradition mentioned above, not more not less, and allows for its translation into pastoral practice.

I have mentioned the Holy See. The Ecumenical Council is another case in point, the only other one, indeed, because there is no other "center" in the Church and both the Council and the Pope are closely intertwined so that one should perhaps speak of only *one* center and not of two.

Some documents in this volume (and the preceding collection) emanate from this "center," some from local Churches and others from Episcopal Conferences. There are also some coming from individual persons in an official context.

It seems fairly obvious that one ought not to expect absolutely the same from all of these documents, or that they all must be read in exactly the same way.

There are, I assume, two perfectly legitimate "horizons of interpretation" (if I am allowed this technical expression of the hermeneutical science), in which the documents in question should and do differ, inside the unity of the Catholic apostolic tradition.

The first "horizon," or dimension, if you wish, is the vertical one, to wit, the difference of outlook, and of course responsibility, just outlined, between the center of the Catholic Church at large and the center of any local, or particular Church, whether episcopal conference or diocese. Such differences as mentioned may imply a difference of thematization, not to mention concrete regulations or norms. This is why not everything found in documents published by local sources is identically found in documents published by the central office, and vice versa. This is also why, in the final analysis, paragraph 4 of *Nostra Aetate,* which was before a chapter of the Decree on Ecumenism, passed through such an agonizing process of revision and rewriting right to the end—not only, and not mainly, because of "progressives" and "conservatives" pushing each toward their own side, but because of the deeply experienced need and (at least in some quarters) the definite will to arrive at a final document acceptable to the largest possible majority of bishops without betraying the essence of its content. For a "first" document of this kind this was particularly necessary so as to avoid divisions in the new matter raised and, on the other hand, ensure faithful and coherent application in thought and practice. "Quod omnes tangit, ab omnibus approbari debet," says an ancient rule of Canon Law.[10] As things went, the majority, I have already said, was astounding even to those who were more optimistic.

The second "horizon"—if one may go on with such a spatial terminology—is the "horizontal" one. Churches local or particular have their own needs and problems and pastoral priorities. There is no use pretending that Judaism is a major pastoral challenge in Bangladesh or Burkina-Faso (ex-Cameroons), where Christians probably know very little even about the present existence of the Jewish people. Contrariwise, relations with the Jews are an issue of foremost importance in the United States, England, France, and even Argentina and Brazil.

This accounts not only for different emphases and orientations, but also sometimes for the presence or absence of local documents referring to matters Jewish.

Having said this, I want to stress immediately that, from the *ad intra* point of view (i.e., the point of view of the internal needs of Christians), *all* Churches are, or should be, equally concerned with, for instance, a true and honest presentation of Jews and Judaism in Catholic teaching, not to mention the rejection of antisemitism. But, even in those quite common fundamental concerns, accents and emphases may not be always the same, according to history, local tradition and, last but not least, presence or absence of definite dangers.[11]

If I may give here a concrete example, the State of Israel is extremely important for a great majority of Jews, however they may look at its present political, social and international difficulties and the ways and means to overcome them. This, in principle, must be acknowledged by all Christians concerned with Jews, as their brothers and sisters. But it does not necessarily follow that the reference to the State should occupy exactly the same place or even any place, at least explicitly, in each and every document published by any source in the Catholic Church on relations with Judaism. *Nostra Aetate*, n. 4, chose not to do it—nor did the "Orientations and Suggestions for the Implementation of the Conciliar Declaration." Instead, the French and American episcopates chose to mention the State of Israel in their documents, and also, more recently, the Brazilian Episcopal Conference.

Are they thereby "correcting" the Council or the Holy See? The drafters and voters of these documents would be extremely surprised to learn of such an interpretation. They simply thought, and rightly so, that in their time and place the reference to the State of Israel was convenient or necessary. So has the Holy Father done, on more than one occasion,[12] right from the center of the Church, again because time and circumstances seemed to invite such a reference. It would be, I believe, bad hermeneutical method to explain away all silences (or all references) as inspired by "political" expediency.

I leave out here an extended discussion of a third possible "horizon," namely the one concerned with time, not to make this paper grow disproportionately long. But it should be clear to all that *time* is an important factor in discerning the content and import of documents, and this because men take the place of other men (and women), but also because, as Qohelet says (3:1ff), there is a time for this and a time for that—"this" and "that" being possible different emphases, in different times, of a common basic kerygma and commitment of the Catholic Church regarding Jews and Judaism.

Accordingly, there are limitations in the documents that follow. "Limitations" is a very relative concept. It implies a criterion for judgment grounded in content, place, time, origin and (in the case of these particular documents) coherence with the apostolic tradition. In this sense, there are limitations indeed. One could ask, however, if there are at all documents without limitations, and then which. The main point of the explanation above, on "horizons," is to place some, at least, of the possible limitations in a proper hermeneutical perspective. Others perhaps do not find adequate justification, and these would be *true* limitations (i.e., intrinsic). Others finally are no limitations at all, as when Church documents are criticized because they hold fast to the Word of God as interpreted in the apostolic tradition, and do not go wild in ecclesiology, Christology, or whatever. But this is quite another matter.

In one of our meetings of the Holy See Commission with the International Jewish Committee on Interreligious Consultations (IJCIC), held in Madrid and Toledo, in 1978, I attempted to synthesize in a kind of framework the *doctrinal* content of most of the official documents published in the Catholic Church up to that date. This paper was only a private one and such it has remained till now. If it were to be published in its entirety it would badly need updating and perhaps refining here and there. However, it may still give a useful idea of how and what the documents in question, up to 1978 (but mainly also afterward), have contributed to a new teaching, albeit truly traditional, on Jews and Judaism in the Catholic Church.

I take therefore the liberty of quoting extensively the two last pages of this paper.

1. There are, in the official teaching of the Church and the Churches, some general principles and some orientations on how to present in RC teaching, at all levels, the Jews, Judaism and the relation of both to Christianity.

2. The general principles indicate in terms of the true spirit of Christianity and the true reality of Judaism what lines this teaching should respect if it is to be faithful to both.

3. The orientations are both negative and positive. The negative ones indicate some dangers and extremes to be avoided. The positive ones show the concrete paths to be followed.

4. We can now synthesize the *negative* orientations in this way:

—the Jewish people should not be presented as repudiated, cursed or rejected by God;

—the Jewish religion must not be said to be one of fear and retributive justice only, diametrically opposed to the New Testament religion;

—post-biblical Judaism is not a decadent form of religion, without any positive values at all. "Jews" in the New Testament do not necessarily have a pejorative connotation. The same must be said of Pharisees and Pharisaism;

—Jews are not collectively responsible for the passion and death of Christ, neither those of his time nor those who came after;

—antisemitism in all its forms stands condemned and the Holocaust is to be seen as a grim consequence of its malignant nature.

5. The *positive* orientations raise those points which we enumerate now:

—a "spiritual bond" exists between Judaism and Christianity, manifest in different historical, biblical, liturgical and doctrinal aspects;

—the Old Testament (or Hebrew Scripture) has not been superseded by the New; it is always the true Word of God and belongs to the integrity of the Bible and thus of divine Revelation;

—the Judaic roots of Christianity should be made present, either in the founding personalities, starting with Christ himself, or in the language, teaching and general atmosphere of the New Testament and primitive Christianity;

—Jews are "dear to God" because of their fathers; their election and mission has a permanent validity and they play a decisive role in the religious history of mankind;

—finally, two of the documents (the American Episcopal Statement and the Orientations of the French Episcopal Commission of 1975 and 1973, respectively) recognize in a positive way the relation of the Jewish people to the land of Israel, without, for that matter, adopting a political stance in the present controversies affecting that part of the world.

6. As many, if not all, of the above principles and orientations are founded in Holy Scripture and Catholic tradition, or in the self image of the Jewish people, it can be said that:

—for what regards the points which touch on the interpretation of Scripture, the Catholic teacher has here the true norm for reading Scripture when it refers to Jews and Judaism;

—the same Catholic teacher has also here at his disposal a basic outline of Catholic theology regarding Judaism. A development and deepening of this basic outline is now needed. Remarkable efforts have been made in that direction;

—the main principle of dialogue has been frequently applied in the documents, namely, as stated by the Guidelines and Suggestions for Implementing the Conciliar Declaration *Nostra Aetate* (n. 4), by the Vatican Commission for Religious Relations with the Jews, that we "strive to learn by what essential traits the Jews define themselves in the light of their own religious experience."

The principles and orientations thus exposed must then, as a matter of Christian and Jewish identity, constitute the main content and the basic framework of Catholic teaching on Jews and Judaism.

NOTES

1. A study which, I believe, remains to be made. A first important approach may be found in Hugo Schlesinger and Humberto Porto, *Os Papas e os Judeos,* (Petropolis: Vozes 1973).

2. The best account of these proceedings is found (to my knowledge) in an unpublished lecture of Miss Maria Vingiani, of the *Segretariato Attività Ecumeniche,* in Italy, which I take the liberty of mentioning. The account, may I add, is not only first-hand but first-rate.

3. There seems to be no other report of the audience.

4. T. Herzl, *The Diaries of Theodor Herzl,* ed. Martin Löwenthal (New York: Grosset and Dunlap, 1962), pp. 419–422. The audience with Pope Pius X is on pp. 427–430. For another audience with Cardinal Merry del Val of a collaborator of Herzl

cf. Amos Elon, *La rivolta degli Ebrei* (Milano: Rizzoli, 1979), pp. 470–472, esp. note 9, where the author refers, for the conversation of the cardinal with Heinrich York-Steiner, to Christopher Sykes, *Two Studies in Virtue* (London, 1954).

5. Cf. *Codex Iuris Canonici,* can. 337 §1.

6. Cf. Dogmatic Constitution on the Church, n. 25.

7. Some practical decisions have been taken by medieval Councils, like Lateran IV, whatever we may now feel about such decisions.

8. *Nostra Aetate* had a remarkably low count of negative votes: 88 against, 2221 for.

9. Cf. Declaration (Notificatio) read by the Secretary General of the Council, in General Congregation 123 (Nov. 16, 1964), which I transcribe here in the original Latin text: "Ut de se patet, textus Concilii semper secundum regulas generales, ab omnibus cognitas, interpretandus est." This is followed by the Declaration of the Doctrinal Commission, of March 1964, also published in the *Acts* of the Council: "Ratione habita moris conciliarii ac praesentis Concilii finis pastoralis, haec S. Synodus ea tantum de rebus fidei et morum ab Ecclesia tenenda definit, quae ut talia aperte ipse declaraverit. Coetera autem, quae S. Synodus proponit, utpote Supremi Ecclesiae Magisterii doctrinam, omnes ac singuli christifideles excipere et amplecti debent iuxta ipsius S. Synodi mentem, quae sive ex subiecta materia sive ex dicendi ratione innotescit, secundum normas theologicae interpretationis." This second quotation, in a rough translation, would read as follows: "Taking into account conciliar tradition and the present Council's pastoral aim, this Holy Synod only defines as a matter of faith and morals what it openly presents as such. For other matters, also taught by the Synod, as the doctrine of the supreme teaching authority, all and sundry Christian faithful are obliged to receive and accept them, according to the intention of the Holy Synod, manifest either in the content or in the style of proclamation, with due attention to the theological rules of interpretation."

10. "What concerns everybody must be approved by all"—one of the rules in the sixth book of the *Decretales* of the ancient *Corpus Iuris Canonici.*

11. Cf., *inter alia,* John M. Pawlikowski's remarkable article "The Evolution of Christian-Jewish Dialogue" in the July/August 1984 issue *"The Ecumenist."*

12. As in the allocution to the representatives of the German Jewish community in Mainz, Nov. 17, 1980 (*John Paul II, Addresses and Homilies on Ecumenism 1978–1980,* ed. John B. Sheerin C.S.P. and John F. Hotchkin, U.S. Catholic Conference, 1981, p. 153), and more recently, in the Apostolic Letter "Redemptionis Anno" on the city of Jerusalem (*L'Osservatore Romano,* English edition, April 30, 1984, pp. 6f), to quote only two examples.

2
A Christian Problem:
Review of Protestant Documents

Alice L. Eckardt

Alice L. Eckardt is Professor of Religion Studies at Lehigh University. She is author and co-author of books and articles on Christian-Jewish Relations. Her latest publication is "Long Night's Journey into Day" (Detroit, 1982).

There is no question but that it took the German Nazis' "Final Solution" to make Christians begin to be aware that the so-called Jewish problem is in reality a Christian problem and that it has always been so.

This does not mean that Jews have not had and do not now have a problem, but it does mean that theirs is quite different from the one Christians have. For Jews the issue has been an existential one—survival: how to survive as a community despite catastrophes and crises in threatening or homogeneous non-Jewish environments. Threats to survival have ranged from the hostility of a religiously different majority that sought the disappearance of Jews through conversion, to the extreme of German National Socialism that planned the physical destruction of every last Jew regardless of the individual's religion or cultural/political affiliation. In recent years (*since* World War II) attacks on Jewish survival include the mixture of cultural genocide and antisemitic policies practiced by the Soviet Union and the various attempts to delegitimate and ultimately to destroy the State of Israel, engaged in by many nations and hostile groups. And still the threat of a "spiritual Final Solution" remains in the open societies of the West, embodied in the various Christian "missions to the Jews."

The Christian problem is not one of survival. It is much more complicated than that. At stake is the church's moral and spiritual integrity. A complex of issues is involved: (1) Christian identity, which almost inevitably is defined in terms over against and in contrast to Jews and Judaism; (2) theology, which faces the challenge of how to proclaim the Christian confession of faith and hope without denigrating other religions, but particularly that of Jews; (3) interpretation of the Scripture shared with Jews (Tanakh/Old Testament), which is all too often used to "prove" the authenticity of the church and the inauthenticity of the synagogue or other forms of Jewish existence; (4) the Christian portion of the Bible, the New Testament, many portions of which can be used (directly or indirectly) to confirm the church's negative presentation of Jews and Judaism, and its traditional teaching that Christians have replaced Israel as God's people; (5) the mission or calling of Christianity, which is still overwhelmingly understood as the responsibility to bring all others to confess Christ as Lord; (6) the question of God's role in history, which is traditionally interpreted as having been definitive and final in Jesus the Christ; (7) the historical record with respect to Christian responsibility for initiating hostility, legislative discrimination, oppression, and various forms of violence against Jews long before Adolf Hitler.

All of these issues were exacerbated for the churches by the challenges and experiences of the Hitler years. Moreover, they remain at the heart of Christian-Jewish relations as well as of Christian introspection, as a perusal of the church statements shows.[1]

The Nazi Holocaust showed how easily the anti-Jewish policies and laws of Christendom could be emulated and utilized by a regime that deliberately set itself to abolish the old restraints and to carry the logic of reprobation and exclusion to an end the church had been unwilling to condone.[2] It also revealed how thoroughly the predominant Christian tradition regarding Jews and Judaism had come to comprise a teaching of contempt[3] which left little room for compassion toward its object. We are forced to this observation because the institutional churches did so little to try to "put a spoke in the wheel"[4] of the machinery of discrimination and murder (or even commiserate with the victims), and because the theology of deicide, curse, and displacement continued to be proclaimed at the very same time that the trains were carrying their human cargo to the gas chambers.[5] Even the crying human needs were insufficient to overcome the theological-historical tradition and the current form of antisemitism to any significant degree, though the individuals and occasionally whole communities who dared to act are the seeds of hope for many today.

In the years since 1945 Christian communities (synods/dioceses, denominations, regional church conferences, national and international organizations) have been struggling with some or all of the issues listed above, attempting to find some way to move Christianity out of the *Adversus Judaeos* morass. The present volume of officially adopted statements attests to the on-going church efforts to respond responsibly to the *Shoah* and contemporary forms of antisemitism, and (though to a lesser degree) to the reestablished State of Israel and a Jewish renaissance. The new scholarship in biblical studies, rabbinics, and history, new ventures in Christian theology,[6] and the interfaith dialogue have made it possible.

There is considerable significance in these attempts to cleanse Christian teaching of its anti-Jewish aspect. Important questions are lifted up for careful and prayerful consideration. What is the relation of faith and history? How has Christianity's particular affirmation of faith influenced history and the gener-ations of people who lived in that faith and those who lived alongside it? (To what extent was it a beneficial influence? To what extent was it a harmful in-fluence?) How has history, especially particular historical events, shaped the Christian faith? And how should (or may) historical events *continue* to inform and condition faith and the way it is proclaimed.[7]

Generalizing, we may say that Christianity has by and large built its af-firmation on the singular event of the life, death, and resurrection of Jesus of Nazareth, confessed as Christ and Lord, which was seen as the culmination of the process of redemption God had begun long before. With the exception of the visitation of the Holy Spirit at Pentecost, which was understood as an ex-tension of God's work in Jesus, no other historical event is assigned or ex-pected to have revelatory or salvational significance until the final act of holy history: the Second Coming of Christ, the Parousia.[8] Fully in keeping with this perspective, the church has understood its history as one of progressive victory in carrying out its assigned task of bringing the world to Christ in the interim period between Resurrection-Pentecost and Second Coming-Kingdom of God. Only now, after the *Shoah,* are some Christians considering whether the church doesn't need to be more aware of God's continuing activity and reve-lation in history (and the community), and *not* only in ways that confirm Chris-tianity's traditional theology. They ask: Isn't there a need to recognize how God-in-history reveals to us our human fallibility and our false absolutes?

The singular significance of such statements as the ones included in this volume (and its predecessor) may be determined by the degree of readiness their authors and supporters show in being open to new understandings gained through awareness that "revelation is the encounter with God in experience . . . learned in multi-dimensional experience."[9] For only then are we liberated from a too literal reading of Scripture and from a too absolute conviction of the completeness of our own tradition, both of which have locked the church into a triumphalist and adversary position vis-à-vis Judaism and the Jewish people.

There is another important aspect of all these efforts. The very process of considering and debating the questions and their many ramifications enables and even forces the persons involved to think about theological positions (and the supporting arguments or data) that they have heretofore taken as givens (or "gospel truth"). In such situations people *do* theology perhaps for the first time, instead of just accepting what they have been taught as if there were no alternatives.

The final products of this confrontation with theology in the light of a simultaneous confrontation with its historical consequences probably should be seen as new "epistles to the churches" at the start of what we may hope will be a new era.[10]

Having pointed to the significance (at least potentially) of the church statements, we need also to consider their limitations. Such limitations extend beyond the particulars of any single document (whether all the issues are addressed, how adequately, etc.), and beyond the intentions of their framers. The crucial question is: To what extent do the thinking and implications of the contents permeate the regular preaching, teaching, and life of the denominations and individual congregations? The answer so far appears to be: very little. Unless the wider Christian community enters into the process of critical reexamination, and does so with a sense of urgency,[11] the most ideal reformulation of Christian beliefs must remain a buried treasure, an unused resource for a transformation that could be spiritually liberating and genuinely redemptive for both parties.[12]

When we look at the Ten Points of Seelisberg of 1947 and then at some of the later documents, we find a significant growth in awareness of what is involved in this undertaking. At that pioneering gathering, the Protestant and Catholic churchmen, together with their Jewish colleagues, were primarily concerned with the terrible force of antisemitism, not only as it had reached its apogee in the Third Reich but as it was still manifesting itself in other societies as well. They focused on ten issues which they believed the churches needed to emphasize in order to avoid "false, inadequate, or mistaken presentations or conceptions . . . of the Christian doctrine," and to promote "brotherly love towards the sorely-tried people of the old covenant." Although an apologetic note was immediately apparent with the statement that "the Christian churches have . . . always affirmed the anti-Christian character of antisemitism,"[13] the ten point program was certainly a fundamental corrective to New Testament texts and the classical presumption of Christianity as the "new Israel" over against reprobate, deicidal Israel. Had all the churches incorporated these propositions into their teaching and preaching ef-

forts as suggested, much greater progress would have been made in the eradication of Christian anti-Judaism and Christian antisemitism.

Some of the specifics of Seelisberg are to be found in expanded form in
some of the recent declarations. For example, point 5 (avoid disparaging biblical or post-biblical Judaism in order to extol Christianity) is fleshed out in
eleven paragraphs of "Ecumenical Considerations" of the World Council of
Churches' Executive Committee (section 2:1-8, 12-14). Some other emphases
of Seelisberg such as concern over aspects of the gospel accounts of Jesus' trial
and crucifixion and how the Passion story is presented (7 and 8) are considered
only in two of the recent Protestant documents (the British Working Group and
the Evangelical Churches of Switzerland). Presumably such omission is to be
understood as meaning that the churches have moved beyond the point of need-
ing to mention this subject. Yet the fact remains that each year congregations
build up to the climax of Passion/Holy Week and Easter. They are in dire need
of guidance about how to present the New Testament texts so that the traditional anti-Jewish emphasis is not reiterated. All the affirmations about the permanent election of the Jewish people or about the vitality of Jewish faith do
little to eradicate the ongoing negative effect of this annual public reassertion
of Jewish perfidy.[14] Since some of the statements published here represent a
first-time declaration on the relation of Christianity and Judaism, it would
seem that some space should have been allotted to the thorny issue.

The positive aspect of the omission of the subject of Jesus' crucifixion is
that Jews and Judaism are being thought and spoken of as living contempor-
aries whose traditions have been constantly evolving and whose presence testifies to the dual faithfulness of God and His people, and to the survival of
messianic hope.

A further testimony to an increasing awareness by the churches of the
Jewish people in their present reality is to be found in the inclusion of references to the State of Israel. The three statements that give greatest attention to
it are the British Working Group, which refers to it in three contexts (I.3; II.3;
IV.3), the Evangelical Churches of Switzerland, which gives it a very full section (VI) and one additional reference (in III.2), and the Council of Churches
in the Netherlands, which has an extensive and most helpful analysis of changing Christian attitudes toward the State of Israel, as well as suggestions about
what Christians can do and cannot do about the conflict in that part of the
world. It is most surprising to find no mention of the State of Israel in the Texas
Conference of Churches statement, though, to be sure, the overall subject of
that document is dialogue.

The most thoroughly theological of the Protestant documents in this collection is that of the Protestant Council of Belgium. It espouses a provocative

analysis of the meaning of "remnant." The American Lutheran Church's affirmation is the only one to acknowledge that "Jewishness is both a religious and a cultural phenomenon which is exceedingly hard to define. . . . Not all Jews necessarily believe in Judaism. . . . We must . . . allow Jewishness to be defined by Jews. . . ." The Lutherans also insist that Jewish practices and beliefs should not be "judged different from those of any minority group." Moreover, "Jews and Lutherans need not share a common creed in order to cooperate . . . in fostering human rights." The European Mennonites speak from their particular perspectives and experiences: recognizing the need of a people to be able to create their own community and to maintain an independent existence; confessing their silence during the Holocaust and the efforts of Jews to rebuild the State of Israel.

The one issue that most frequently divides the authors of these statements is that of mission and witness. Proselytism or "unwarranted" or "coercive" proselytism is readily rejected. But whether Christians should bear witness of their faith to the Jewish people, and if so how, usually is left unresolved (see "Authentic Christian Witness," World Council of Churches Consultation on the Church and the Jewish People, 4; "Guidelines for Jewish-Christian Dialogue," WCC Sub-Unit on Dialogue with People of Living Faiths and Ideologies, 3.5; "Reflections" of the Evangelical Churches of Switzerland, V). However, in two of our documents we have unequivocal rejection of Christian mission to Jews: the Texas (USA) Conference of Churches and the Synod of the Protestant Church of the Rheinland. The latter states that "in their calling Jews and Christians are always witnesses of God in the presence of the world and each other. Therefore . . . the church may not express its witness toward the Jewish people as it does its mission to the peoples of the world . . ." (4.6). The former is a complete statement on dialogue as an alternative to proselytization and needs to be read in its entirety. With regard to Jews and Judaism, the churches have a "singular relationship" which makes "dialogue and shared mission" the appropriate posture (IV.B).

Of all the Protestant statements the two just mentioned are the most outstanding. It is gratifying to have the church of the most populous synod in West Germany take an unambiguous step "Toward Renovation of the Relationship of Christians and Jews." Years of dedicated study, consultations, and discussions preceded this achievement. One correction should be made in its wording, for it has caused much misunderstanding and criticism. In 4(3) the text reads: "We confess Jesus Christ the Jew, who as the Messiah *of* the Jews is the Saviour of the world. . . ." The authors insist that the text is meant to say "Jesus Christ the Jew, who as the Messiah *from* Israel. . . ."

The special contribution of the statement by the Texas Conference of

Churches is its sense of movement and change. It proclaims its conviction that "the Spirit of God is once again moving" to create "light out of darkness, life out of death," and that the Spirit "moves among us through the events of our day." The Texas churches are summoning us to new awareness and new understanding so that together we may take new steps and build new relationships. The hallowing of God's name in the world, the insistence on respect for the dignity and worth of each person, and the active pursuit of justice and peace are the tasks for which Christians and Jews must jointly strive, in the shared hope of a messianic age.

In addition to the present documents, there are others that are in various stages of consideration—one, a major study by an American denomination—which, if adopted, will be further "stepping stones" on the path of reconciliation and recovery of Christian integrity.

NOTES

1. An analysis of the Protestant documents in this volume reveals that each of them is concerned with almost all of the seven issues listed here, and several deal with all of them.

2. Cf. Yosef Yerushalmi, "Response to Rosemary Ruether," in *Auschwitz: Beginning of a New Era?*, Eva Fleischner, ed. (New York: Ktav, 1977), pp 98f.

3. This descriptive phrase was first coined by the French historian Jules Isaac as a result of his in-depth investigation of the roots of antisemitism while in hiding from the Nazis who had already deported and killed his wife and daughter.

4. See Richard Gutteridge, *Open Thy Mouth for the Dumb* (Oxford: Basil Blackwell, 1976), p. 93.

5. See, e.g., Charlotte Klein, "Vatican View of Jewry, 1939-1962," in *Christian Attitudes on Jews and Judaism*, 43 (August 1976), pp. 12–16. The church commemoration of the Slaughter of the Innocents (under King Herod) continued each year without the occasion being used to cry out against the contemporary slaughter of the one and one-half million Jewish innocents (H.J. Richards, "The Crucifixion and the Jews," London: Sisters of Sion, 1966, p. 12).

6. The work of numerous individuals underlies much of the new thinking that is revealed in these statements; they and their writings lie outside the scope of this volume.

7. Generalizing, we find that out of necessity Judaism traditionally has been more attentive to both of these questions than the church. The many sufferings along with renewals required constant consideration of the existential questions that these events posed. How did they correlate with Judaism's understanding of God in covenant with Israel? Were they in some sense revelatory events or a form of divine pedagogy? Should they be ignored, or incorporated into the faith? Was the Covenant imposing an unrealistic burden on its adherents? Was one or another form of Jewish faith to be seen as a dead end or a side road that led the people away from a productive life of serving

God's positive goals? Out of this anguish of questioning emerged new insights, new answers to ancient—but persistent—queries, and new modes of life and worship.

8. The Reformation, even for Protestants, is considered to be merely a human recovery of the pure truth of the apostolic church; it was not a new act of God in history. With regard to suffering, the early and intermittent periods of persecution were interpreted as opportunities to witness to the good news that those who believed in Christ would be raised from death even as he had been.

9. Monika Hellwig, in Lawrence Boadt, Helga Croner, Leon Klenicki, eds., *Biblical Studies, Meeting Ground of Jews and Christians* A Stimulus Book (New York: Paulist Press, 1980), p. 186.

10. A Symposium held in 1974 and the volume of papers from that Symposium bear the title "Auschwitz: Beginning of a New Era?" (cf. n. 2 above).

11. Cf. Monika Hellwig, *ibid.*

12. The absence of statements or study documents within some churches or the defeat of submitted drafts must be taken as a negative attestation: changes in church positions are held to be unnecessary or even a denial of the gospel. Changes that are made in early versions often reveal an attempt to water down or cancel out the new voices.

13. What definition of the term were they using? Certainly not "hostility to Jews"!

14. No reference is to be found among this collection of Protestant statements to the problems posed by Passion plays, of which Oberammergau is the most world famous example. Yet, concern about the impact of these dramatizations is being widely expressed these days, in the press and by individuals.

3
The Dialogue, Touching New Bases?

Mordecai Waxman

Mordecai Waxman is a Rabbi of the Temple Israel of Great Neck, N.Y. He is President of the Synagogue Council of America.

The idea of assembling and setting side by side major statements by significant Catholic and Protestant bodies on the question of Christian-Jewish relations is important in itself. The accomplishment does justice to the intention. From these documents it becomes clear that, in the last thirty years or so, a revolution has been taking place among major Christian groups regarding their attitude toward Jews and Judaism. The insistent and consistent use of the term "dialogue," which implies equality and sharing, is at once the statement of a key concept and a repudiation of prevalent Christian thinking and behavior over the past eighteen hundred years, in regard to Jews and Judaism.

Changes which have been taking place must be measured against that history. The documents are essentially self-critical assessments, but in calling for remedial actions and thinking, they make it clear what they are repudiating. According to a Talmudic saying, one may hear the No in the Yes.

Almost all of the papers suggest that it was the Holocaust which spurred Christians to re-examine the relationship between Christianity and Judaism. Clearly, the fact that the events under Nazi rule took place in what is commonly called "Christian" Europe, and, further, that the churches were largely silent or indifferent, nagged at the conscience of many Christians. It led them not alone to feel that Christian teaching had failed, but to examine the role Christian theology and church teaching had played in creating the atmosphere that made the Holocaust possible. This sense of responsibility can only be heightened by recent revelations of callousness to, even complicity in, the events, by major and minor statesmen and bureaucrats of Western democratic powers.

Another significant cause for the re-examination of Christianity's Jewish policy is implied in these statements, namely, the fact that in the post-World War II era and with the development of new nations Christians became increasingly involved with millions of people of other faiths or communist ideologies. That situation necessitated an examination of standard Christian doctrine and the assessment of ecumenical possibilities. Inevitably in this context, the nature and role of Judaism had to be examined as well.

Certain propositions on desirable patterns of Christian-Jewish dialogue are stated and restated in virtually every document, often in similar words. This is readily understandable in the Catholic statements, most of which are based upon the Vatican II Declaration *Nostra Aetate*. But it is quite evident, too, in a number of Protestant documents which are largely independent of one another. They all indicate a change in attitude after World War II, which took fifteen to twenty years to develop and reflects a new climate of opinion. Also evident is the recognition of a changed Jewish reality, that is, a post-Holocaust Judaism which includes the state of Israel, the development of modern biblical studies among Jews, and a Jewish community more willing to pursue interfaith dialogue and better organized to do so.

Common themes sounded in the various documents are:

1. Antisemitism in every form must be repudiated by the churches, and Christians must become aware that Christian theology and concomitant actions have created antisemitic attitudes and behavior.

2. The churches must re-examine and largely reject their own teachings about Jews and Judaism in the past. The deicide charge leveled against Jews must be repudiated. This, it is recognized, implies that certain anti-Jewish passages in the New Testament, as for instance in the Gospel of John, must be explained as applying exclusively to some Jews of that particular time, rather than to all Jews through the ages.

3. Another and necessary aspect is the emphasis on Christianity's Jewish origins, underlining the idea that Christianity is a branch grafted on the trunk of Judaism.

4. The assertion that God repudiated the Jews and elected a new Israel in their place is put aside. Paul's statement in Romans that God has not repudiated His covenant with the Jewish people is emphasized. While Christianity has a covenant with the God of Abraham to whom it has attached itself, the covenant of the Jewish people remains as an act of God's grace. For that reason, many of these statements assert, Christians should not attempt to proselytize Jews. While that raises problems for the Christian idea of mission and witness, it is suggested that proselytizing among adherents of other faiths does

apply, with the sole exception of the Jews. In relation to Jews, mission and witness are taken to mean that Christians should, by their actions, testify to Christian teachings.

5. Judaism should now be understood as a separate approach which, "after the parting of the ways," continued to have a vital and creative existence. Christian failings included the insistence on Judaism's lack of development beyond the time of Jesus; rabbinic and subsequent developments were ignored; and the high level of spirituality achieved by Jews was overlooked. In this context, the role and meaning of the Pharisees should be redefined and Christians are bidden to study the Talmudic and Midrashic sources, and later Judaism.

6. Such study should lead to the recognition that language and concepts should be changed. The characterization of Judaism as a religion of law and Christianity as one of love and similar contrasts intended to exalt Christianity at the expense of Judaism, it is recognized, misrepresent Judaism and contribute to antisemitism. Even the terms Old and New Testament carry freights of negative meaning, and suggestions for a new vocabulary are abroad.

7. The key to understanding now becomes that Judaism must be seen in its own ways and not in terms of Christianity as its successor. That, it is asserted, is the required basis for dialogue. It means that Judaism should be studied and its attitudes, goals and hopes properly understood.

In the major re-evaluation reflected in these documents, two fundamental issues are dealt with rather loosely. The first is the role of Jesus, which clearly differs for the two faiths. Almost all of the papers stress the Jewish background of Jesus; some suggest that he worked within the rabbinic tradition of his day; others, while asserting that he continued the prophetic line of Israel, stress that he is the beginning of something new. Still others are content to say that, for Christianity, the Messiah has come, while Jews are still awaiting him. Direct theological confrontation is thereby avoided and the resolution of the question left to history.

The second issue is the role of the state of Israel. No one suggests that the return of Jews to Israel represents a theological problem. On the contrary, it fits neatly into the theological outlook of some Protestant groups. Nearly all of the papers support "the right of Israel to exist" but find it necessary to refer to or stress the rights of Palestinians, too. The role of the state of Israel is seen as supremely important to Jews, both in terms of the Holocaust background and in regard to the Jewish vision. Yet, none of the documents suggest a resolution of the matter and few unequivocally endorse the state of Israel without the proviso that there are two claims to be reconciled. There exists, for many, a lurking assumption that, despite everything, Israel is actually a political rather than a theological issue. As a result, ambiguity replaces the clarity and forthright quality of some of the other theological statements, an attitude reflected in the churches' quiescence during the wars of 1967 and 1973, in the failure to condemn terrorism, and in the rise, as one of the Dutch statements suggests, of "increasingly negative sentiments toward the state of Israel."

The final concern of most of the papers is how to translate the changed perception of Judaism into different attitudes and behavior on the part of clergy and laity, and how to conduct dialogue with Jews. The specific suggestions range from attendance at Jewish services to inviting Jews to Christian services, to interfaith services in which great sensitivity is shown to Jewish feelings and in phrasing of prayer. A variety of suggestions on the study of Jewish history and doctrine, the formation of dialogue groups on the local level, care in what is preached and how, are offered to clergy and laity. It is interesting to note that it is mainly in the Catholic diocesan statements (rather than Protestant ones) that the attempt is made to translate general propositions, many formulated by Vatican II, into specific modes of behavior involving the programs described above, as well as joint social action.

One issue dealt with specifically and in detail by several Catholic bodies is that of intermarriage between Jews and Catholics. Revealing sensitivity to Jewish objections to intermarriage on the grounds of survival, the Catholic statements nonetheless recognize the natural right of the couple to marry and, therefore, feel that the Church is called upon to witness the marriage. They set forth the manner in which such marriages may take place, deal with the question of rabbinic participation, and face the question of religious education of offspring. On the whole, treatment of the problem shows a spirit of dialogue, abandonment of past rigidities, and recognition that intermarriage between Jew and Catholic is different from that between Catholic and Protestant.

The far-reaching changes mirrored in these papers represent the attempts of Catholics and Protestants to reconsider their positions and roles in respect to Jews and Judaism. That may in large measure be due to changes in the cultural climate of the last century and a half, the decline of state religions, the increased impact of American thinking and practice upon the church bodies, as well as to the shock effect of the Holocaust. One further cause, not mentioned in the documents, is that the great Jewish texts, such as the Talmud and Midrash, as well as more recent Jewish scholarship, have been rendered into languages which Christians can understand. All of these elements, together with an increasing interchange on relevant themes between Christian and Jewish scholars and the frequency of interfaith conferences, with special groups devoted to furthering them, have contributed to creating a spirit of dialogue which is both new and welcome.

It is pertinent at this point to raise the question how the Jewish community perceives these developments. Jews who are in professional contact with Christians are aware of recent changes. The average Jew, however, is not as yet particularly cognizant of the new climate which, after all, arises out of the esoteric realm of theology. In this regard he is probably in a similar position to the average Christian to whom theological formulations must seem remote. But Jews know, as probably many Christians do as well, that in the past thirty-five years there has been a decline in antisemitism and increased contact between churches and synagogues.

It must be recognized that the middle-aged Jewish adult, with memories of the Holocaust and pictures of Catholic and Protestant attitudes and teachings derived from his youth, remains apprehensive that these new Christian perceptions may be temporary or may not siphon down to the local level, no matter how they are viewed in Christian theological circles. It cannot readily be forgotten that the history of Christian theological teaching and Christian persecution of Jews is eighteen hundred years old while the process of new thinking has barely twenty years behind it.

Nonetheless, Christian re-evaluation of relations to Jews and Judaism is very welcome. It comes appropriately at one of the great watersheds in Jewish history, at a time when Jews, as a people, have re-entered history and are in a position and faced with the need to make autonomous decisions about their destiny and beliefs. It comes appropriately, too, at a time when many Jews are at home both in the Jewish intellectual, religious and scholarly worlds as well as in the world at large. Only a generation or two ago, that was a rare phenomenon. The beneficial result is that dialogue can now take place between Jews who authentically mirror the Jewish world and Jewish thought and Christians who are open, for the first time, to Jewish insights. It seems that a dynamic process has been set in motion whose long-range effects within sacred history cannot be predicted. A necessary condition of effective dialogue, however, is to reach beyond blandness toward genuine confrontation with the issues on which Jews and Christians agree and disagree, and to feel free to do so without fear of reprisals. After all, intolerance had been for millennia the characteristic posture of the world and of the Christian environment. Tolerance is a new virtue yet to be learned and cultivated.

From the Jewish point of view, however, a central reality of contemporary Jewish existence has not been properly dealt with by the Christian churches. The existence, significance and meaning of the state of Israel to the Jewish people cannot be overestimated. In the Jewish theological and religious assessment the State represents a fulfillment of Jewish history, a validation of the ongoing covenant, and the major creative response to the Holocaust. In the political sense, the State represents insurance to Jews who found the doors of other states barred during the Holocaust—insurance that there is a place to which they may repair by right.

Granted the inadequacies of the state of Israel, granted its precarious political position, Jews nonetheless see its existence as the beginning of a great overturn in Jewish history and as the opening to new developments in sacred history. Christians apparently cannot share this vision nor the psychology and history which have created it. Fundamentalist Protestants, who are not represented in these documents, seem to have a view of the major role of Israel, but within the context of an apocalyptic theology not shared by Jews. Catholic and mainline Protestant groups, whose moderated theology and interest in dialogue are acceptable to Jews, seemingly cannot bring themselves wholeheartedly to understand the Jewish point of view. The niggling statement, "Israel has a right to exist," conveys no sense of religious and theological grandeur and recognition. It is the reluctant admission of foreign-office bureaucrats, not of churchmen reared in the Judaeo-Christian tradition. Nor has the reaction of Christian religious bodies, in the opinion of most Jews including those most deeply committed to dialogue, been adequate to recurrent threats to Israel's existence in the last thirty-seven years.

Most Jews recognize the need to find a peaceful solution to the problem presented by Palestinian Arabs, and they expect Israel to seek and find one. They cannot, however, accept as legitimate the open or tacit endorsement by Christian churches of the Palestine Liberation Organization and the terrorist tactics it pursues. Obviously, people with moral concerns have a stake in the moral resolution of political problems, and that is why the Christian churches are entitled to urge and offer advice; but they should not make their support conditional.

If it is, indeed, the new posture of dialogue to understand Jews as they understand themselves, then the touchstone of a fruitful relationship may well be the ability of Christian churches to see the state of Israel with the eyes of Jews, namely, as a stage in the reaffirmation of the covenant with Abraham and his descendants. This should be the beginning of a process for which support and love must be unconditional while, at the same time, the commitment to moral goals must be unending.

Another aspect of Jewish reactions to the guidelines is whether the Jewish community, or communities, have any guidelines of their own to offer, which are addressed to fellow Jews.

It has been argued that Christianity needs a theology of Judaism in order to define itself, while Judaism does not have to define itself in terms of Christianity. The first proposition is unquestionably true, whether Christianity considers itself the successor or replacement of Israel, or as co-existing with Israel. The second proposition is only partially correct. True, Judaism can independently define its origins which precede Christianity, its continued being which is co-existent with Christianity, and its future goals which are conceived differently from Christianity. Still, Judaism can no more deny a relationship with Christianity than parents can deny that with a child. Moreover, sheer reality demands that Jews in the past and present have had to recognize Christianity as the dominant religion of the world in which they live. Operative guidelines of relationship have therefore been formulated, even if they were not reduced to formal statements.

Jews have clearly rejected the notion that Christianity, by the will of God, came into existence as a successor to Judaism. Equally, they deny that salvation comes through belief in Jesus. They have not accepted the New Testament as a new revelation nor acceded to the antinomian position of early Christianity. On the contrary, Judaism since the first century indicated awareness, first of the Christian position and then of Christian power and dominance, while continuing on its own way. The normative way was to accept the authority of the Torah and to translate it, by means of rabbinic interpretation, into a system of actions and behavior called *Halakha*. Judaism has insisted that its own monotheism left no room for a divine role of Jesus. It did, however, in the formulations of Maimonides, Halevi and others, recognize Christianity as a religion fulfilling monotheistic principles and, in its own way, leading toward the Messiah. The more modern version of Franz Rosenzweig that there are parallel covenants can equally, in one of various forms, be accepted by Jews. In sum, Judaism can readily live in harmony with Christianity as a monotheistic religion, with its own theology and view of the Messiah.

Jews see no need to seek to convert Christians, for their own salvation or anyone else's. But by the same token, Jews desire that Christians view Judaism as a faith predicated upon the Torah and covenant, with its own view of Jewish destiny, with its own vision of the Messiah and of the means of salvation. Jews accept the notion that Christians are called upon to bear witness to their view of God and their faith. Jews are even required to do so. The Kaddish, the basic Jewish prayer which closes every section of the prayer service, is precisely devoted to "magnifying and sanctifying God in the world which He created"—an obligation that is placed upon every Jew.

Judaism, in short, wishes neither to compel nor to be compelled. And since it is a religion based upon historical premises, it can afford to live with a tension between belief and ultimate truth, leaving it to God, in His own good time, to establish His truth. The *Bat Kol,* the Voice from Heaven, which spoke so long ago to resolve a dispute between the Schools of Hillel and Shammai by announcing that "both are the words of the Living God," is the position adopted by Judaism vis-à-vis Christianity, and which it would prefer Christians to accept in relation to Judaism.

In view of Christian attempts in the past to convert Jews by force and to compel them to hold public debates, certain Jewish groups prefer to avoid any dialogue with Christians. Others are quite willing to discuss social issues and philosophies as well as joint social action but would eschew theological discussion. Many Jews living in the Christian world are both willing to engage in dialogue and to discuss theology. Let it be observed, however, that by and large they know more about Christianity than Christians know about Judaism. Jews would like to trade information so that there may be mutual acceptance of people and of faiths living side by side. Jews hope that antisemitism, which for so long has played upon Jewish life and existence, may thereby be reduced and its theological underpinnings removed. Theological discussion, however, is a task for specialists.

One of the great virtues of this volume is that it brings together material which establishes that many Christian groups today are wrestling with the problem of Judaism, seeking to create the atmosphere in which fruitful dialogue can flourish. The great challenge now is for church and synagogue to translate this spirit from paper to life, to begin a new era in the relationship between two great faiths sharing a biblical history and biblical vision.

4
The Ten Points of Seelisberg

published by the International Council of Christians and Jews in 1947

1. Remember that One God speaks to us all through the Old and the New Testaments.

2. Remember that Jesus was born of a Jewish mother of the seed of David and the people of Israel, and that His everlasting love and forgiveness embraces His own people and the whole world.

3. Remember that the first disciples, the apostles and the first martyrs were Jews.

4. Remember that the fundamental commandment of Christianity, to love God and one's neighbour, proclaimed already in the Old Testament and confirmed by Jesus, is binding upon both Christians and Jews in all human relationship, without any exception.

5. Avoid distorting or misrepresenting biblical or post-biblical Judaism with the object of extolling Christianity.

6. Avoid using the word *Jews* in the exclusive sense of the enemies of Jesus, and the words *The Enemies of Jesus* to designate the whole Jewish people.

7. Avoid presenting the Passion in such a way as to bring the odium of the killing of Jesus upon all Jews or upon Jews alone. It was only a section of the Jews in Jerusalem who demanded the death of Jesus, and the Chris-

tian message has always been that it was the sins of mankind which were exemplified by those Jews and the sins in which all men share that brought Christ to the Cross.

8. Avoid referring to the scriptural curses, or the cry of a raging mob: *His Blood be Upon Us and Our Children*, without remembering that this cry should not count against the infinitely more weighty words of our Lord: *Father Forgive Them, for They Know not What They Do.*

9. Avoid promoting the superstitious notion that the Jewish people are reprobate, accursed, reserved for a destiny of suffering.

10. Avoid speaking of the Jews as if the first members of the Church had not been Jews.

I. ROMAN CATHOLIC DOCUMENTS

A) STATEMENTS AT GATHERINGS IN THE VATICAN

5
Study Outline on the
Mission and Witness of the Church
[from SIDIC]

The following translation from the original Italian is based on the revised version of the study paper prepared by Professor Federici and includes a preface by the author.

PREFACE

The following study outline on "The Mission and Witness of the Church" was presented at the sixth meeting of the Liaison Committee between the Roman Catholic Church and the International Jewish Committee for Interreligious Consultations, held in Venice at Casa Cardinal Piazza March 27 to 30, 1977. It was the basis of discussion between the two parties. In all meetings it is usual to have one or two unofficial papers from either side that serve to orientate the discussion on a given theme, which is chosen in advance by common consent of the parties themselves.

The outline here published was drawn up by Tommaso Federici, consultant member of the Commission for Religious Relations with the Jews, which has its office in the Secretariat for Christian Unity. The author submitted it to the other consultant members of the said Commission, whose observations he noted and embodied in the final version presented in Venice. For part three of the outline, entitled "The Catholic Church in Dialogue", with its presuppositions and technical aspects, a greatly appreciated collaboration was given by Monsignor Pietro Rossano, secretary of the Secretariat for Non-Christians and consultant of the Commission for Religious Relations with the Jews.

The author wishes to state that any other version than the present study outline on "The Mission and Witness of the Church" which may in any way have been published, whether in part or apparently complete, whether in daily newspapers or in periodicals, in any language whatever, is to be considered unauthentic and therefore unauthorized.

TOMMASO FEDERICI

INTRODUCTION

A. Present-Day Renewal in the Catholic Church

1. By now no one can be unaware that the Catholic Church is in an irreversible phase of profound renewal.

Various factors have contributed to this historical moment, among them, by divine Providence, the so-called "modern renewal movements". Hence we speak of an authentic beginning of "return to the sources".

2. Among these "movements", first and foremost should be noted the *biblical* movement, that proposes anew the study and living of Scripture as a necessary substratum of the Church's life and action in the world. The *liturgical* movement, with its insistence on the biblical "history of salvation" to be lived in the community of faith, leading once more to the central significance of the cult of the One God as "memorial" and thanksgiving for all the marvels he worked in the history of his people, as "blessing" of him who performed them, and praise and glorification of him in himself. The *patristic* movement has brought us again to the vital, global and pastoral manner of the Fathers of the Church, which nourishes the people with continuous Scripture reading lived in communitarian liturgy and in life. The *pastoral* movement is concerned with study and action for community life. The *catechetical* movement deals in particular with the content and technique of the Church's ongoing teaching, based necessarily on Scripture. The *missionary* movement has given fresh impetus to the evangelizing action of the Church among the peoples and cultures of the world, following accurate study of multiple connected questions. The *spirituality* movement seeks to deepen and diffuse the biblical and vital contents of a living faith. The *ecumenical* movement has rediscovered the factors that led to the age-old divisions between groups of Christians, studies their causes and remedies, and urges along the difficult way to a rediscovered unity, showing again that there is no ecumenism without authentic and on-

going renewal (*Unitatis Redintegratio* 6–8). *Dialogue* with the various religions and emerging ideologies requires that Christians listen to the deep questions of men of our times, and share with them their own experience as men and believers in the building up of the "society of love" illumined by "God's light". A renewed sense of *history*, read in the light of Scripture, today leads to a deeper knowledge of the origins and vicissitudes of the Church, her insertion in the world and among different peoples and cultures, the biblical plan of salvation and its actualization in the midst of the events involving men of all times.

3. The Second Vatican Ecumenical Council (1962–1965) came about at the happy meeting place of these "movements" and other complementary ones, begun and carried forward by a few increasingly successful pioneers. It sanctioned the intuitions, desires, studies and efforts of past decades, analyzed and synthesized their provisional results, while finally giving fresh impetus to the main, vital contents.

On its side, urged on by pressing demands for renewal, the Council undertook a tremendous effort of re-thinking and deepening of the whole life of the Catholic Church, in herself and in so far as her life is lived in the midst of the world among peoples and cultures, and in the unfolding of concrete history. All this is set down in the sixteen official Council documents, which will be the indispensible future basis of modern action in the Church.

4. It is, however, not a closed basis, as numerous "documents for application" have already shown. These have exposed various pressing points in the conciliar documents, or have raised fresh ones from recent events and have laid down guide-lines for the programme of the ecumenical Council to be carried out thoroughly and coherently. The magisterium of the popes, too, who directed the work of Vatican II, and orientated its application, shows this irreversible will for renewal. Hence, ten years after the end of the Council, it is possible to note not merely the phases of its actualization, but also real progress, as also much that remains to be done either in the near future or in future generations.

5. Therefore, it is a question of real and irreversible acquisitions or reacquisitions, gained by the peaceful efforts of the Catholic Church in her internal life and in her relations with other churches or other religions of the universe, particularly with Judaism, or any other human groups.

6. Neither should it be overlooked that we are speaking of a solid undertaking, guided by the Pope and the bishops, but carried out by degrees. There are certainly many external and internal difficulties, but it goes forward irreversibly with hope and trust in the divine will.

B. Biblical "Return to the Sources"

The present phase of renewal in the Catholic Church is marked by a careful and by now more and more universal and continuous "return to biblical sources".

1. This has come about among Christians either through pioneers, first Protestant and then Catholic, or by means of official efforts of the Catholic Church, with the foundation of specialized institutes for high level biblical studies. But a very particular aspect of this "return to the sources" came with the present liturgical reform. This not only obliged and continues to oblige to the study of the biblical and Jewish origins of the Christian liturgy, but in the new Roman Lectionary of the Mass and other celebrations it has recovered the whole of the priceless reading of the Old Testament, and consequently the vital sense of the historical dimension of the cult of the One God and the co-extensive salvation of man. Furthermore, numerous programmatic pontifical documents, as well as those the Council drew up (notably *Sacrosanctum Concilium*, the Constitution on the Sacred Liturgy, and *Dei Verbum*, the Constitution on Divine Revelation), and finally, documents concerned with their implementation, have given this "return" a universality in extension and depth.

2. Study and continual contact with the sources have gradually intensified the movement towards a total re-discovery of divine Revelation set down in Scripture as "sacred history", history of divine salvation ceaselessly coming about among men, divine design of universal salvation in the world and in the complex vicissitudes of men and peoples of the earth. This plan takes place and is actuated in the exemplary choice of an historical people, Israel, and from it goes forth to spread throughout the universe. There is better understanding of the salvific definitive value of the divine Word which, bestowed as exemplary, irreversible and faithful promise to the fathers (cf. Gen 12:1–3 for Abraham as model), was continually proclaimed to the people in worship that it might also be lived in their life. It was confirmed by the prophets, and in essence "remains eternally" (Is 40:8). Better understood is the pressing necessity Christ lays on his disciples of all times, when he teaches in person and thereby sends the disciples themselves to scrutinize the Scriptures (cf. Luke 24:25–27 and 44–47; texts which were taken up again in the context of *Dei Verbum* 14–17 on the Old Testament in the life of the Church today), Scriptures that were then, in practice, the Old Testament with its permanent value, in view of a life to be lived. Hence the apostle Paul, demonstrating the historical basis of the event of Christ's death, clearly states that it was "according to Scripture" (1 Cor 15:3) and so also for the resurrection

of Christ that is "according to the Scriptures" (vs. 4), at that time consisting only of the Old Testament. Already then acute problems of interpretation, confrontation and actuation were posed, whereby it is easy to understand the sound reasons behind the Vatican Council's reminder that the whole Church should firstly evangelize herself with the Word (cf. on this in particular *Sacrosanctum Concilium; Dei Verbum*). In-depth scriptural study reveals ever more clearly the salvific paschal historical thread, so that, while the Church recognizes herself as a "pilgrim on earth" (cf. *Sacrosanctum Concilium* 2,8; *Lumen Gentium* 48,68; *Dei Verbum* 7; *Unitatis Redintegratio* 2,6; *Ad Gentes* 2; *Christus Dominus* 16), that is, while she carries into action her "paschal exodus", her prayer and action once again are ever more impressed with the paschal event, in a continual "memorial" of the paschal act, in permanent blessing, thanksgiving and praise to the Lord. Hence, authoritative voices have stated very precisely that the greatest Christian re-discovery of our times has been that of the paschal event, and Christian life will be increasingly specifically marked with a clear *paschal spirituality*. In the same official documents, and this should be noted, the thought of the Church on the various questions dealt with is more and better expressed with numerous and adequate biblical citations.

3. In a relatively short space of time, but particularly since Vatican II, within the Catholic Church there has come about a change of mentality among the leaders and the faithful, in spite of lags and resistances. By now it is no longer possible in practice to ignore facts and realities; a closed necessarily reductive "reading" is not possible. Internal and external relationships in the Church can no longer be based on anything but inductive, realistic and more complete analysis, taking into account situations, other men and their requirements, interpersonal relationships. And all this adhering ever more fully to the divine will as expressed in the biblical revelation to men in history, concretely to the people chosen by God.

4. This makes it easy to foretell that in the fairly near future the Catholic Church's relationships with other human, cultural and religious groups, are destined to enter into an improved, more open and realistically available phase.

5. Very favorable for this is both the earlier and more recent ecumenical experience that has taught and clarified a new method of analysis of reality and its resulting relationships.

6. It was necessary to state all this in order to present the theme of this study in complete and firm adherence to the Catholic faith.

I. THE BIBLICAL PRECEPT OF MISSION TO THE PEOPLES OF THE EARTH

The Catholic Church does not conceal the fact that the basis of her mission in the world, among the peoples of the earth and through their cultures, is to be found exclusively in the revealed will of God. In no way has she any human motive based on power, preeminence or conquest. On the contrary, she claims a mission of service to the One God, and co-extensively of fraternal service to the peoples of the Earth.

Already in the Scriptures of the two Testaments this echoes like an imperative precept. And the Church feels called and solicited directly and continually by both Old and New Testaments. She looks on the Old Testament as a concrete reality that is hers rather than something foreign, almost accidental and distant, even if it is to be studied on the basis of the plenitude brought by the New Testament. For this reason she has always reaffirmed and still maintains her links with the Jews.

A. *The Specific Precept of Mission*

1. The Church is firmly conscious of having as her own the great precept of the Old Testament, fulfilled and renewed by the New Testament, of making known the Name of the One God among the peoples of the earth in all eras (cf. *infra*). The Lord in his infinite majesty as in his goodness has himself revealed his one true Name, the only authentic one (Ex 3:15), the one that is to be worshipped and to be invoked with fear and faith as well as with love (Ex 23:13). Hence, the people he chose for himself will be distinguished from every other people by their calling upon the Name in praise, commemoration, invocation and petition. It is a "terrible" Name (Deut 28:5), eternal (Ps 135:13), all holy (Ps 99:3,5,9), sanctified (Is 29:23), praised, thanked and invoked (Ps 7:18), loved (Ps 5:12). To invoke the divine Name, but not in vain (Ex 20:7; Deut 5:11), that means the attainment of salvation (Joel [Hebrew] 3:5; [RSV] 2:32).

2. It is therefore necessary that the people God himself chose for his merciful plan should carry to other peoples, but always and only through the sole grace of the One God, "to invoke the Name of the Lord and serve him with one shoulder (adoration)" (Zeph 3:9). This is the universalist opening that rings forth from the Old Testament, whether in the Torah of Moses (for example, in the "covenant of brotherhood" of Abraham the common father: Gen 12:1–3), or in the Prophets (cf. Is 2:1–5; 10:33–11:10; 25:6–12; 49:1–6; 56:1–

8; 60; 66:7–23; Jer 16:19–21; Jon and others), or in the wisdom books and the psalms.

3. But the Lord himself has sent out severe and clear prophetic warnings that he will not tolerate on any account that his people "make his name blasphemed" among the nations (cf. Ez 36:16–23; cf. also Deut; other Prophets; and in the New Testament, Christ, for example in Lk 6:17–49; Paul, Rom 2:24, that recalls Is 52:5; 1 Tim 6:1; Tit 2:5; 1 Pet 4:4; Jas 2:7).

4. Because in fact, the mission of the people of God in all ages and on the earth is always to "sanctify the Name (*Kiddush ha-Shem*)" in the world and among peoples (Ex 9:16; Is 29:23; cf. Num 20:23; cf. Is 8:13; Ez 20:41; 28:22,25; 36:23; 38:16,23; Mal 1:11,14).

5. In the New Testament the person of Christ, Lord and God (Jn 20:29) is represented both as the continuing of the prophetic line of the Old Testament, and as something new, so that he is central and stands as the source of the very complex and heavily weighted historical and spiritual consequences. Christ himself, in the wake of the Old Testament, places the precept "hallow the divine Name" in first place in the Lord's prayer or "Our Father", when he taught it to his disciples (Mt 6:9; Lk 11:2; see also the synagogal parallel in the liturgical *Kaddish*), which is then made more explicit by apostolic men (thus in Heb 13:15; see also Rom 9:17; in the difficult context of "the mystery of Israel", actually quoting Ex 9:16; cf. texts like Eph 3). Christ makes known the fullness of the divine Name in a new way to his disciples of all times, the divine Name that is "the God and Father of our Lord Jesus Christ", ineffable and tremendous object of adoring love (cf. for example, Jn 17, the whole chapter; and the "incipit" (openings) of the Pauline epistles).

6. The person of Christ, Lord and Master, together with his teaching and that of the apostles, commit Christians of all times, therefore, to consider themselves in the historical and prophetical line of the biblical covenant, and in a perspective above nationality, as "a chosen race, a royal priesthood, a dedicated nation, and a people claimed by God for his own to proclaim his triumphs . . ." (1 Pet 2:9, which is a re-reading of Ex 19:5–6, with Old Testament parallels).

7. Both before and after his resurrection, Christ ordered his faithful disciples to continue his self-same mission: to proclaim the Name of God and Father, and all the salvific reality that springs from it as from a unique, prodigious source: his justice and mercy, his kingdom of salvation through love, the fraternity among all men, the return to the home of the common Father in a spirit of conversion of heart (*teshuvah*, Greek *epistrophê; niham*, Greek *metánoia*), and the receiving of a neverending gift of divine grace, as in the promise made to the fathers (cf. Mk 1:14–15; Mt 28:16–20; Mk 16:15–20; Acts 1:8

and other texts). Therefore the Lord gives his spirit (cf. Lk 24:2; Acts 2:1–11; Jn 20:21–23).

8. Basing ourselves on the latest analysis of New Testament texts, we can state that primitive missionary methodology was founded on the fact that Christ himself and therefore the apostles, conscious of belonging to their people, the chosen people of God, had at first wanted to involve and associate Israel in the mission of universal salvation among the nations, understood emphatically as unique in the divine plan. The Church has never wanted to operate alone. Hence she had first to turn to the house of Israel (Mt 9:35–11:1, Christ's messianic ministry and "missionary discourse" addressed to his apostles, cf. especially vss. 10:5–10; Acts 2:13–40; 3:16–26; 7:1–53; 13:14–41 and 44–47; 18:4–9; 22:1–21; 28:17–28, and others). Only afterwards they would have turned to the pagan peoples who stood outside the covenant with the fathers in the renewal brought about by Christ (cf. Mt. 28:16–20; Acts 10:34–48; 13:46–52; 14:15–17; 17:16–34; 19; 20; 26:1–23; 28:30–31).

9. The best-known New Testament missionary experience, that of Paul, enabled him, however, to get to the bottom of the difficult problematic of relationships between the new community of the faithful, the Church, and historical Israel, that came up immediately in dramatic terms. This problematic is to be found in the fundamental text of Romans 9:1–11,36 (which, however, should be read in the global context of many other New Testament texts), but has often not been sufficiently explored in its presuppositions, its dynamic reality and its ultimate consequences. When re-examined, the Pauline text allows us to conclude respectfully and with all reserve due to possible ulterior exploration and acquisitions, that the mission of the Church to Israel consists rather in a Christian life lived in total fidelity to the One God and his revealed Word, so that Jews and Christians emulate each other in their turning to God (cf. e.g. Rom 11:11,14), and this is the universal salvation of the Jews and all peoples. In brief, Paul admonishes his churches that the Israelites, because of the irreversible divine election given by the faithful and living divine Word, to the fathers (cf. 9:4–5), are God's "beloved" (Rom 11:28), because—unlike men who are always sinners—God is unchangeably "the Faithful One" to himself and therefore towards Israel. "God's gifts and call are without repentance" (Rom 11:29). Hence the Church in the course of ages, and today with the emerging of various principles and avenues of research, has felt and feels towards the Jews a variety of attitudes: respect for their mission, desire to find common forms of testifying to the divine Name in the world, particularly in the modern world that is losing every feeling of the divine and of transcendence; in other periods, for a long time, the desire to embrace Israel through conversion to Christianity. Today in the Church there is a renewed

feeling that in any case the people God has chosen for himself is "the people of divine praise" (cf. for example *Ad Gentes* 2, on the mission to non-Christian peoples).

10. Here it should be emphatically stated as is affirmed in many contexts (cf. *Lumen Gentium* 16; *Dei Verbum* 14–16; *Nostra Aetate* 4; *Guidelines and* *Suggestions for Implementing the Conciliar Declaration "Nostra Aetate" No. 4*, espec. par. III), and more and more studied by various ecclesial currents, that no inspired Christian sources can warrant our supposing that the Lord's covenant with his people Israel has been abrogated and almost reduced to nothing (cf. above, B 2). And this, even if the events of the Christian Easter and Pentecost, for example in Luke's intense view, have given the Church—that for Luke is Israel—the deep conviction of having obtained, in its beginnings but very really from God, the object of Israel's messianism.

B. Mission to Peoples and Cultures in History

1. The Church, therefore, has obeyed the powerful precept of her Lord to proclaim the Name of the One God to the world and all peoples, up to this very day. This has been an incredible two-thousand-year effort that has been substantially uninterrupted in spite of adverse human events. Paul VI's pontifical exhortation *Evangelii Nuntiandi* (8 Dec. 1975) traces clearly the perennial conditions of the Church's mission starting from Jesus Christ the Lord, in its necessary adaptation to the situation of today's world.

2. The Church has always proclaimed to the world the God she worships, the God of Israel, the God of Abraham, the God of Isaac, the God of Jacob, the God of Moses (Ex 3:6; cf. quotation made by Jesus, Mk 12:26–27 and parallels), the God of David, the God of the Suffering Servant, the God of Jesus Christ. He is the hidden Lord, the Lord of Israel, the Savior (Is 45:15). He is the Lord Creator, Provider, Father, "compassionate and gracious" (Ex 34:5–8; Ps 103:8) "He gives food to all his creatures; his love endures for ever" (Ps 136:25, the great Paschal *Hallel*), who maintains his promise to the fathers (Ps 105:42–45; 106:45–47) in a continuous divine "memorial", perpetually realizing it for his people and extending it to the gentiles, but carrying it out and propagating it most of all through Jesus Christ servant, poor, meek and humble (Acts 10:34–43; 13:16–41).

3. In the course of centuries, then, the Church has brought innumerable peoples, kingdoms and human cultures to faith and love of the only living Lord, who ever manifests that he has acted and acts with great and terrible deeds in the history of his people, "with efficacious actions and with his words" (thus in *Dei Verbum* 2). And that the Lord has also acted and acts in

the history of the nations of the earth, in the periods of the Old and New Testaments, and in the course of worldly events, according to his inscrutable wisdom. These are efficacious acts of goodness and mercy, pardon and calling, the recovering of the lost and entry into the messianic kingdom of those God himself has saved; and there are also severe but just "signs" to call to the needed conversion of heart. The Church would have operated more widely in the world had it not been for repeated historical obstacles, particularly in the East. But also and no less harmful were the irreparable schisms, the behavior involving ambiguity, compromises, errors of realization, intemperance and cruelty, which nearly always slowed down, and often wholly frustrated, the urgency and efforts of the mission, causing obvious infidelity to the authentic way of "proclaiming the divine Name".

4. Without triumphalism, but only conscious of her own mission, it can be stated that the Church meditates on the revealed but ineffable mystery of the divine goodness, by which throughout the ages not only did many people reach the adoration and sanctification of the Name, but this Name is at least known in the whole world. And the substance of the biblical message, centered on Christ, Son of God and Son of Man, who died and rose for love, is therefore a message of justice, goodness, humanity, wisdom, liberty, equality, fraternity, total peace, aspiration to a full development of men and human societies, which has become a universal patrimony, even though many, whether cultures or individuals, do not realize it.

5. In this uninterrupted mission, even through insurmountable obstacles, men have been offered the laborious but sure way that, through the saving proclamation of the death and resurrection of Christ, carries all the brethren united among themselves by a common bond of solidarity, towards the one God and Lord, to love, recognize, thank and adore him. And this salvific dynamic faith has manifested and will manifest the complete liberation of man, with effective results even in the field of social relationships. This has been reaffirmed also in Paul VI's recent apostolic exhortation *Evangelii Nuntiandi* (8 Dec. 1975), that is a kind of "summa" of missionary action and witness of the Catholic Church today in the world.

6. It can be stated that besides this, the Church does not ignore that according to the revealed divine global plan, Israel has an important fundamental work to do, which originates in the "sanctification of the Name" in the world.

7. And she knows with certainty that the "honor of the Name" is conditioned by the salvation of the Jewish people who are the original nucleus of the divine plan of salvation.

8. And because of her fidelity to Jesus Christ the Lord, which she can never relinquish, the Church must proclaim to the world that Christ himself,

with his life, his word, his works, his death and resurrection, has not made void the divine plan, but rather, coming in his humility and meekness, in poverty and service, he is the living, efficacious synthesis of the divine promise to give the Spirit of God to man.

C. Christian Life as Witness

1. Today, in spite of every existing temptation to the contrary, in the Catholic Church it becomes clearer that the mission received from her Lord and Master is before everything else a life lived in fidelity to God and men; it is unity in love, respect for all brethren, service excluding no one, sacrifice and goodness, as is clear from the biblical announcement, confirmed by the Master the very evening he accepted to die for all men (cf. Jn 13:1–17:26).

2. Hence, obviously, there is a severe rejection of and denial of inauthentic missionary methods which, while proclaiming the Lord and his Kingdom to men, fail to urge the herald of the proclamation and the witness to live already according to this same reality (cf. Paul's stern remarks in 1 Cor 9:27). In this lack of effort there is not the awareness of having to ask pardon of the common Father and men our brothers, every time that in the course of history our neighbor has suffered from our wrongful actions.

3. It seems as if today, when individuals or groups from various Christian milieux are asserting an increasing fidelity to the Lord and his revealed word, with greater awareness of being and acting in the world, and desire of renewal, faithful Christians better understand the fundamental need to lead a life lived to the full.

4. In the same way today we have to realize and continually remind all Christians, that it is the faithful Jews, who "sanctify the divine Name" in the world, living in justice and holiness and causing the divine gifts to bear fruit, who are a true witness to the whole world to the destiny of the Jewish people. Hence today in the Church deep research is being done on the permanence of the Jewish people according to the divine plan (cf. above n. I, A, 10, conciliar texts).

D. Witness as a Vital Necessity

1. From the divine plan of salvation, contemplated in faith and love, adoring the divine inscrutable wisdom and majesty, the Church derives the awareness of the absolute necessity constitutive of her mission in the world among peoples. She shares the anxiety that already existed in the earliest beginnings of the Church itself (cf. 1 Cor 9:16: "Woe is me if I do not announce

the Gospel!''), which is never absent, and has been reaffirmed clearly by Vatican II (cf. *Lumen Gentium; Ad Gentes; Christus Dominus; Dei Verbum; Gaudium et Spes,* and other documents, like *Evangelii Nuntiandi,* e.g. 21,26,41,76).

2. There is first the life lived, and then the messianic missionary proclamation to those who have not yet received the divine salvific Word, or those who unfortunately have not for various reasons responded, and lastly those who, having received it, do not live it and even despise and fight it. But it must be made clear to everyone that, as has often been said, the Church preaches first to herself the reality she has to live, and then carries it to others (cf. above, 1 Cor 9:27; *Evangelii Nuntiandi* 15), so that the mission may not be contradicted by facts.

3. It cannot be denied that the Church's mission, though coming from the divine will and gifted and guided by divine grace, is carried out by men, and so will never be perfect because of the possible behavior of Christians: their erroneous judgments on facts and men and methods, and the activities that the centuries have shown to contradict the mission itself; their betrayal of the original mission, self-interested view of the mission, lack of respect for the interlocutors and their cultures, and blindness to values in other religions (cf. above, I, B, 3).

4. Vatican II has explicitly examined these facts, recognized prevarications and insufficiencies, excluded what does not correspond with the original biblical mission, urged new methods and behavior more in line with the actual situation of the Church and men of today. She has more than once, especially in the declaration *Nostra Aetate*, expressed her esteem for the values of other religions and the urgent need to know them and dialogue with them (cf. above).

II. UNWARRANTED PROSELYTISM IS REJECTED

A. *Unwarranted Proselytism*

1. Many Christians, especially during and after the last war, and with the conciliar experience, have awoken to the fact that after two millennia of misunderstanding, particularly of contempt, and moral, spiritual and physical persecution, the attack on the very existence of the Jewish people as such and because they were Jews, with deliberate diabolical intent (in which Christian responsibility cannot be passed over), make it urgent that a fresh study be made, not only of the destiny, permanence and mission of the Jewish people,

but also of general anthropology. Previous contacts with the Jews, and now in a renewed climate the developed possibilities of collaboration in social fields, open up new perspectives that should not be neglected.

2. On October 28, 1965, the Second Vatican Council promulgated the declaration *Nostra Aetate* on the relations between the Catholic Church and non-Christian religions, in which section 4 is dedicated to relations with the Jews. It is of great importance as the first document of its kind, and its contents definitively approved, though still open to improvement, have given rise to an irreversible movement.

3. On December 1, 1974, this same Commission for Religious Relations with the Jews published its first document to implement *Nostra Aetate* 4, entitled *Guidelines and Suggestions for Implementing the Conciliar Declaration "Nostra Aetate" No. 4*. After an introduction this document deals with: Dialogue, Liturgy, Teaching and Education, and Joint Social Action. We refer to this document and to *Nostra Aetate* 4, as the only complete context. With this, then, a new phase in the relations and action of the Church towards the Jews has opened, geared above all towards eliminating, as far as it is possible today, the numerous and persistent misunderstandings in this field.

4. Here we wish to make a few points on the difficult question of proselytism that has alienated and still alienates so many people.

5. Already, on May 1, 1970 the Joint Working Group between the Roman Catholic Church and the World Council of Churches had published their Third Official Report with two annexes: I. Report on the Common Activities of the Joint Working Group, and II. Study Document on Common Witness and Proselytism. It is Appendix II which interests us most. Though dealing with proselytism among various Christian groups, it gives by analogy a good basis for treating every kind of proselytism, with accurate analyses and a new working method. We refer to this document also because for various reasons it had not the effect its importance deserved, and up to now has not had sufficient influence (cf. *Service d'Information* published by the Secretariat for Christian Unity, No. 14, avril 1971/II, pp. 14–24, especially pp. 19–20).

6. Ecumenical experience of the past few years has among other problems brought to the surface the most serious of all, that is, proselytism among Christian Churches themselves and then in relationship to other religions and religious groups.

7. Vatican II itself, especially with its Declaration on Religious Liberty, *Dignitatis Humanae*, and then in the decree on ecumenism, *Unitatis Redintegratio*, in the Pastoral Constitution on the Church in the Modern World, *Gaudium et Spes*, and in other documents, has studied the problem of proselytism, which ruins relations with other religious groups.

8. First we must distinguish clearly between mission and "Christian witness" (cf. above, on the mission to the world), and "proselytism".

9. "Witness" signifies a variety of realities. From Scripture itself derive various terms that reveal particular aspects of the proclamation of the Gospel in word and act, for example "evangelization", "kerygma", "announcement", "message", "apostolate", "mission", "confession", "testimony", and others. For the abovementioned Joint Working Group, the most suitable term seemed that of "witness". By this is understood the permanent action in which the Christian or a Christian community proclaims the action of God in history, and tries to show how with Christ has come the "true light that enlightens every man" (Jn 1:9). Hence, the whole of life: worship, responsible service, proclamation of the Gospel, all, in brief, that is done by Christians under the inspiration of the Holy Spirit for the salvation of men and to gather them together in the one and only body of Christ (cf. Col 1:18; Eph 1:22–23), tends only towards the gaining of eternal life, which is to know the living God and his messenger Jesus Christ (cf. Jn 17:3). But today even Christian witness leads to possibilities of common action in the limitless sphere of "social" action, where there are endless opportunities for collaboration, so that Christians show in their deeds the face of Christ the Servant (cf. e.g. *Unitatis Redintegratio* 12; *Guidelines and Suggestions IV*).

10. Such witnessing that Christians of various denominations tend now to regard as common, runs up against the problem of religious liberty. This expression "religious liberty" is not used here with its full biblical significance (e.g. Rom 8:21; cf. also Gal 5:1). It concerns the primordial inalienable right of physical persons and the community to enjoy social and civil liberty in religious matters. Every person and community has the right to be exempt from constriction on the part of other persons or groups or any human power, whether cultural, economic, political or religious. No person or community should ever be forced for any motive whatever to act against his convictions and his conscience, nor should he ever be prevented from manifesting his faith by teaching, worship, publications, social action. Here we refer to the Declaration of Human Rights of the United Nations (1948) especially article 18.

11. The term "proselytism" in certain linguistic, cultural or denominational contexts has assumed, when unqualified, a pejorative sense. In other contexts, however, when "proselytism" has kept its original meaning of zeal for the propagation of the faith, it should always be qualified, and in the unacceptable sense it should be specified with expressions such as "unwarranted proselytism" or similar terms that indicate clearly reprehensible attitudes and ways of acting that are to be rejected.

12. Here by "unwarranted proselytism" we understand an attitude and

action that stands outside Christian witness. It includes, in fact, anything that forces and violates the right of every person or human community to be free from external and internal constrictions in matters of religion, or else embraces ways of proclaiming the Gospel that are not in harmony with God's ways when he invites man to respond freely to his call and to serve him in spirit and in truth (cf. *Evangelii Nuntiandi* 39).

13. Therefore, the Church clearly rejects every form of unwarranted proselytism. Excluded, then, is every kind of testimony and preaching that in any way becomes a physical, moral, psychological or cultural constraint on the Jews, as individuals or as a community, that could in any way destroy or even diminish personal judgment, free will, full autonomy to decide, either personal or communitarian.

14. Excluded also is every kind of disqualifying judgment, contempt or prejudice that could be levelled against the Jewish people or individual Jews as such, or against their faith, their worship, their culture in general and their religious culture in particular; against their past and present history, their existence and the meaning of their existence. Excluded also are odious types of discussion, especially those harmful forms already condemned by *Nostra Aetate* 4 and by *Guidelines and Suggestions,* which try to exalt the Christian religion or Christianity as such by discrediting Jewish religion and Judaism, whether past or present.

15. We are reminded also of the rejection of any action that aims at changing the religious faith of the Jews, whether in groups, minorities, or individual persons, by making more or less open offers of protection, legal, material, cultural, political and other advantages, using educational or social assistance pretexts. Particularly excluded is any such action or behavior directed towards children, old people, the sick, or adolescents still searching for their place in society. Still more is excluded every kind of threat and coercion even when it is indirect or concealed. Liberty of conscience as an inalienable right of the human person and human groups, should therefore be guaranteed from every possible attack and coercion at every level, exterior and interior, physical and moral.

16. Although the times and methods of forced conversion of Jews, of obligatory catechesis and compulsory preaching imposed by the surrounding Christian majority have irreversibly ceased, and indeed have been rejected and deprecated, nevertheless there remains in the religious press and Christian behavior the ever-present latent danger of pressure exercized on individuals or groups of Jews. In a contradictory and blameworthy manner, "conversion" is still expected of them, while at the same time we ourselves are not prepared to strive after "conversion of heart" to God and our brethren.

17. Today, in fact, it is openly acknowledged in the Church, as Vatican II has repeatedly and insistently stressed, that "conversion" understood as the passage from one faith or religious denomination to another is included in the inalienable statute of liberty of religious conscience, as an intangible process in which there is interaction between divine grace and man's response. Indeed no "conversion" is authentic if it does not result in a spiritual deepening in the religious consciousness of the one who, never without distress, takes such a step.

18. For this reason, the temptation to create organizations of any kind, especially for education or social assistance, to "convert" Jews, is to be rejected. On the contrary, we should encourage every effort to gain greater knowledge of the history of Israel, beginning with the Bible, and to explore in depth the existence, history and mission of Israel, her historical survival, her election and call, her privileges recognized in the New Testament (cf. again Rom (9:4–5; 11:29), in the light, if one is a true Christian, of God's message of love and mercy brought by Jesus Christ in the Spirit of God, never failing to listen to what the Jews themselves say (cf. below, on dialogue: *Guidelines and Suggestions,* Introduction, 5).

19. All this is openly expressed, without mental reservations, in the series of official Church texts (cf. above). Thus should the works be visible and glory be given to the Father (cf. Mt 5:16), so that men may finally discover the face of their brother, bearer of the one common image and likeness of the Omnipotent Lord, who is kind and a rewarder of men (cf. Gen 1:26–27).

B. *New Christian Attitude*

1. Once more we recall the need the Church has to bear witness, to announce and carry out her mission, as outlined above. This is to be understood and performed with the explicit Christian biblical proclamation (cf. *Evangelii Nuntiandi* 22; 29), without ever being tempted to diminish this proclamation (cf. *Evang. Nun.* 32), and with neither ambiguity nor obscurity (cf. *Evang. Nun.* 32). This operation is carried out solely in view of the Church's goal which is the glory of the One God, who is in his turn the unique salvation of mankind. *Lumen Gentium* has set forth clearly for all Christians the theocentric and salvific purpose of the People of God in this world (cf. all *Lumen Gentium* II).

2. The gift of Christian faith, hope and charity cannot be hidden, but by its works all should perceive the divine Glory, with the Christian awareness that every man who adores the One God is the object of the grace of the Spirit of God, and is not concerned with mere human success.

3. The Catholic Church, therefore, aware of her mission, appears today renewed in spirit and attitude. She is prepared to trust men openly, as she is ready to receive them in actual fact. Her sons desire to be "servants of truth" (*Evangelii Nuntiandi* 78) and they want to carry out their Christian mission for pure love (*Evang. Nun.* 79).

4. The already perceptible renewal in action, as has been recalled above, is destined to grow and become more universal, deep and accelerated in the coming years. On the level of organisms set up by the Church for relations with other religions, it is possible to grasp the real intentions of the Church herself. The grassroots will be more and more vitally influenced.

III. THE CATHOLIC CHURCH AND DIALOGUE

1. Among the most important "novelties" in the Catholic Church today, emerge very clearly the will and attitude of "dialogue" whether with other Christian churches, or the adorers of the God of Abraham (Jews and Muslims), or with the followers of other world religions and—with the necessary distinctions—even with atheists. This will of the Church was set out clearly after the pioneers had done their work in Vatican II assemblies, and it was summed up by Paul VI in his first encyclical, *Ecclesiam Suam* (1964). Study and action have brought it to what is now an advanced stage. The principles for initiating dialogue were already set down in detail in *Nostra Aetate* 4, and then more analytically and practically in *Guidelines and Suggestions,* especially in the introduction and paragraph I on dialogue.

2. Basic presuppositions for dialogue are respect and acceptance of the "other" in his intangible human, cultural, historical, spiritual and religious reality.

3. Decisive for the development of dialogical awareness between Christians have been the substantial contributions of Jewish thinkers (above all Martin Buber). Their assiduous frequentation of the Bible and hassidic spirituality showed and deepened the meaning of faith in a personal God, creator and savior, from whom alone comes the dignity of the human subject and the reality of his ontological relation with the "other", the community and God.

4. This aura of interpersonal relationships of which the Hebrew Bible is full is not absent in the Chrisatian sections of the Bible itself; in fact it becomes universalized, describing every interhuman relationship in cogent terms of fraternity and service. To respect another man's conscience, above all if it is weak, to carry his burden, feel oneself his debtor, accept him in his existential condition, to meet his deepest desires, respond to his demand for growth

and affirmation, all these are categorical imperatives of New Testament morality, which bring dialogue into the very order of existence and daily behavior.

5. It is evident, however, that in such imperatives there is an implicit will to testify and communicate, which is not abstract and doctrinal but very concrete, which does not take the form of dictating or conquest, but is response and participation. It offers men through existential experience the specific contribution of the Christian being. This is to obey the invitation we read of in the New Testament: "Always be ready to give a reason for the hope that is in you, gently, with respect and a sincere conscience" (1 Pet 3:15–16).

6. In this way dialogue becomes one of the main types of communication of the Church with the men of our time. Indeed, it has been noted authoritatively that dialogue is the way of communication par excellence of adult society. Hence it is neither betrayal nor disguise of the essential constitutive mission of the Church and the whole people of God to bear witness to the Glory of God in the world, "to sanctify the Name". Dialogue co-exists, however, with other forms of communication in the Church, such as the permanent evangelization of herself, the proclamation, catechesis, pastoral activity (see above) and mission of evangelization in the strict sense, that is, directed to the building up of a new community of adorers and glorifiers of God in spirit and in truth. But dialogue is essentially an action of giving and receiving, of attentive listening and full response, total respect and generous offering, the whole already expressed in existence before being uttered in words (see above). It is quite clear that this is carried out and developed on various levels that extend from a "thaw" in relationships to sympathy, to deepened knowledge and collaboration in common aims and objectives. Among these last, many practical questions necessary in the social and international fields can be usefully stated and resolved in common dialogued agreement. Hence a long trajectory has begun in which exchanges and interaction should be assiduous, and a clear vision of reciprocity and intercommunication (*partage*, sharing).

7. Dialogue, to be sincere, demands authentic self-discipline. Every temptation to exclusivism must be eliminated as also any imperialism or self-sufficiency. On the other hand there must be fidelity and dedicated personal searching, avoiding any form of relativism and syncretism that would try artificially to combine irreconcilable elements. Once the spiritual identity of the one and the other is guaranteed, there must be mutual esteem and respect (theological as well), and the conviction that every growth and bettering in the spiritual field comes about with the other's contribution. In this process it sometimes happens that dialogue with the other helps to discover new dimensions and valencies of one's own faith, and above all it teaches how to live it

in humility and docility of spirit, looking to the "riches God has given to men" (*Ad Gentes* 11).

8. A knotty problem inherent in dialogue is the question raised by Paul VI in his discourse on the opening of the Synod of Bishops (September 19, 1974): "How can we reconcile respect of persons and civilizations and sincere dialogue with them . . . with the universalism of the mission Christ entrusted to the Church?" On this point, existence and experience can offer sincere, realistic words and deeds. In general the evangelical message has no intention of destroying what is valid and typical in the religious experience of men of all faiths. It is presented with various biblical images, among others, that of grafting. As such, it does not alienate nor depersonalize, but confers a new dimension that restructures all that has gone before. Besides this, it demands of Christians at the same time conversion and breaking off, while teaching that it is difficult to foresee how there can be peaceful confrontations and separations, restructuration without triumphalism, unless in the knowledge that "he who wants to save his life will lose it, and he who loses it will save it" (cf. Mk 8:35).

9. The central intuitions of other religious faiths may in their turn enrich the Christian, offering him fresh possibilities of expression, arousing in him valencies and potentialities that were formerly latent. But this can come about still more in contact with the Jewish tradition and its exegetical, liturgical and mystical treasures, its religious and philosophical thought.

10. If this is true of other religions in relationship with Christians, how much more is it with the Jewish religion, to which Christians are and remain united by so many unbreakable ties. For this reason, of all dialogue, that with the Jews is and remains for Christians one of singular and exemplary value. Moreover, when Christians enter into dialogue they take up a new attitude, made up mainly of the will and capacity of listening to the Jews who want to speak of themselves and of their vision of reality, and letting themselves be taught, wanting to learn with a grateful heart. Thus will be avoided the harm, even involuntary, of trying to understand Judaism by interpreting it through the projection of categories alien to it.

6
Catechetics and Judaism:
1977 Synod
[from SIDIC]

On October 18, 1977, during the deliberations of the Roman Catholic bishops gathered in Rome for the Synod on catechetics in our time, Cardinal Willebrands (President of the Secretariat for Christian Unity) made a written presentation on the subject "Catechetics and Judaism".

For many Christians the Synod of 1977 was to have been a door opening up for catechetics the possibility of embarking on the broad lines traced by the Council, such as a scriptural deepening on the part of Christians and renewed dialogue with Jews. "The New Testament is profoundly marked by its relation to the Old", stated the Vatican Guidelines *of December 1, 1974, and "Christians must therefore strive to acquire a better knowledge of the basic components of the religious tradition of Judaism; they must strive to learn by what essential traits the Jews define themselves in the light of their own religious experience".*

The Synod was disappointing in this regard, for it made no allusion to the necessity of reinserting the Bible into catechetics, the Bible in its totality and its dynamism. It is in this context that the intervention of Cardinal Willebrands is important: as a reminder of the basic points in the Guidelines, *and as a warning to pastors of the danger flowing from the official silence.*

It seems important that, in a discussion on catechetics, especially for young people and children, as is going on in this assembly of the Synod, the question of the image of Judaism in catechetical teaching be raised. The reason is twofold: on the one hand, it is impossible—theologically and practically—to present Christianity without referring to Judaism, at least as it is found in the pages of the Old Testament, and also as it really was at the time of the New Testament. And, on the other hand, because the image of Judaism used to illustrate Christianity in Christian teaching is seldom exact, faithful and respectful of the theological and historical reality of Judaism.

For these reasons it seems useful to offer some material, taken from official documents of the Church, on how to present Judaism in our catechetical teaching.

The Second Vatican Council, after a general presentation of the relations between Christianity and Judaism, states: "All should see to it then, that in catechetical work and in the preaching of the Word of God they teach nothing save what conforms to the truth of the Gospel and the spirit of Christ" (*Nostra Aetate,* No. 4). This principle appears as a conclusion of the previous developments in which some very practical points emerge, which are also taken up by the recent *Guidelines and Suggestions for Implementing the Conciliar Declaration "Nostra Aetate" No. 4,* published by the Commission for Religious Relations with the Jews, dated December 1, 1974 (issued in January 1975).

1. A first point of great importance is the relation of one Testament to the other. A catechesis which would not found the revelation of the New Testament upon the revelation of the Old Testament would be a false one. Indeed, it would be in serious danger of falling into the Marcionite heresy because, as the Second Vatican Council says: "Thus the Church of Christ acknowledges that, according to God's saving design, the beginnings of her faith and her election are found already in the patriarchs, Moses and the prophets" (*Nostra Aetate* No. 4). And the *Guidelines* (par. III) say specifically: "The Old Testament and the Jewish tradition founded upon it must not be set against the New Testament in such a way that the former seems to constitute a religion of only justice, fear and legalism, with no appeal to the love of God and neighbour (cf. Deut. 6:5; Lev. 19:18; Mt. 22:34–40)". In fact: "The New Testament is profoundly marked by its relation to the Old." The *continuity* of both Testaments in God's plan, with all respect for the plenitude found in the New Testament, must be a guiding principle in catechesis.

2. Another point of great practical value regards the presentation of Judaism in the time of the New Testament and as a necessary background for the interpretation of the gospels. On these points the *Guidelines* state: "Judaism in the time of Christ and the Apostles was a complex reality, embracing many different trends, many spiritual, religious, social and cultural values." Therefore, all simplification in the presentation of the facts, groups and persons mentioned in the New Testament must be carefully avoided. The *Guidelines* say in another place (par. II): "With respect to liturgical readings, care will be taken to see that homelies based on them will not distort their meaning, especially when it is a question of passages which seem to show the Jewish people as such in an unfavourable light." And, in a note (1), two important

references are made: ''Thus the formula 'the Jews', in St. John, sometimes according to the context means 'the leaders of the Jews' or 'the adversaries of Jesus', terms which express better the thought of the evangelist and avoid appearing to arraign the Jewish people as such. Another example is the use of the words 'pharisee' and 'pharisaism' which have taken on a largely pejorative meaning.'' Apropos the last question, scholars distinguish at least seven classes of Pharisees for the time of the New Testament.

3. There is still another delicate point regarding the interpretation of the New Testament which was taken up by the Council and the *Guidelines,* that is, the responsibility for the death of Jesus. This point comes out necessarily in any catechesis on the life of Our Lord or on the history of redemption. On this the Council has this to say: ''True, the Jewish authorities and those who followed their lead pressed for the death of Christ (cf. John 19:6); still, what happened in his passion cannot be charged against all the Jews, without distinction, then alive, nor against the Jews of today'' (*Nostra Aetate* No. 4). And it goes on to say: ''Besides, Christ underwent his passion and death freely and out of infinite love because of the sins of men in order that all might reach salvation'', thus giving the exact theological meaning of the death of Our Lord. The *Guidelines* (par. III) repeat the first quote as one of the ''facts'' that ''deserve to be recalled''.

4. As a consequence of this last point, another reference made by the Council is quite worth recalling here for the use of catechesis. It deals with the question of the image of the Jews for Christians. The text says: ''Although the Church is the new People of God, the Jews should not be represented as rejected by God or accursed, as if this followed from Holy Scripture'' (*Nostra Aetate* No. 4). Already the Dogmatic Constitution on the Church, *Lumen Gentium,* had said (par. 16): ''In the first place there is the people to whom the covenants and the promises were given and from whom Christ was born according to the flesh (cf. Rom. 9:4-5). On account of the fathers, this people remains most dear to God, for God does not repent of the gifts He makes nor of the calls He issues (Rom. 11:28-29)''. On this the *Guidelines* comment appropriately (par. III): ''The history of Judaism did not end with the destruction of Jerusalem, but rather went on to develop a religious tradition. And, although we believe that the importance and meaning of that tradition were deeply affected by the coming of Christ, it is still nonetheless rich in religious values.'' Therefore, Judaism should not be presented as a dead or useless religion.

Grounded upon these facts, the Commission for Religious Relations with the Jews, created by the Holy Father in November 1974, tries to relate to the Episcopal Conferences to serve them in this important matter of the implementation of the conciliar declaration *Nostra Aetate* No. 4. But it also has tried to relate to Judaism in an official way so as to bring about the desired reconciliation between both religions which have so much in common. To this end a Liaison Committee was created, even before the existence of the Commission itself, with the main Jewish organizations, which is already in the sixth session. Many important questions have been discussed frankly and fraternally in these sessions. It is relevant to note for the present discussion, that the following meeting, fixed for next year, has as its main subject the image of each religion in the teaching system of the other.

We sincerely hope, with the help of Our Lord, that these facts and ideas will promote a better image in the catechetical teaching of the Roman Catholic Church as well as a growing and more fraternal relationship among all the "sons of Abraham" (cf. Rom. 4:11–12).

7
Intervention of Roger Cardinal Etchegaray of Marseilles at a Plenary session of the Synod of Bishops on Reconciliation, Rome, October 4, 1983 [from SIDIC]

In the course of this Synod, my thoughts are turning especially towards the Jewish people because it is certainly this people amongst all peoples which must be the first beneficiary of the double mission of reconciliation and of penitence from the Church in a strictly religious way, because of the original bond which unites Judaism and Christianity.

OUR MISSION OF RECONCILIATION WITH THE JEWISH PEOPLE

We already read in Isaiah 19:25 this extraordinary promise of the Lord:

"Blessed be Egypt my people, and Assyria the work of my hands, and Israel my heritage".

And we see this prophecy accomplished beyond all hope, when St. Paul gives to the Ephesians the most spectacular sign of reconciliation which is the Christ himself.

". . . that he might create in himself one new man in place of the two,[1] so making peace, and might reconcile us both to God in one body through the cross. . ." Eph. 2:15

---

1. That is, Jews and Gentiles.

The Pauline image in the Epistle to the Romans (11:16-24) of the true olive which is Israel on which have been grafted the branches of the wild olive, which are the pagans, allows us to grasp better the privileged nature of our relations with Judaism.

> "Do not boast over the branches. If you do boast, remember it is not you that support the root, but the root that supports you". Rom. 11:18

We have to admit that we have forgotten this Jewish root, which remains holy,

> "For the gifts and the call of God are irrevocable". Rom. 11:29

The great, nay the inevitable question which is put to the Church is that of the permanent vocation of the Jewish people, of its significance for Christians themselves. It is not enough to discover the riches of our common patrimony. Little by little, following the Second Vatican Council, the Church, without losing anything of its originality, is becoming aware that it is all the more flourishing in proportion as it lives from its Jewish root. The perpetuity of the Jewish people does not only carry, for the Church, a problem about external relations which need improving, but an internal problem which touches on its own definition.

Is not this connection, which can only be lived in a peaceful tension, one of the elements of the dynamism of the history of salvation? As in the parable, it recalls that neither of the two sons can gain possession of the entire inheritance; each one is for the other, without jealousy, a witness to the gratuitousness of the Father's mercy. It is also a demanding emulation between the one who awaits a Messiah to come and the one who awaits his return. Franz Rosenzweig, after quoting the Midrash which says:

> "At the death of a Jew, he will only be asked one question: did you hope for redemption?"

used to add:

> "All other questions are for you Christians. From now until then let us prepare ourselves together in faithfulness to appear before the heavenly Judge!"

Such perspectives are somewhat unfamiliar to our minds, even to our ecclesiology. But it is there, it seems to me, that we must advance on a level of exegesis which is difficult to explore. If not, this Judeo-Christian dialogue will remain superficial and full of mental reservations. In proportion as Judaism remains exterior to our history of salvation, we shall be at the mercy of anti-semitic reflexes. We must also consider the break between Israel and the Church as the first schism, the "prototype of schisms" (Claude Tresmontant) in the heart of the people of God.

OUR MISSION OF PENITENCE FOR OUR ATTITUDE TOWARDS THE JEWISH PEOPLE

After defining the limits of our mission of reconciliation with the Jewish people, we must also take seriously our mission of penitence, of repentance for our secular attitude in its regard. No opportunist calculation, no risk of political backlash can force us to conceal from ourselves this duty of justice which, if rightly taken up, must, on the contrary, help us to be in solidarity with all those who come from the same affiliation with Abraham. As the Bishops of a city which contains an important equal number of Jews and Moslems (80,000 of each in a port of one million inhabitants), I can bear witness that both live together in a good understanding and that with the two communities I enjoy good human and pastoral relations.

Let us learn how to ask forgiveness of the Lord and of our brothers who have so often been overwhelmed by the "teaching of contempt" (Jules Isaac) and plunged into the horrors of the Holocaust. Let us set to work so that all may be repaired that must be repaired.

Let us remember the prophets and psalmists, and all the poor of the Lord who, in the long succession of generations, end in Mary, the Daughter of Sion.

But let us remember also their present descendants today, of those who by their fleshly and spiritual understanding of Scripture, by their rejection of idols and so often by their martyrdom, give support to our own faith in the thrice-holy God.

May we, together with God, become a consolation for the Israel of God, his "first-born son" and, by our fidelity, may we obtain the grace to hasten the day of their plenitude and our own, which will be like "life from the dead" Rom. 11:15.

And you yourselves, brothers and sisters who are listening to me here, forgive me for taking you so far and with so much boldness into the "mystery of Israel" glimpsed by a Jew who became the Apostle of the Gentiles.

"O the depth of the riches and wisdom and knowledge of God! . . . For from him and through him and to him are all things. To him be glory for ever. Amen". Rom. 11:33,36

B) U.S. STATEMENTS

8
Guidelines of Archdiocese Galveston-Houston, 1975

I. ON ANTI-SEMITISM IN THE WORLD TODAY

A. Mindful of the rich patrimony we share with the Jews, Catholics should be the very first to decry all forms of hatred, persecution and displays of anti-Semitism directed against Jews at any time and by anyone.

B. It is important for Catholics to see Christian-Jewish relations today in the context of a long history of misunderstanding and even persecution of the Synagogue by the Church. (For information on this subject we suggest the book, *The Anguish of the Jews* by Edward Flannery, Macmillan Pub. 1965; new edition, A Stimulus Book, Paulist Press, 1985.)

C. Catholics should be educated to develop a sharp sensitivity to remarks, policies and practices which are anti-Semitic in nature and be particularly alert to such prejudices in themselves. They should do all in their power to root out such prejudices from our society. For the purposes of these guidelines we define prejudice as the pre-judging of every member of a group assuming of them anything bad we know of some individual members of that group.

D. Disagreement, whether of a religious or political nature, with a Jew or group of Jews need not and should not be construed as anti-Semitism. Dialogue and unity are not served by obscuring our differences but rather by honestly and lovingly sharing and examining them. Dialogue demands that we be in touch with our true feelings and express them openly to each other without fear.

II. ON THE HOLOCAUST

A. It would be impossible to understand the attitude and feelings of the modern Jew without remembering the killing of six million Jews by the Nazis during the II World War. This atrocity, so recently perpetrated, has been fittingly called the Holocaust. The Holocaust has left an indelible mark on the mind and memory of the Jewish people and Christians should share in this remembrance in their effort to understand and love their Jewish brethren. The memory of this tragedy when not only Jews but many Christians and other innocent persons were put to death should motivate us to work together to insure that such violations of human dignity and freedom will never happen again.

B. We deplore the Holocaust and the prejudices and horrors connected with it; nevertheless, we must not live in the past. Our understanding of ourselves as a pilgrim people calls us to learn from the past, live in the present, and prepare for a future without allowing undue guilt feelings to keep us from creating a new and different world.

III. ON THE STATE OF ISRAEL

A. While we have in our own diocesan family many Catholics of Arab descent, we should also become very sensitive to the religious and historic Jewish longing for a nation and a land of their own, a longing reinforced by the tragedy of the Holocaust. We recognize the right of the State of Israel to exist along with other nations of the Middle East who gained their independence as a result of World Wars I and II. Such recognition of these nations does not necessarily imply an endorsement of every political activity and position of their respective governments.

B. Catholics should be mindful of the complexity of the situation in the Middle East and remain respectful of both Arab and Jewish rights and feelings, and look forward to and pray for the day when peace can come.

IV. ON THE COMPARISON AND CONTINUITY OF THE JEWISH AND CHRISTIAN TRADITIONS

A. The II Vatican Council teaches: ''God holds the Jews most dear for the sake of their Fathers; He does not repent of the gifts He makes or of the call He issues.'' (Nostra Aetate, #4) This means that great care must be taken in religion classes and in liturgical celebrations to show that Christianity is deeply rooted in the Jewish religion. On the other hand, it must always be made clear that God did not terminate his special relationship to the chosen people with the advent of Christianity.

B. The Jewishness of Jesus must be constantly kept in mind. He was born of the Jewish people, as were his Apostles and a large number of his first disciples. When he revealed himself as the Messiah and Son of God, the bearer of the new Gospel message, he did so as the fulfillment and perfection of the earlier covenant. And, although his teaching had a profoundly new character, he nevertheless, in many instances, took his stand on the teaching of the Hebrew Scriptures. Jesus also used teaching methods similar to those employed by the rabbis of his time. (Vatican Guidelines)

C. Concerning the Sacred Scriptures, we believe that the New Testament brings out the full meaning of the Old, while the Old and New illumine and explain each other. Concerning the Hebrew Scriptures, the II Vatican Council teaches: "These books give expression to a lively sense of God, contain a store of sublime teachings about God, sound wisdom about human life, and a wonderful treasury of prayers, and in them the mystery of our salvation is present in a hidden way. Christians should receive them with reverence." (Dogmatic Constitution on Divine Revelation, #14,15) When commenting on biblical texts, emphasis should be laid on the *continuity* of our faith with that of the earlier Covenant, without minimizing those elements of Christianity which are original. We believe that those promises were fulfilled with the first coming of Christ. But it is none the less true that *we still await* their perfect fulfillment in his glorious return at the end of time. (Vatican Guidelines)

D. The history of Judaism did not end with the destruction of Jerusalem but rather continued on to develop a religious tradition.

E. The Old Testament and the Jewish tradition founded upon it must not be set against the New Testament in such a way that the former seems to constitute a religion of only justice, fear and legalism with no appeal to the love of God and neighbor. All untrue and unfair comparisons between the two Covenants should be scrupulously avoided, e.g. love and fear, mercy and wrath, gentleness and severity, other-worldliness and this worldliness. It is not enough to shun such ill-founded antitheses used to characterize the two traditions; we must try to see their kinship. For all their differences, Christianity and Judaism are so deeply related that their various attitudes or qualities more often than not supplement each other. They can do so because they have a common patrimony, because they have been shaped by the same spirit.

V. ON PRAYER AND WORSHIP

A. In whatever circumstances as shall prove possible and mutually acceptable Catholics are encouraged to participate in a common meeting with Jews in the presence of God, whether by prayer or by silent meditation.

B. Prayer is a deeply personal reality both for Catholic and Jew and great sensitivity should be exercised in engaging in common prayer with another person. Some will prefer a more conversational style of prayer while others may experience prayer as a silent attention to the Divine Presence.

C. Catholics are encouraged to attend Jewish services on occasion whether for reasons of friendship or education. A visit to a synagogue is an excellent way to learn more about the Jewish religion and worship.

D. Jewish people should be invited to visit Catholic services whether for reasons of friendship or education, but great care should be taken that:

1. There is no appearance of proselytizing during the services or in connection with them.

2. Nothing is said or done during the services which would be offensive to the Jewish people.

E. Interfaith services in which Christians and Jews worship together can be very helpful in strengthening the bond of faith and in asking divine assistance in undertakings of a social nature. Such ceremonies, however, should be carefully pre-planned by representatives of both religions.

F. On occasion a Catholic is asked to offer a prayer at a public gathering, e.g. a meeting of a P.T.A. In such situations great care should be taken in composing the prayer so as to avoid any expression which would offend or exclude the Jewish people or other religious persons present at such public gatherings. An example of such a prayer would be:

> "Almighty and Eternal God, our creator and Father, we ask your blessing on this assembled people. Fill us with your Spirit that we may seek justice and peace in our times. Guide us in our deliberations and empower us to the doing of your Holy Will. Amen."

VI. ON THE NEED FOR DIALOGUE WITH THE JEWISH COMMUNITY

A. Catholics are urged by the recent Vatican Guidelines to make every effort to establish contact and dialogue with the Jews of their community. "To tell the truth, such relations as there have been between Jew and Christian have scarcely ever risen above the level of monologue. From now on, real dialogue must be established." (Vatican Guidelines)

B. Dialogue assumes that there is no conversionary intent in sharing our different traditions as well as our rich common heritage. Catholics should avoid any words and actions of a proselytizing nature in our dialogue with the

Jewish people. It is true that the Church has received from Christ a mandate to bring the gospel to all nations; this universal mission of the Church, however, should never obscure the fundamental rights of religious liberty. "Lest the witness of Catholics to Jesus Christ should give offense to Jews, they must take care to live and spread their Christian faith while maintaining the strictest respect for religious liberty in line with the teaching of the II Vatican Council." (Vatican Guidelines) The fundamental value of freedom in religious faith is given emphasis in the Conciliar document, "Declaration on Religious Freedom," in these words: "Of its very nature the exercise of religion consists before all else in those internal, voluntary, and free acts whereby man sets the course of his life directly toward God. No merely human power can either command or prohibit acts of this kind." (#3)

C. One common pitfall in religious dialogue of any kind, especially between Christian and Jew, is ignorance of the terminology being used by the other party. (Cf. *A Dictionary of the Jewish-Christian Dialogue,* A Stimulus Book, Paulist Press, 1984.)

D. In view of the emphasis of the recent Vatican Guidelines it is recommended that steps be taken immediately to establish in every parish, school and other Catholic institutions structures for dialogue with Jews.

VII. ON THE LITURGICAL PROBLEM

A. The existing links between the Christian liturgy and the Jewish liturgy will be borne in mind. The idea of a living community in the service of God, and in the service of men for the love of God, is just as characteristic of the Jewish liturgy as it is of the Christian one. To improve Christian-Jewish relations, it is important to take cognizance of those common elements of the liturgical life (formulas, feasts, rites, etc.) in which the Scripture holds an essential place. (Vatican Guidelines)

B. With respect to liturgical readings, care will be taken to see that homilies based on them will not distort their meaning, especially when it is a question of passages which seem to show the Jewish people in an unfavorable light. Efforts will be made so to instruct the Christian people that they will understand the true interpretation of all the texts and their meaning for the contemporary believer. In this regard, we call attention to three specific areas of possible misunderstanding:

1. In John's gospel the formula "the Jews" sometimes according to the context means "the leaders of the Jews," or "the adversaries of Jesus," terms which express better the thought of the evangelist and avoid appearing to ar-

raign the Jewish people as such. Obviously, one cannot alter the text of the Holy Scriptures but adequate explanation can be given to the people concerning the true meaning of the passage.

2. For the Jewish people the Pharisee movement in the time of Jesus was a good and positive effort to help the people understand the true meaning of the Law. The words "pharisee" and "pharisaism" therefore should not be used carelessly or indiscriminately as though always applying to hypocritical or evil persons.

3. In many parishes the Passion is read during Holy Week by the celebrant, two lectors and the congregation, each taking a part in the ancient narrative of Jesus' Passion. Care should be exercised to avoid an undue emotional or dramatic tone when reading passages which concern the Jewish role in the Passion.

VIII. ON RESPONSIBILITY FOR THE DEATH OF JESUS

A. Catholics should all avoid all language or impressions which would imply that we hold all the Jewish people collectively, whether past or present, responsible for the death of Jesus. The II Vatican Council teaches: "What happened in Christ's Passion cannot be charged against all the Jews, without distinction, then alive, nor against the Jews of today." (Nostra Aetate, #4)

B. We ask forgiveness of our Jewish brothers and sisters if in the past or present we have consciously or unconsciously contributed to anti-Semitism in the world by attributing to them the guilt for the crucifixion of Jesus.

C. In parochial schools, CCD programs and liturgical celebrations Catholics must be ever alert for references to the Jewish people which would hold them responsible as a people for the death of Christ or otherwise precipitate prejudice. (For more information, we recommend the book, *Catechetics and Prejudice* by John T. Pawlikowski, Paulist Press 1973)

IX. ON INTERMARRIAGE

A. Catholics, and especially priests, should be mindful that in the Jewish community the majority of rabbis and lay people are strongly opposed to intermarriage. When working with a couple of Jewish and Catholic faiths the priest should be very mindful of this fact and do everything possible to assist the couple in meeting the sensitivities and rights of both families. He must also take care that nothing is done to cause a Jewish person to act contrary to his conscience or to alienate himself from his religious community.

B. Both Jews and Christians view marriage as a sign or symbol of the sacred covenant between God and his people. This common heritage should be the basis of a shared religious life between a Catholic and Jew in marriage.

C. The ceremony of an interfaith wedding should be carefully planned beforehand so as to provide a celebration which is in keeping with both traditions and offensive to neither.

D. Rabbis are frequently unwilling to participate in interfaith marriages with a Christian minister for the reason given in A. Priests should keep this in mind when considering the possibility of co-officiating at an interfaith wedding.

E. Concerning the religious upbringing of the children of an interfaith marriage the same principles apply as in an ecumenical marriage:

1. The priest should assist the interfaith couple to reach an agreement which is mutually acceptable to both partners and respectful of the conscience of both partners. If such an agreement cannot be reached in preparing for the wedding, there is reason to at least question the advisability of proceeding with the plans.

2. The Catholic party will be asked to promise that he/she will do all in his/her power to share his/her Christian faith with the children by having them baptized and reared as Catholics. When this is unacceptable to the Jewish partner, a dispensation may be sought from the Holy See, provided no prior agreement has been made that would exclude the possibility of rearing the children in the Catholic faith; and that the Catholic accepts the responsibility to raise the children as Catholics, if possible.

3. In reaching a concrete decision concerning the religious education of children, both partners should remember that neither thereby abdicates the fundamental responsibility of parents to see that their children are instilled with deep and abiding religious values. The religious education of children is the right and responsibility of both parents; it cannot be totally given to one parent and denied to the other.

4. In the event that the children are reared as Christians, care should be taken that they have ample opportunity to visit the synagogue and learn the values and traditions of the Jewish parent.

X. ON RELIGION IN THE JEWISH COMMUNITY

A. Believing Jews in our country follow generally three traditions of religious expression and practice:

1. *Orthodox Judaism*—the more traditional of the three, it regards both the written law of Moses and the oral law of the Rabbis as authoritative and binding and considers that every question facing man today can be answered in the light of these ancient, divine teachings. Orthodox Jews are known for their strict adherence to the beliefs and traditions of the past.

2. *Conservative Judaism*—the religious movement of the center, it attempts to steer a middle course between adherence to the traditions of the past and accommodation to the demands of modern times.

3. *Reform Judaism*—the more liberal of the three groups, it began in the middle of the 19th century, chiefly in Germany and America, as a radical answer to the new discoveries in science, history and comparative religion. Reform Jews seek to be faithful to the principles of Judaism but feel it unnecessary to observe the ancient practices of their people.

B. Many religious Jews practice strict dietary laws. Catholic institutions (hospitals, retreat houses) and hosts should be prepared to take into consideration these dietary laws at any function to which Jewish individuals or guests are invited.

C. In relating to modern Jews it is important for Catholics to be keenly aware that there are today individual Jews who were born of Jewish parents yet who do not believe in God or who question God's existence; who might observe many, a few, none of Judaism's traditions and rituals; and yet who consider themselves, and who are considered by the Jewish community, to be Jewish. These individuals while still considering themselves Jews, have abandoned the religious undergirding which originally set the tone of their lifestyle. In addition, there are those individuals who even have rejected a culturally Jewish life, who are acculturated to the point of assimilation and yet, who still feel themselves a part of the Jewish peoplehood. Catholics, therefore, should not assume that all Jews are religious persons but should be mindful instead of the pluralism and diversity within the American Jewish Community.

XI. ON COOPERATION IN SOCIAL ACTION

Jewish and Christian tradition, founded on the Word of God, is aware of the value of the human person, the image of God. Love of the same God must show itself in effective action for the good of mankind. In the spirit of the prophets, Jews and Christians will work willingly together, seeking social justice and peace at every level—local, national, and international. (Vatican Guidelines) At the same time, such collaboration can do much to foster mutual understanding and esteem.

XII. ON BEING A PILGRIM IN THE WORLD

In their great common patrimony both Jew and Christian can easily identify with the way of the pilgrim. The Jews live in great hope for a future messianic age which is so beautifully described by the prophet Isaiah. Christian prophetical vision also looks forward to the second coming of Christ, a time in which God's Law will be fully revealed and obeyed. ''This is God's dwelling among men. He shall dwell with them and they shall be his people and he shall be their God who is always with them.''

9
Los Angeles Guidelines:
Jewish-Catholic Dialogue, 1977
[from SIDIC]

The following text is an excerpt from Guidelines for Ecumenical and Interreligious Affairs *published by the Archdiocese of Los Angeles, 1977.*

6. Los Angeles has one of the major Jewish communities of the world in terms of size and influence. The Church of Los Angeles has enjoyed a long and deep sense of mutual respect with this community.

7. We acknowledge that the Jewish community has its own sensitivities and concerns. Catholics in dialogue with Jews should be mindful of the following sensitivities which seem to be growing concerns in many portions of the Jewish community:

a. The Holocaust: The mass murder of six million Jews by the Nazis is a painful memory to many American Jews;

b. The State of Israel: To American Jews, Israel is not "their country" but the Israelis are part of "their people";

c. Anti-Semitism: Some view Jews as inferior or reprobate;

d. Proselytizing: Efforts to convert Jews to Christianity; or views of Judaism as an "incomplete faith" are considered unacceptable;

e. Interfaith Marriage: As a small minority, Jews are concerned with preserving a distinct living faith.

8. While these are not intended to be all-inclusive, they are agenda concerns we must sensitively consider. As Catholics we ought to be aware that these issues will influence all dialogue in which the Jewish community becomes involved.

LOCAL DIALOGUES

9. Three distinct local dialogues are encouraged:

Priest-Rabbi Dialogue: In these dialogues priests and rabbis may gradually explore areas of mutual concern and sensitivity. With our scriptural heritage having such a mutuality, it is highly recommended that joint scripture exploration between scholars and clergy of both faiths be encouraged. The Council reminds us that "since the spiritual patrimony common to Christians and Jews is great, this sacred Synod wishes to foster and recommend that mutual understanding and respect which is the fruit above all of biblical and theological studies, and of brotherly dialogue" (*Declaration on the Relationship of the Church to Non-Christian Religions,* 4). St. John's Major Seminary and local rabbinic seminaries are ideal centers for student exploration of our heritage. In addition, homiletic and liturgical studies could counteract a sometimes anti-Semitic Gospel interpretation and do much to develop mutual richness in music, festival and symbol. Since marriage and family life are of extreme concern in both communities, joint study, understanding and action might well aid the struggle in which these institutions find themselves.

Education: Dialogue is a reality that looks both to the present and to the future for a measure of success. The well-developed parochial and secondary religious education systems of the Jewish and Catholic communities in Los Angeles offer a unique opportunity to continue the positive achievements of the Jewish-Catholic dialogue. By exposing students to the religions and by elaborating on the sources common to both, the success of today's dialogue may be assured for the future.

Parish and Synagogue Interaction: If the dialogue between Catholics and Jews is to be thorough and significant, it must also include a grassroots exchange between Catholic and Jewish congregations. Certainly the Easter-Passover liturgical convergence, while presenting some inherent difficulties, does offer an opportune time for interchange. Times such as Thanksgiving present another excellent opportunity for mutual sharing. However, as in any other dialogue, great care, patience and understanding are required. It is suggested that priests and rabbis participate in dialogues on their own level as preparation for a congregational dialogue.

10. In exploring such parish-synagogue interactions, priests and rabbis might find it beneficial to seek suggestions from the Interreligious Commission of the Archdiocese and the Committee on Interreligious Affairs of the Board of Rabbis. There are basic pastoral needs which need careful attention to properly implement the goals of these dialogues:

a. Selectivity in Scripture texts: While the entire Hebrew Scripture or Old Testament is part of Catholic tradition, the New Testament is not part of the Jewish Testament. To avoid offense and mutual misunderstanding, texts for liturgical services or joint scripture study must be selected very carefully.

b. Liturgical Interchange: Such an interchange could consist of attendance at a Catholic or Jewish worship service or a joint prayer service cooperatively and sensitively developed by both traditions.

c. Trinitarian Formulas: While a prayer to the God of Abraham, Isaac and Jacob, the One God of Creation and the Universe, is part of the Catholic experience, the Catholic formulas referring to the Trinity or Jesus as Lord are foreign to the Jewish expression.

d. Correct use of the Seder Service: The Seder Service can be an enriching experience for the Catholic if it is conducted in accordance with authentic Jewish Tradition. We must avoid turning it into a bogus Last Supper meal.

e. Correct Awareness of Holy Days: To insure a clear understanding of the meaning of Holy Days and Sacred Seasons in the context of the respective faiths. Hanukkah must be understood in the light of Jewish History: it is not a Jewish Christmas. Easter must be understood in the light of the Christian belief in the Resurrection: it is not a Christian Passover.

f. Centrality of the Person of Christ: Because of the centrality of Christ in our faith Catholics may experience a sense of shock when exposed to Judaism, in which Christ plays no role. Conversely, the centrality of Christ can be a shock to Jewish observers. Priests and rabbis should be aware of this possibility and should prepare their congregations for these differences.

g. Christian Call to Witness: The obligation to witness our faith may be interpreted by non-Christians as an attempt to denigrate their religious beliefs. In our manifestations of witness, we must be particularly sensitive to avoid any semblance of proselytism. Jews are disturbed when members of so-called "Jesus Movements" (such as "Jews for Jesus") disturb their privacy in the name of Christianity. The Archdiocese is not connected with these movements and recognizes the animosity they may cause.

11. The religious experience connected with the pastoral sacraments and rites of Baptism, Marriage, Confirmation, Bar Mitzvah and Burial should be explored. The ability to express appropriate sentiments on these occasions is one of the basic signs of authentic understanding and respect. Because of its many ecumenical dimensions, we shall explore in detail the official Catholic and Jewish positions regarding marriage.

CATHOLIC-JEWISH MARRIAGES

12. When a Catholic and a Jew decide to enter into marriage, the priest who is helping them prepare a marriage ceremony should be sensitive to the religious conviction and customs of both parties. Neither party to the marriage should be asked to violate the integrity of his or her faith.

13. Priests of the Archdiocese should be aware that the Jewish community is officially in opposition to mixed marriages; they are a prime area of concern and sensitivity within the Jewish community.

14. The official statement of the Board of Rabbis of Southern California, made in response to an inquiry from the Archdiocesan Commission on Ecumenical and Interreligious Affairs, highlights this concern:

> Our Board of Rabbis has issued a statement, as of February 28, 1974, in which we called upon members to refrain from officiating at mixed marriages. This is in accordance with the decision and guidelines established by each of our three rabbinical associations and is in keeping with our on-going Jewish tradition.
>
> Similarly, all of our rabbinical bodies have reaffirmed the historic view of Judaism that Rabbis should not participate with clergymen of other faiths in the performance of marriage ceremonies. Hence Rabbis who do participate with ministers of other faiths in such ceremonies are violating Jewish doctrine and practice and are doing so without the sanction of tradition or the approval of their rabbinic bodies.
>
> Our committee, of course, recognizes that the Catholic religious community establishes regulations for the guidance of its own constituency, but

in the matter referred to us it also seems to touch upon concepts and rites treasured by the Jewish community. The official religious leadership of the Jewish faith would therefore welcome Catholic cooperation in helping to keep intact our accepted standards and views concerning rabbinical participation in Jewish-Catholic marriages.

These regulations should be shared with a Jewish-Catholic couple seeking pastoral advice concerning marriage. The priest should also advise the couple that the Catholic Church does not encourage such marriages; indeed, the Church greatly desires that Catholics marry Catholics. This position stems from a concern for the marital union and the good of the family.

15. If the priest is still asked to assist after sharing this with the Catholic-Jewish couple, the following avenues may be pursued:

a. A priest may officiate at the wedding of a Jew and a Catholic, with a dispensation from the impediment of disparity of worship, in the sanctuary or other part of the Catholic Church, or in any suitable building on the parish grounds.

b. A dispensation from the Catholic form of marriage may be sought so that the Catholic party may marry in a religious ceremony before a rabbi in a temple, or other sacred or private place.

c. If neither of these options is possible, then the Ordinary is prepared to dispense the Catholic party from the Catholic form of marriage so that a public ceremony that is civilly valid will be accepted by the Catholic Church as both licit and valid.

16. Jews may be admitted as witnesses and attendants at a marriage ceremony in a Catholic church. Catholics may act as witnesses and attendants at the wedding of friends who are Jews.

17. When a priest or deacon is invited to participate in the marriage ceremony of two Jews conducted by a Rabbi, he may offer prayers for the couple and invoke God's blessing on them.

18. When a Rabbi is invited to participate in the marriage ceremony of two Catholics conducted by a priest, the Rabbi should be offered a place of honor in the sanctuary and may offer prayers for the couple and invoke God's blessing on them.

10
Archdiocese of Louisville, 1979
Seder Guidelines:
A joint statement of archdiocesan offices

Parishes which choose to hold a Seder Meal to foster a knowledge of the rituals of our Jewish neighbors should be careful:

A) that a study of contemporary Judaism precedes the occasion so that your parishioners understand that this is a living ritual meal, not something of the past or replaced by the Eucharist;

B) that you consider seeking the help of a Jewish couple/family to conduct the ritual correctly; caution should be used in attempting to create any direct ties between Seder and the Last Supper;

C) that the changes you make in the ritual are not destructive to the rite of a true Seder Meal or contrary to the authentic Jewish traditions;

D) that if you are not using an authentic Jewish ritual for the Seder, but are having a Parish meal to celebrate the beginning of the Easter Triduum on Holy Thursday, that you call your meal by another name, e.g., an Agape, which means 'love feast.'

11
Catholic-Jewish Relationship Guidelines Diocese of Brooklyn, November, 1979 [from SIDIC]

INTRODUCTION

1. The term "interreligious" refers to our relationship as Christians with those who are not part of the Christian tradition. These relationships are developed theologically in Conciliar documents such as the *Declaration on the Relationship of the Church to Non-Christian Religions.*

(NOSTRA AETATE)

2. One aim of interreligious dialogue is to foster a deeper understanding of, and respect for, the integrity of other peoples and faiths. Another aim is to identify the basic principles which are the common heritage of the world's great religions. However, it should be clear that interreligious dialogue does not promote homogenization, which may be defined as an attempt to create one religion out of the diverse traditions and sanctities of many religions.

3. In the document alluded to above, the Fathers of the Council made a momentous declaration regarding Judaism and Islam, Hinduism and Buddhism: we are urged to recognize these religions as positive forces with which the Church can and should enter into dialogue. The *Declaration* states: "Let Christians, while witnessing to their own faith and way of life, acknowledge, preserve and encourage the spiritual and moral truths found among non-Christians, also their social life and culture. (*Nostra Aetate, n. 2*)

DIALOGUE

4. Thus, the Church in dialogue is sensitive to the concrete forms in which man is seeking God. The quest for the Absolute and man's experience

of the Absolute is manifold. Through our sensitivity to this diverse richness we can also come to appreciate the special relation of Judaism and Islam to Christianity and the History of Salvation, based on the uniqueness of God's self-revelation through the Law, the Prophets, and His Son.

5. It is important for us to understand the meaning of dialogue. The responsibility to be involved in dialogue does not diminish the mandate of the Church to proclaim Jesus Christ to the world.

> "In virtue of her divine mission, and her very nature, the Church must preach Jesus Christ to the world." *(Vatican Commission—Guidelines, 1974, I).*

Evangelization therefore is a primary responsibility of the Catholic Church.

6. Dialogue does mean that the Church recognizes her duty to foster unity and charity among individuals *(NOSTRA AETATE, N. 1)* and mutual understanding between religious traditions. This means that the Church will show great sensitivity to the concerns of our Jewish brothers and sisters.

> "Lest the witness of Catholics to Jesus Christ should give offense to Jews, they must take care to live and spread their Christian faith while maintaining the strictest respect for religious liberty in line with the teachings of the Second Vatican Council." *(Vatican Commission—Guidelines, 1974, I).*

Even outside the context of official dialogue, the Church respects and esteems non-Christian religions because they are living expressions of the soul of vast groups of people.

CATHOLIC CONCERNS

7. In fairness to our Jewish brothers and sisters we should express to them areas of special sensitivity that flow from our Catholic tradition. There is a wide spectrum of concerns and sensitivities within the Catholic community due to various ethnic and national values, but several are common to all:

a) Respect for life at all its stages. Life itself has value and is to be supported and defended. As Catholics we make no distinctions about respecting one mode of human life more than another.

b) Coupled with this we have a strong regard for the quality of life and a long social doctrine tradition that is now being expressed in terms of liberation from hunger, disease, oppression and ignorance.

c) Moral values and religious teaching is something that is a right of all persons to experience and know. Education is a concern of the family and the state has no monopoly over the children of society. The state should not penalize by double taxation the Catholic family that seeks to exercise the right to educate children in Catholic schools.

d) While the state has many rights it is not society. The demands of the common good limit the actions of government as do the clear rights of individual citizens.

e) A long tradition calls for the acceptance of all people into our community. The alien is to be regarded not as an enemy but as a subject who is to receive welcome and be given hospitality.

f) Voluntary agencies by which love and concern are expressed to people in need are to be fostered and assisted by individual charity and also by government assistance.

JEWISH CONCERNS

8. We should be aware of the special concerns and sensitivities of the Jewish Community. Although there is a very wide spectrum of opinion within the Jewish community, the following concerns are shared by all:

a) *The Holocaust:* The wanton murder of six million Jews by the Nazis weighs very heavily and painfully upon all Jews.

b) *Anti-Semitism:* On the basis of centuries of Jewish suffering and martyrdom at the hands of some who styled themselves as Christians, many Jews cannot escape the fear, either conscious or unconscious, that anti-Semitism, which is so deeply embedded in Western culture, may yet erupt in lesser or greater degree. In dialogue Jews and Christians should be encouraged to probe their deepest feelings toward each other. Sources of interreligious animosity should be identified with openness and candor, and an earnest effort should be made to reach a mature understanding of each other's convictions. Hatred of our neighbors is a grievous sin against the God in Whom both Christians and Jews believe.

c) *State of Israel:* American Jews feel a very strong bond of kinship to Jews throughout the world, and especially to Jews in the State of Israel.

Though American Jews have no political allegiance to Israel, they take very great pride in its accomplishments, in the holy city of Jerusalem, in the new life Israel has made possible for the survivors of the Holocaust and for those Jews who have obtained permission to emigrate from the Soviet Union. To many Jews, indeed as to many Christians, the establishment of the State of Israel represents the fulfillment of the Divine promises set forth in Scripture. American Jews will do whatever is in their power to ensure the security of Israel. Almost all of them contribute to the welfare of the people of Israel through the United Jewish Appeal and other philanthropic agencies.

d) *Proselytizing:* Jews are always highly sensitive to activities that, to them, appear to encourage conversion. It must be remembered that Jews are mindful of the time when overly zealous churchmen used to compel them to attend services in which Judaism was belittled and condemned; in the past forced conversions were not infrequent. Therefore, from the Jewish perspective, efforts to convert Jews to Christianity, whether overt or subtle, or the implication that Judaism is an incomplete faith, are unacceptable and destructive of dialogue. Our conversations with one another should be regarded as forums wherein each side freely expresses its views in the hope of attaining mutual knowledge and understanding. The motivation of dialogue is not conversion.

e) *Interfaith Marriage:* Jews are greatly concerned with preserving the Jewish people and Judaism as its way of life, and experience has demonstrated that intermarriage will inevitably lead to the diminution of the Jewish community.

While the foregoing five topics are not intended to be all-inclusive, they call for careful preparation. As Catholics we ought to be aware that these issues are likely to emerge in every dialogue with members of the Jewish community.

OPPORTUNITIES FOR DIALOGUE

9. a) *Priest-Rabbi Dialogue:* In these dialogues, priests and rabbis will explore areas of mutual concern. Since we share a common scriptural heritage through the Hebrew Bible, the study of Scripture by scholars and clergy of both faiths is highly encouraged. The Second Vatican Council reminds us that "since Christians and Jews have such a common spiritual heritage, this sacred Council wishes to encourage and further mutual understanding and appreciation. This can be obtained, especially, by way of biblical and theological enquiry and through friendly discussions." (*Nostra Aetate,* n. 4)

b) *Seminaries:* Seminaries are ideal centers for student exploration of our heritage. In addition to homiletic and liturgical instruction, care should be given to implementing the 1974 Guidelines of the Vatican Commission for Religious Relations with Jews. Such instruction could counteract a sometimes anti-Semitic Gospel interpretation and do much to develop mutual richness in music, festival, and symbol.

> "With respect to liturgical reading, care will be taken to see that homilies based on them will not distort their meaning, especially when it is a question of passages which seem to show the Jewish people as such in an unfavorable light. Efforts will be made to instruct the Christian people so that they will understand the true interpretation of all the texts and their meaning for the contemporary believer". (*Vatican Commission Guidelines,* 1974, II).

c) *Marriage and Family:* Since marriage and family life, justice and morality are of extreme concern in both communities, joint study, understanding and action might well prove of mutual benefit. It is important that priests and rabbis participate in dialogues about these issues on their own level as a preparation for congregational dialogue.

d) *Education:* The well-developed parochial and secondary religious education system of the Jewish and Catholic communities in Brooklyn and Queens offers a unique opportunity to continue the positive achievements of the Jewish-Catholic dialogue. By exposing students to the religious traditions and by elaborating on the sources common to both, today's dialogue will ensure future good.

e) *Parish and Synagogue Interaction:* If the dialogue between Catholics and Jews is to be thorough and significant, it must also include a grassroots exchange between Catholic and Jewish congregations. However, as in any other dialogue, great care, patience, and understanding are required.

In exploring such parish-synagogue interactions, priests and rabbis might find it beneficial to seek suggestions from the Diocesan Ecumenical Commission and the Catholic-Jewish Relations Committee.

12
Guidelines:
Diocese of Cleveland
1979

One of the most beneficial results of interfaith dialogue has been a greater appreciation by the Catholic Church of its unique relationship to the Jewish people and the Jewish religion. Though it is a fact of history that Jesus himself was Jewish and came to his unique ministry within the People of the Covenant, the positive significance of Judaism for Christianity has not always been acknowledged. History bears witness to fierce past conflicts as well as to present misunderstandings between these two religions.

The best contemporary theology and pastoral practice recognizes that the Church not only finds her roots in God's revelation to Israel on Sinai, but she continues to enrich her own self-understanding by dialogue with the Jewish tradition. Since the Church considers herself as sharing in Israel's election, in Christ (Gal. 3:26-29), Christians should enter dialogue with Judaism with more than a general good will. For by a better understanding of God's relationship to the Jews, they will better understand the relationship of the same God to Christianity.

Our respect and regard for Judaism, therefore, is not for an ancient relic of the distant past. It is God himself who made the Jewish people his own and gave him a divine and irrevocable vocation. So we must recognize that even today the Jewish people "remain most dear to God, for God does not repent of the gifts he makes, nor of the calls he issues." (Lumen Gentium, 16)

Catholic Christians must be called to genuinely repent all forms of anti-Semitism that may survive from unfortunate past polemics, stereotypes and insensitive efforts to proselytize the Jewish people. No one who reverences the name of Christ can harbor even a vestige of bias, hatred, or ill will toward the Jewish people. Priests, Sisters and all those in positions of leadership and influence upon young people must work to counter attitudes that would perpetuate anti-Semitism in subtle social and ethnic practices or expressions.

SPECIFIC POINTS OF IMPORTANCE

1. There should be no derogatory references to Jewish people as "usurers" or "Christ-killers" in any Catholic communication or educational materials.

2. Blaming the Jewish people for the suffering and death of Jesus is both a theological and an historical error. The Church clearly teaches that the sins of all are the reason for Christ's passion and death.

3. Neither the New Testament nor the Church teaches that the Jewish people have been deprived of their divine election.

4. In this light, Catholics must be aware that the Jewish people have a particular and permanent vocation as a "community and covenant with God."

5. It is incorrect to contrast Judaism as the religion of fear with Christianity as the religion of love.

6. In dialogue both Catholics and Jews must be allowed to give full expression to their faith. Differences and tensions in the way each tradition approaches the one Lord of humankind should not be glossed over.

7. Catholic leaders should be knowledgeable of such movements as "Jews for Jesus" and the Jewish response to them.

8. Catholics should be sensitive to the very deep feelings which Jewish people have toward the State of Israel. They should also seek to be correctly informed concerning the complex political differences between Arabs and the people of Israel.

9. The facts and implications of the Nazi attempt to exterminate European Jewry (i.e., The Holocaust) should be well known to Catholics. This tragic event has had a great impact on Jewish people and all people everywhere. We can never forget that this horror took place in what was thought to be "Christian" Europe. We must honestly face the implications that the Holocaust may have on Jewish-Christian relations today.

10. In the joint study of Scripture, points of continuity between the Christian faith and Judaism should be noted. However, key elements that are original to Christianity or those which are unique and of permanent value to the Jewish tradition should be addressed as well.

13
Ecumenical Commission—
Archdiocese of Detroit, 1979
[from SIDIC]

CATHOLIC-JEWISH RELATIONS

1. Attitudes Inconsistent with the Spirit of Christ

a) Cliches and stereotypes derived from past centuries of hostility must be eliminated. Anti-Judaism is a heritage from the ancient world, but it has been increased in Christian times by pseudo-theological arguments. Depicting Jews as "usurers," "conspirators" or even "deicides" is, sadly, still current today. Such charges, whether stemming from hate-groups or found imbedded in Catholic teaching materials, should be denounced.

b) The repeated teaching of the Church has reminded us that to blame the Jewish people for the passion and death of Jesus is a theological and historical error (e.g., the Catechism of the Council of Trent). Although a few Romans and some Roman appointed Jewish "leaders" historically participated in the events surrounding Jesus' death, the Church holds that "Christ underwent his passion and death because of the sins of all."

c) The New Testament does not state that the Jewish people have been deprived of their election. The Scriptures urge us to recognize God's eternal faithfulness to the Covenant He established with the Hebrew people on Sinai (Gen. 12, Ex 21). Therefore, from the Christian viewpoint (cf., Rm 11:1–2), Judaism is to be seen, not "as a relic of a venerable and closed past, but as a reality living on through time." (Statement of French Bishops, Nov. 1973).

d) It is false to contrast Judaism as a religion of fear with Christianity as a religion of love. The fundamental article of Jewish belief, the *Shema Israel,* states, "Thou shalt love the Lord thy God." (Dt. 6:4ff). Equally fundamental is the command to love the neighbor (Lv. 19:18). It is to these same passages that Jesus appeals in his own summation of the essence of the Torah (Mt. 22:34–40).

e) It must be affirmed that contrary to well established reactions, the doctrine of the Pharisees is not opposed to Christianity. The Pharisees strove to make the Law a principle of life for each Jew by interpreting its prescriptions so that they could be adapted to the different circumstances of daily living. Contemporary research has clearly shown that fundamental to the Pharasaic approach was the principle of *Kavanah* (inner meaning, intention, spirit of the Law), a principle fundamental to the writings of the Talmud as well.

When Jesus denounced the attitude and formalism of the teaching of certain Pharisees, he was not questioning this awareness. Indeed, the Talmud itself, much in the manner of Jesus, makes some charges of "Hypocrisy" and "Legalistic" against certain types of over-zealous Pharisees. The very closeness between the Pharisees and the first Christians may be one of the main sources of the friction between the two movements.

2. *Right Understandings of Judaism*

Christians must strive to acquire a better knowledge of the basic components of the religious tradition of Judaism; they must strive to learn by what essential traits the Jews define themselves in the light of their own religious experience. (Vatican Commission for Religious Relations with the Jews, Jan. 3, 1975).

a) A real Christian catechesis should affirm the value of the whole Bible. The first Covenant has not been rendered void by the New. The first Covenant is, in fact, the root, the source, the foundation and a continuing promise of the New. While for us the Old Testament can be fully understood only in the light of the New, this fact in itself presupposes that it should be welcomed and recognized in its own right (see Tim. 3:16). Jesus, after all, was as man a Jew and fulfilled His ministry within the people of the Covenant by His obedience to the Torah and by His prayer. The "Our Father" remains today a particularly apt expression of both Jewish and Christian longings for the final coming of the Kingdom of God, with each component part having clear Rabbinic parallels.

b) Acknowledgement should be made by Christians of the particular and permanent vocation of the Jewish people as a "community and Covenant with God." An essential element of synagogue prayer, for example, is called in Jewish tradition "the sanctification of the Name." The idea of sanctifying the name of God through public worship and ethical living is a biblical concept which Christians should deeply honor, since it is a basic element of the Lord's Prayer, viz., "Hallowed be Thy Name." Through it the Jewish people, invested with a sacerdotal mission (Ex. 19:6), offer all human creation to God and give Him glory. This vocation makes the life and the prayer of the Jewish people a blessing for all the nations of the earth (Gen. 12).

c) Jewish laws should be seen not as mere constraining practices but as gestures which remind those who observe them of the sovereignty of God. Faithful Jews receive as gifts from God the Sabbath and the rites destined to sanctify human acts. They transcend the literal prescriptions of these rites and find in them light and joy on the road of life. (Ps. 119).

d) In meetings between Christians and Jews, the right of each to give full witness to one's faith must be recognized. Christians need not apologize for or seek to cover over differences in the way each approaches the one Father for all humankind. The mystery of God's Divine Will in electing first the Jews and then the Church as bearers of His Will, while revealed in essence, has not yet been resolved in all its details. Humility and openness are signs of dialogue.

e) The dispersion of the Jewish people and the present ingathering into the Land of Israel should be understood in the light of Jewish history and Jewish perspectives.

f) It is difficult to make a clear theological judgment on the return of the Jewish people to its ancient land. Scripture witnesses most strongly to the Promise of this Land to this People (Gen. 12:7, 26:3–4, Is. 43:5–7, Jer. 16:15, Zeph 3:20 *et al.*). Therefore, Christians as well as Jews are faced with the question: Will the ingathering of the Jews effected under the constraint of persecution and the interplay of vast forces be one of the channels of God's Justice for the Jewish people, and at the same time for the Arab populations of the area, and indeed, for all the peoples of the earth, or will it not? Together Christians, Jews and Moslems must face this great challenge as together they are the "People of the Book."

Catholics should be sensitive to the deeply held feelings which American Jews hold for the State of Israel. In a statement put forth by the National Conference of Catholic Bishops promulgated on November 13, 1973, the Bishops state clearly the need for "recognition of the right of Israel to exist as a sovereign state with secure boundaries" as well as "recognition of the rights of the Palestinian Arabs, especially the refugees."

g) Catholics should be well grounded in the facts and implications of the Holocaust, that is, the Nazi attempt at extermination of European Jewry. This terrible event, unparalleled in human history, has had a profound impact on Jews throughout the world. It must never be forgotten that these events took place in presumably "Christian" Europe. The implications of the Holocaust for Jewish/Christian relations must be honestly faced today.

3. Practical Guidelines

In order to implement the above understandings and following the Guidelines promulgated on January 3, 1975 by the Vatican Commission for Religious Relations with the Jews, the following steps are recommended:

a) Joint Prayer and Social Action

Common meetings in the presence of God in prayer and silent meditation, in mutual study and celebration of our common traditions and differences should be established on a regular basis, especially on the parish level. Action for justice and peace, seeking to fulfill both Jewish and Catholic needs as well as the needs of the larger community, is encouraged on all levels.

b) Reconciliation

As Catholics we need to discover to what extent the responsibility for past and present misunderstandings and injustices is our own, to admit that responsibility in a spirit of humility and openness of heart, and to deduce practical conclusions for the future.

c) Liturgy

When commenting on biblical texts, emphasis should be laid on the continuity of our Faith with that of the Jewish Covenant without minimizing either those elements of Christianity which are original or those of the Jewish tradition which are seen as of permanent value to the Jewish people. Care should be taken to see that homilies based on liturgical readings do not distort their meaning, especially when it is a question of passages which seem to show the Jewish people as a whole, or major groups such as the Pharisees, in an unfavorable light. The formula, "the Jews," for example, as used in St. John is a theological rather than an historical category. The full meaning and context of such phrases must be carefully explained, where necessary, in homilies, introduction to biblical readings, Prayers of the Faithful, and commentaries printed in missals. It may be advisable to select a member or members of the parish liturgical and catechetical teams to assume special responsibility for the carefulness of expression and historical accuracy which should characterize all liturgical and paraliturgical events.

d) *Education*

Information and clarification concerning Judaism is important to all levels of Christian instruction. The effective use of the sources of information available on parish and diocesan levels, such as catechetical instructions, textbooks, and the mass media presupposes the thorough formation of all those involved, whether in schools, religious education programs, seminaries or institutions of higher learning.

14
Guidelines for Ecumenical and Jewish-Catholic Relations: Trenton, New Jersey [from SIDIC]

In 1980 the Diocese of Trenton, New Jersey published a booklet containing its Guidelines for Ecumenical and Jewish-Catholic Relations. *They deal with the topic in great detail under many headings and from different aspects. We publish here those sections which directly concern Jewish-Catholic Relations. In particular, this document looks realistically at the delicate problem of mixed marriages, attempting to deal with it with all possible tact and respect for the religious convictions of the Jewish partner.*

Chapter I
Catholic Principles—Jewish-Catholic Relations

1] BACKGROUND INFORMATION

a) Spiritual bonds and historical links between the Church and Judaism, as well as personal dignity, condemn all forms of anti-semitism and discrimination. (GS)[1]

---

1. GS—Guidelines and Suggestions for Implementing the Conciliar Declaration *Nostra Aetate*, December 1, 1974. cf. *Stepping Stones to Further Jewish-Christian Relations*, Helga Croner ed. (London/New York: Stimulus Books, 1977) pp. 11 ff.

b) It is important to acknowledge common elements in the liturgy (formulas, feasts, rites, etc.) in which the Bible holds an essential place (GS).

c) Facts to be recalled:

- The same God speaks in both old and new covenants.
- Judaism in the time of Christ and the Apostles was a complex reality with many trends and values.
- The Old Testament and Jewish tradition do not constitute a religion of only justice, fear, and legalism with no appeal to love of God and neighbor.
- Jesus and many of his followers were Jewish. His teaching, though profoundly new, reflects the teaching of the Old Testament and uses rabbinical methods.
- Christ's passion cannot be blamed on all Jews then living nor on Jews of today.
- Even after Jerusalem was destroyed, Judaism developed a tradition rich in religious values.
- The Church awaits the day when all men will serve the Lord in unity. (GS)

2] INTERRELIGIOUS EFFORTS ARE FOR ALL THE FAITHFUL

Because the Church encounters Israel as she ponders her own mystery, Jewish-Catholic relations remain an important problem even where no Jewish communities exist. More, the return to origins of Christian faith helps the ecumenical movement. (GS)

3] POSSIBLE COURSES OF ACTION TO PROMOTE UNDERSTANDING

Suggested practical steps: Dialogue; care in handling and interpretation of Scripture, liturgical texts, prayers of faithful, commentaries; attention to catechisms, religious texts, histories, mass media; social action; prayer together. (GS)

Chapter VI

WORSHIP IN COMMON

Catholics with members of the Jewish Religion

At present, elements of worship in common would, practically speaking, be restricted to the areas of spiritual care and of marriages between Jews and Catholics.

1] SPIRITUAL CARE

a. A Catholic priest may offer prayers at the bedside of a Jewish person and may, if such is desired, dispose him in his last moments. This should be done only if requested by the sick person himself or by a member of his family with his presumed permission.

b. Authorities in charge of Catholic schools and institutions (e.g., hospitals, nursing homes) should offer rabbis every facility for spiritual ministration to their adherents. Means should be used to notify Jewish leaders when a member of their congregation is present.

2] MARRIAGES

a. Preparation for Marriage.

1) When a Catholic and Jew decide to enter into marriage, the priest who is helping them prepare a marriage ceremony should be sensitive to the religious convictions and customs of both parties. Neither party to the marriage should be asked to violate the integrity of his or her faith.

The priest should advise the couple that neither the Catholic Church nor the synagogue encourages mixed marriages; indeed, both the church and the synagogue greatly desire that Catholics marry Catholics and that Jews marry Jews. In counseling the interfaith couple the priest should remind them of the likelihood that the extended family of each party may be reluctant to accept their child's or sibling's spouse, and that tensions frequently arise as family ties are stretched to the breaking point.

2) All other provisions for the marriage preparation will be the same as those for marriages of Catholics with Protestants.

b. The Marriage Ceremony.

1. The regulations for marriages between Catholics and Protestants all apply with equal force to the marriages of Catholics and Jews.

2) Additionally, in exceptional cases, the dispensation from form may be granted to permit a civil ceremony; however, some public form of civilly recognized celebration is required. (SIMM # 11)[2]

---

2. SIMM—Statement of Implementation of *Matrimonia Mixta*, January 1, 1971.

c. *Recording Marriages.*

Requirements here are the same as for marriages between Catholics and Protestants.

d. *After the Marriage.*

Priest should show continued concern and readiness to assist the couple and their children. (SIMM # 3b)

Suggestions for Pastoral Practice in Marriage Between a Catholic and a Jew

INTRODUCTION

1. Preparing for marriage when one partner is a Catholic and the other a Jew presents certain difficulties not usually found in marriages between a Catholic and another Christian. Catholic and Jewish partners come to the priest with questions about their own and others' attitudes toward such a marriage; when, and how an appropriate wedding ceremony can be arranged; the religious faith and upbringing of children of the marriage; and the proper pastoral care and follow-up for themselves after the marriage.

2. The following suggestions for pastoral care are meant to address these concerns. Without replacing the Common Policy for Marriage Preparation or substituting for the Guidelines for the Practice of Ecumenism, these suggestions are offered to assist the priest with the most frequently expressed special concerns that arise when a Catholic wants to marry a Jew.

ATTITUDES

(a) *Of Clergy*

3. Because of their concern for the preservation of Judaism, which historically has never approved of the intermarriage of Jews and non-Jews, most rabbis absolutely will not officiate at a marriage between a Catholic and a Jew. The priest should make certain that the couple is aware of this fact. While the bride and groom may wish to seek out a rabbi willing to officiate, they should be certain this officiant is indeed a rabbi, and avoid agreeing to exorbitant fees

for his services. Certainly the priest himself should not offer nor attempt to engage the services of a rabbi for this occasion.

(b) Of Families

4. For many reasons, the families of both the Catholic and the Jew may be opposed to the marriage. The Jewish family may not accept the marriage of their son or daughter to a Catholic because in the new family unit Jewish faith and practice could be lost. A Catholic family might well express similar concern. To a degree, the effort of each spouse to learn about the teachings and traditions of the other's faith will help promote harmony between them; but both the couple and the priest involved need to understand that the intermarriage itself creates a family unit that is not considered Jewish. Thus Jews conclude that intermarriage weakens Judaism itself. Without the conversion of the Catholic partner to the Jewish faith, this fundamental Jewish objection to intermarriage can never really be resolved; indeed, in preparing a couple for marriage the priest may well discover that the Jewish partner is being pressured to choose between marrying the Catholic and retaining his or her own Jewish family ties. The priest should take the time to find out and evaluate the reasons for family objection, especially objection of a religious nature.

(c) Of Couple Themselves

5. Frequently the Catholic and Jew desire marriage so strongly that they do not forsee how differences in belief and practices, not to mention cultural conditioning, may seriously interfere with their effort to sustain a married life. Preparation, then, should include an exploration of these differences.

(d) Of the Catholic Church

6. While officially discouraging such intermarriage, the Catholic Church recognizes that the natural right of the couple to marry requires us to witness the marriage of a Catholic to a Jew, provided the basic principles are observed. (MM p. 1[3], SIMM, Introduction.) To offer more effective preparation of such couples, it would be helpful for the priest to establish contact with local rabbis either directly or through area ministerial associations, and communicate from time to time with them. If this cannot be done locally, the priest may contact the Diocesan Office for Ecumenical and Interreligious Affairs for assistance in establishing this line of communication.

---

3. MM—*Matrimonia Mixta,* March 31, 1970.

THE WEDDING CEREMONY

7. Since two separate ceremonies and the combining of rituals are expressly forbidden, and family objections to the wedding are likely, determining the place for the ceremony, the officiant, and the type of ceremony usually will require special care.

(a) Place

8. In accord with the requirements for the valid marriage of a Catholic, a priest or deacon is ordinarily the officiant at the wedding of a Catholic with a Jew, and the wedding may take place in the sanctuary of the Catholic Church, or in a chapel or other suitable place on the Catholic parish grounds. A rabbi may participate in accord with the Diocesan ecumenical guidelines. This option should be offered the couple first, and its advantages clearly set forth. If, to avoid family alienation, it is necessary to have the wedding in another place, the Diocesan guidelines call for the use of some other sacred place, a synagogue or more likely a nondenominational chapel (as the use of a synagogue is likely to be as "unacceptable" as the use of a Catholic church may be, in view of the danger of family alienation). Less preferred, though at times necessary, is the inside of the private home of one of the spouses, or courtroom or public hall in which a civil official might witness such a marriage. Without denying the appeal of other settings, such as parks, restaurants, gardens, and auditoriums, the priest should help the couple understand that these are not acceptable in the Diocese of Trenton because they often distract the couple and their family and guests from the fundamentally religious understanding of marriage in the community of faith whose prayer and blessings the couple seeks. Finally, if the marriage is not to take place within the Diocese of Trenton, the priest should immediately contact the chancery of the diocese where the marriage will take place, to determine the special guidelines that may apply to the weddings of Catholics with Jews.

(b) Officiant and Ceremony

9. Resolving the question of where the ceremony should take place may well depend on determining who will officiate, and what type of ceremony will be used. If the Catholic clergyman will officiate, the most appropriate place will be the Catholic church, and the ceremony to be used is that from the Catholic ritual for marriage between a Catholic and an unbaptized person. This ceremony is very often acceptable to all concerned in the intermarriage, and

offering its use to the couple may lead to the acceptance of the Catholic church as the appropriate place for the ceremony. As pointed out earlier, a rabbi may participate in accord with the diocesan ecumenical guidelines. If a rabbi is to officiate, the ceremony to be used is the Jewish one and the dispensation from canonical form must be obtained. The synagogue would seem preferred, but more likely the couple will need to find a non-denominational chapel or other acceptable place for the ceremony. Finding the acceptable place may not be easy, but in practice a non-denominational chapel in the bride's or groom's community is more likely to be acceptable to all concerned as well as providing adequate space. If the rabbi officiates, the priest may participate in accord with the diocesan ecumenical guidelines. Again, if the marriage is to take place outside the Diocese of Trenton, and the rabbi has invited the Catholic's priest to be present, the priest should find out the policy of the Diocese with regard to such marriages. In practice, where a priest and rabbi are both to be present, the wedding to take place other than in a Catholic Church, and the priest supposed to officiate, the dispensation from form could be obtained *ad cautelam* to avoid embarrassment in the event the rabbi insists on officiating.

10. Sometimes the resolution of the issues that arise over the wedding ceremony will require that a magistrate, mayor or other civil official witness the marriage. While this suggests the use of a courtroom, public hall or the like, the priest should keep in mind and discuss with the couple the possibility of the civil official witnessing the marriage in one of the other acceptable places, and the opportunity for the priest and even a rabbi to offer some prayer of blessing. Of course, the dispensation from form would be required in this instance, even if the Catholic priest were to be present, because the priest would not be receiving the wedding vows of the couple, nor acting as the official witness of the Church to this wedding.

11. Finally, in seeking to prepare a wedding celebration that is faithful to the spouses' religious traditions and truly an act of worship, the priest and couple should keep in mind that there are a number of ways in which place, rite or ceremony, and officiant can be combined within the guidelines in force in the Diocese of Trenton. Questions about this may be addressed to the Diocesan Commission on Ecumenical and Interreligious Affairs or to the Chancery Office, as we cannot anticipate all the possible alternatives here.

THE CHILDREN

12. Presuming the couple intend to have children, there will be concern for the children's religious identity and upbringing.

(a) Identity

13. In the Jewish tradition, children find their religious identity, and they are expected to brought up, in the religion of the mother. If the mother is the Catholic, the children would not be recognized or accepted as Jewish unless she herself became a Jew. If the mother is Jewish, her children are not likely to be accepted as Jewish once they have been baptized as Catholics; and the mother's permitting their baptism could well put her at odds with her family even if the marriage itself does not. For these reasons, the questions the couple has about the religious identity and upbringing of the children need very careful consideration. The bride and groom cannot usually make this decision without reference to their families, and the solutions usually suggested when a Catholic marries a Protestant are not often acceptable or workable where the Catholic marries a Jew.

(b) Upbringing

14. When it comes to the "promises" that the Catholic makes in order to obtain the required dispensation for marriage, what appears as "offensive" to Jews is not the fact that the Catholic must make the promises, but rather the fact that, if the Catholic intends to keep this promise, the family is thus "lost" to the Jewish people. Couples will ask, then, whether it is really necessary to make the promises at all, in view of this real danger of family alienation.

15. In such circumstances, the couple may want to opt for what seems to them the easier solution—to promise the families and the church what is necessary for them to marry, but in reality to plan to raise their children without any formal religion until the children are old enough to decide for themselves. While it appears the path of least resistance, it is also the one choice that marriage preparation needs most surely to discourage.

(c) The Decision

16. Since the issue of children reflects so seriously the difference that exists culturally and religiously between the Catholic and the Jewish partner in marriage, this issue should not be avoided or put off. The couple needs to recognize that, when they decide to baptize and educate the children as Catholics, an agreement to teach the children also about Judaism will not really satisfy the requirements of the Jewish faith. Their decision about the religious identity and upbringing of the children, even more than their decision to marry, may well be the point at which they must choose between family ties and their

marriage. The priest needs to help the couple accept the responsibility for making this decision on their own, a decision which comes as an unavoidable consequence of their decision to marry. The couple should clearly understand that the promise to do all in one's power to see to the Catholic baptism and education of the children does not require the Catholic to separate from the Jewish partner if it becomes morally impossible to keep the promise once sincerely made. The priest should explore with the couple the extent to which the Catholic could accept the children being taught about the history and traditions of Judaism. The couple should be encouraged to learn about each other's beliefs and practices, and to meet if possible with a rabbi to find out to what extent their children might be welcome in the Jewish community with which the Jewish partner would want to affiliate.

PASTORAL CARE AND FOLLOW UP

17. All the foregoing involves Pastoral Care, but in addition to the questions of attitude, ceremony and children, there is the matter of following up the preparation of the couple and helping them especially in the early years of their marriage.

(a) Continuing Education

18. Behind the opposition to intermarriage, there is also the matter of prejudice born of centuries of antagonism. It exists on both sides and can do more harm than a staunch devotion to one's religious convictions. The couple needs to be counseled to continue to study and understand each other's heritage and traditions.

(b) Family Contacts

19. The priest involved in the couple's preparation for marriage should make the effort to contact and meet the parents of the Jewish spouse, and his or her rabbi if possible. Often the parents feel more comfortable explaining their objections to the marriage if the priest appears willing to listen, and this attention to their concern often moderates their anxiety about the upcoming marriage. It may even help them accept the decision of their son or daughter about marriage. In meeting with the parents, the priest's effort to understand their feelings should be paramount.

(c) Follow-up for Couple

20. Some plan should be made, during marriage preparation, to contact the couple periodically after the wedding, for at least the first few years, to see how they are doing and to offer such assistance as may be available at the time.

(d) Rabbi-Priest Contacts

21. Prior to the wedding, the priest should contact the rabbi who has been asked to officiate or be present at the wedding, to discuss both the details of the ceremony and the more general issues connected with this couple's decision to marry. An attitude of fraternal cooperation should mark the priest's contact with these religious leaders. The priest should keep in mind that the possibility of intermarriage often presents a much more serious concern and danger in their view that it ordinarily does in ours. Follow-up contacts after the wedding with the Jewish partner's rabbi might be in order if the couple agrees such contact would be helpful. If contact with the rabbi is attempted but unfruitful, the priest can consult with the Diocesan Commission on Ecumenical and Interreligious Affairs for further assistance in this regard.

15
Guidelines for Jewish-Catholic Marriages: Archdiocese of Newark 1983

A. INTRODUCTION

The purpose of these guidelines is to enable a Catholic priest or deacon to respond with pastoral sensitivity to a Catholic-Jewish couple who present themselves to him for marriage. It is not the purpose of these guidelines to promote Catholic-Jewish marriages. Rather, the guidelines presume a Catholic-Jewish couple who have already formed a firm purpose of marriage; they are intended to help those who are confronted with the reality of that decision to respond in a loving pastoral way.

B. PASTORAL CONCERNS

1. The priest or deacon who is asked to minister to a Catholic-Jewish couple should respect their decision to marry. His place is not to judge, but rather to act as a sign of God's loving presence in their lives. The priest or deacon who is helping the couple to prepare for marriage should be sensitive to the religious convictions and customs of both parties. Neither party to the marriage should be asked to violate the integrity of his or her faith.

2. In an interfaith marriage there are three obvious possibilities of faith commitment: (1) both partners may be strongly rooted in their respective religious traditions; (2) one partner may be strong and the other only loosely attached; (3) neither partner may be strongly attached. The priest or deacon should try to understand the particular situation before him in order to minister wisely to the couple's needs. He should be sensitive to the fact that faith is a life-long process, and that the individual's place in that journey may not always be easily discerned or artriculated. In respecting the couple's search for meaning in their lives, the priest or deacon is also respecting the mystery of God's grace.

3. The priest or deacon should be aware that a Catholic-Jewish couple will

probably face some hostility, either from one family or from both, or from their religious congregations, or from many directions. He should be sensitive to the reasons for these feelings so that he can, if possible, become a mediating force. He should realize, for example, that according to Jewish law in its rabbinic interpretation (halakah) only the child of a Jewish mother is considered Jewish (unless the child converts in mature years). From the Jewish viewpoint, therefore, the Jewish man who marries a Gentile woman expresses a decision regarding his future children. The Jewish community, moreover, is especially concerned for the future of its existence after the terrible ravages of the Nazi Holocaust, and is strongly opposed to marriages which do not promise to lead to the continuation of the Jewish people.

4. An interfaith couple frequently feels out of place in both their religious communities. The priest or deacon should realize that what the couple needs most in preparing for marriage, as well as in living it, is a ministering community which will support their commitment to each other. He should support such a community where it exists, and help them to develop one where it does not.

C. PREPARATION FOR MARRIAGE

1. As in the case with all couples preparing for marriage, the priest or deacon should make every effort to explain to the Catholic-Jewish couple that the Church's concern is in helping them prepare for a happy and stable marriage, and not just for the wedding ceremony. The extended preparation for marriage envisaged by the Common Policy on Marriage of the Catholic Church in New Jersey is to be followed, and the options for marriage preparation courses laid down in the Common Policy should be presented to the couple.

2. For the granting of the required dispensation from the impediment of disparity of worship, the Catholic partner must promise to preserve his or her own faith, and to do all in his or her power to share this faith with the children of the marriage. These promises may be made orally or in writing, and the Jewish partner must be informed of these promises.

> In the Jewish tradition, children find their religious identity, and they are expected to be brought up, in the religion of the mother. If the mother is Catholic, the children are not recognized or accepted as Jewish unless she herself becomes a Jew. If the mother is Jewish, her children are not likely to be accepted as Jewish once they have been baptized as Catholics; and the mother's permitting their baptism could well put her at odds with her family even if the marriage itself does not. For these reasons, the questions the couple has

about the religious identity and upbringing of the children need very careful consideration.

Since the issue of children reflects so seriously the difference that exists culturally and religiously between the Catholic and the Jewish partners in marriage, this issue should not be avoided or put off. The priest or deacon needs to help the couple accept the responsibility for making this decision on their own, a decision which comes as an unavoidable consequence of their decision to marry and flows from their natural moral obligation as parents. The couple should clearly understand that the Catholic's promise to do all in his or her power to see to the Catholic baptism and education of the children does not require the Catholic to separate from the Jewish partner if it becomes morally impossible to keep the promise once sincerely made. Both partners must understand that each comes from a religious tradition which recognizes a divine imperative to pass on that tradition from parent to child; however they decide to fulfill their divine obligation to see to the religious upbringing of their children, they should take care that the children appreciate and respect the religious traditions of both parents.

D. THE WEDDING CEREMONY

1. The resolution of the question of where the wedding ceremony should take place may well depend on determining who will officiate, and what type of ceremony will be used. To avoid misunderstanding, it is important that the ceremony be prepared carefully by both the Catholic and the Jewish partners. It is most desirable that the priest and the rabbi both be consulted. The prayers, hymns and scripture readings should be chosen to reflect what is common to both the Jewish and the Christian traditions.
2. All marriages between a Catholic and a Jew require a dispensation from the impediment of disparity of worship.
3. If the Catholic clergyman is to officiate at the wedding, the ceremony to be used is that from the Catholic ritual for marriage between a Catholic and an unbaptized person. The wedding may take place in the sanctuary or other part of the Catholic church or in any suitable building on the parish grounds. For good reason, permission can be given for such a wedding to take place in a private home, place of reception, or other suitable place.

In cases where the priest or deacon is officiating, a rabbi may be invited to participate in the marriage ceremony and he may offer prayers for the couple and invoke God's blessing on them. He may not share in the marriage ritual as such and is not an official witness to the ceremony. He may not request the vows of either party or lead in the recitation of the vows or co-sign a license.

4. Where serious reasons exist which preclude the possibility of a marriage ceremony before a Catholic priest or deacon, a dispensation from the Catholic form of marriage may be sought so that the Catholic party may marry in a religious ceremony before a rabbi in a sacred or private place. If the rabbi is to officiate, the ceremony to be used is the Jewish one and the dispensation from canonical form must be obtained.

> In this case, a priest or deacon may be invited to participate in the marriage ceremony; he may offer prayers for the couple and invoke God's blessing on them. He may not share in the marriage ritual as such and is not an official witness to the ceremony. He may not request the vows of either party or lead in the recitation of the vows or co-sign a license.

5. If for serious reasons it is not possible to have either a Catholic or a Jewish ceremony, the church will reluctantly permit a public ceremony recognized in civil law provided the Catholic party has obtained a dispensation from the canonical form of marriage and provided that all other requirements are fulfilled.

> If a priest or deacon is invited to participate in such a ceremony, he may offer prayers for the couple and invoke God's blessing on them, but he may not share in the marriage ritual as such.

6. The priest or deacon should be aware that Orthodox and Conservative rabbis are forbidden to officiate at mixed marriages. Some members of the Reform rabbinate will officiate at mixed marriages. Of those Reform rabbis who will officiate at mixed marriages, only a very small group will officiate together with a Christian clergyman.

7. Jews may be admitted as witnesses and attendants at a marriage ceremony in a Catholic church. Catholics may act as witnesses and attendants at the wedding of Jews.

8. Once the Chancery office has been informed that the wedding has taken place, the marriage documents, including the dispensations, must be filed in the canonical parish in which the wedding actually took place.

APPENDIX: REFLECTIONS ON
CATHOLIC-JEWISH MARRIAGE

The couple should recognize the religious convictions which Jews and Christians hold in common. These can be explored, both during preparation for marriage and throughout later years. The Jewish partner may be surprised to know how much of Jewish tradition has been absorbed into Catholic thinking and practice, and the Catholic partner will undoubtedly be amazed to discover how much Catholic prayer, liturgy, ethics and Scriptural interpretation is inherently Jewish. The Catholic partner in particular is encouraged to study Jewish tradition openly and lovingly, knowing that such a study will not only bring him closer to his Jewish spouse, but also to his Lord, Jesus of Nazareth. Coming to understand and to value the Jewishness of Jesus can only enrich the Catholic's own faith and at the same time increase his appreciation of his spouse's. An open and wholehearted initiative on the part of both partners to understand each other's religious traditions could well serve to strengthen the unity between husband and wife and also offer a way of unifying and enriching the religious understanding of their children.

The religious sharing of a Jewish-Christian family begins with the Bible. In the Hebrew Scriptures, which Christians know as the Old Testament, they will find the basic roots of both traditions which they can hand on in common to their children: the uniqueness of each human person created in God's image and likeness (Genesis 1:26–28) and called to imitation of God as the epitome of the search for holiness (Leviticus 19:2); the sense of God's presence and providential care of his creatures; the revelation of his Word to the patriarchs, Moses and the other prophets, the psalmists and wisdom writers; the conviction that election is for witness and loving service to others, especially through the keeping of the Commandments; the celebration of God's redemptive work at the Exodus and his covenant at Mount Sinai, celebrated in the great feasts of the Jewish liturgical calendar; the sacred and divinely ordained bond which constitutes marriage; the procreation of children as an intimate cooperation in the work of the Creator; their education as a fundamental privilege and responsibility of parenthood; the honoring of one's parents, caring for them in their old age; concern for one's neighbor and hospitality to the stranger; the works of mercy; involvement in the building of a whole and just and peaceful society. In other words, the basic truths of love of God and love of neighbor derive from the Scriptures which both Christians and Jews hold as a treasured heritage.

Such a base can only enhance any further presentation that may be given to the children of the uniqueness of the person of Jesus. Their reading of the Gospels can only be enriched and illumined by their understanding of their Jewish context.

When a couple have chosen to unite in marriage, they should share the expressions of belief in the one God whose intimate life they share in the Covenant. The Catholic partner can be encouraged to read the Siddur, the Jewish daily prayer book, and to become familiar with how much Jewish prayer and liturgy was adapted by the early Christian church. In particular the Catholic can study and become aware of how the Eucharistic meal is rooted in the Passover meal. The Jewish partner can become familiar with Catholic forms of prayer, and recognize the many ways in which his or her own tradition is reflected in them.

A Catholic-Jewish family can find particular joy and unity in celebrating the yearly Passover Seder. The Catholic can then come to appreciate our belief that the Gentiles were integrated into the family of Abraham when they became one with Christ and children of God (Galatians 3:26–29). Such a couple might well become a source of leadership and inspiration to both the Christian and Jewish communities in which they live, a kind of living bridge between them. There is no doubt that such a common search to live the values of God's Word in a spirit of prayer conveys special graces to the couple and their family. The sanctification of God's Name cannot but be a vehicle of spiritual gifts which raise human life to a new plane, wherein God is present in a mode which indeed transforms the daily efforts of the couple to reflect the divine image upon their home and their world.

TO THE JEWISH-CATHOLIC COUPLE:

1. *Regard your marriage as holy.* To Jew and Christian alike, marriage is a holy covenant, a holy bond which reflects God's covenant with his people. In both traditions husband and wife are considered channels of God's grace to one another, imaging to one another God's lovingkindness, forgiveness and faithfulness.

2. *See your marriage as prophetic.* Know that your interfaith marriage, with its strong bond of love and loyalty, crosses the barriers of centuries, and can be a prophetic sign of God's Kingdom when all people will be one before the Father.

3. *Respect what your spouse regards as holy.* You cannot love your wife or husband as yourself without respecting whatever she or he finds meaningful. Aware that the mystery of God's being transcends all human formulations, make yourself open to the mystery which is mediated through your spouse's tradition.

4. *Learn about each other's traditions.* If you are open to the truth mediated through each other's traditions, you will find your own faith enriched.

The Jewishness of Jesus should be a point of unity for both of you, not a line of division.

5. *Worship God together.* Your interfaith home and marriage should be sustained by family prayer. Emphasize those things which you can share: passages from Hebrew Scripture, the psalms, grace before meals, daily blessings and the yearly seder.

6. *Educate your childen together.* It is important to realize that your child has a right to a religious education. Not to give your child a religious education is unfair to the child and to both faith communities. A divided education—girls raised in one tradition and boys in another—can only create division in the family. The only fair and unifying solution is to educate your children in such a way that they are committed to one tradition with knowledge of and respect for the other. This solution will not be difficult if you are in fact in dialogue with each other; if you are open to one another's traditions, respecting what the other finds holy, you will educate your children in reverence for the transcendent mystery of God's being.

7. *Involve yourselves in service to the world.* The way in which you serve the community together, the world God loves, can be an inspiring sign to others of the reconciliation and unity needed for the building of God's Kingdom.

C) EUROPEAN STATEMENTS

16
Basic Theological Issues of
the Jewish-Christian Dialogue
Workshop on Jews and Christians
Central Committee of Roman Catholics in
Germany
[from SIDIC] 1979

English translation by Elizabeth Petuchowski

I. WHY SEEK THE DIALOGUE?

1. Jews and Cristians have a common ground of hope: the God of Israel who graciously makes Himself available to mankind. Together they expect the complete fulfilment of the hope: the ultimate dominion of God.

Jews and Christians have been challenged to give a common testimony—both on account of what they have experienced of God and on account of the challenge presented by the world in which they are living. Not only to them—so they believe—but to all peoples the call was addressed to find life, home, and peace in the Jerusalem of the life-giving God. (cf. Isa 2. 1-5; Isa 60) As they themselves set out for this Jerusalem as the place of righteousness and faithfulness (cf. Isa 1.26), they feel the obligation to transmit to all of human-kind the liberating power of their attachment to the God who can and who will grant life and future. (cf. Jer 29.11.) God's call enlists them in the service of fashioning the world. It makes them into pioneers of hope, especially for those who have no hope. This call is, at the same time, judgment—by freeing them from any fixation on purely internal interests and fears. Rather, following

God's call, they are to become honest and courageous agents of God's right-eousness and advocates of His mercy.

2. If the obligation to engage in dialogue, which applies in any age, is based upon the fact that Jews and Christians are bound together through the acts of the God of Israel, then the painful experiences of recent history intensify the charge that, in our time, the dialogue be strengthened and deepened as much as possible.

- The past nineteen hundred years of the relationship between Judaism and Christianity have constituted a history of growing apart, the historical con-sequences of which were terrible. In connection with this history of growing apart, one must also view the terrifying occurrence of Auschwitz, the at-tempt to destory the Jewish people completely through Hitler's dictatorship.
- In Judaism as well as'in Christianity, both of which together owe their ex-istence to the Revelation of the God of Israel, there is a gradual awakening of a "spiritual" interest in each other. Jews and Christians acknowledge this common Revelation through just this interest. Consequently, their interest in each other is in itself an act of adoring God.
- Jews and Christians must present a common testimony to a humankind whose very survival in humaneness is at stake, a concrete testimony which must show and prepare concrete ways of righteousness and salvation.

II. CONDITIONS OF A DIALOGUE WHICH CONCERNS THE JEW AS A JEW, AND THE CHRISTIAN AS A CHRISTIAN

As Jews and Christians transmit a common treasure of biblical writings as the basis of their lives, the dialogue has a foundation, the value of which cannot be overestimated. It is the faith in the saving and sanctifying God whose closeness to the Patriarchs the Torah relates, and whose life-promoting teach-ings it proclaims. It is the hearkening to the God of the living and the dead, whose rule in the midst of the people, called by His name, the Prophets an-nounce. It is the cleaving to the near and far God whom the prayerful Psalmists praise, and whose faithfulness they beseech even when everything seems to have been taken from them. It is faith in the Creator God of whose goodness the proverbs and meditations of the sages remind us. Of all of this, Jews and Christians, in their respective ways, give testimony in their divine services and in their lives. But just here, a typical difficulty for the Jewish-Christian dia-logue makes its appearance: Do the identical writings really provide the basis for a common life? To answer this question, it is necessary to bear in mind some fundamental conditions of the Jewish-Christian dialogue:

1. There can be no doubt that, to begin with, Jews and Christians will have to work very hard on behalf of one another, so that they can come to a better mutual understanding. The Jewish image of Christians and the Christian image of Jews, as formed in the course of history and still being formed, should be examined, and should be corrected in an encounter in which, by going back to the common basis, and in the light of the common hope, one interprets his own way to the other. Here in particular the one is not going to wait for the other to approach him in order to "study" him. Rather will he sense the obligation to share what is his own. Conversely, for the sake of the common hope, he will develop an active readiness to listen to the other. By presenting themselves, trusting one another, and revealing themselves to the other both can give the testimony to which they know that God has called them.

2. A Jewish-Christian dialogue cannot succeed if the Christian sees in the Judaism of today merely a memorial of his own past—of the time of Jesus and of the Apostles. But the dialogue will not succeed either, if the Jewish partner can discover in the essential Jewish elements within the Christian faith nothing but the effects of a past condition which did indeed obtain within the first Christian communities, but nowadays no longer obtain. In both of those cases, the one partner does not yet take the contemporaneousness of the other seriously. Instead, he makes him into a mere mirror of his own past. However, contemporaneousness is the condition of any dialogue. The Jewish partner cannot be satisfied if, in a conversation with Christians, he is regarded merely as a surviving witness of the so-called Old Testament and of the period in which the Christian communities originated. Conversely, the Christian partner cannot be satisfied if the Jewish partner thinks that only he has something to say to the Christian which is essential to the Christian's faith, while that which the Christian has to say to the Jew has no essential meaning for the faith of the Jew. From the ecumenical experience of the inner-Christian dialogue, confidence may grow also for the Jewish-Christian dialogue: There, too, both partners have learned to summon the ability and the readiness to listen to the word of the other as a testimony which concerns the listener in his relation to God.

3. The very history which makes today's encounter of Jews and Christians more difficult can also smooth the path towards each other, if only that history be experienced and acknowledged—even if, at first, only in part—as a really common history which concerns us actually now.

   When, in a prayer on Easter Eve, the Christian pleads for "the dignity of Israel" to be bestowed upon all peoples, he cannot forget—he can, at most, suppress it to his own hurt—that the Israel of which he speaks has existed to this day, an Israel which to this day has remained the bearer of the "dignity of Israel". The Christian Church, calling herself "People of God", must not forget that the present existence of Judaism is testimony to the fact that, still today, the same God is in faithfulness committed to that Election through which He became Israel's God, and through which He had made Israel His people. That is why the Christian does not adequately understand his own dignity and election if he does not take notice of, nor seek to understand the dignity and the election of the Judaism of today. But in order to do so, he needs to familiarize himself with the Jewish faith and the Jewish existence to which his Jewish partners in the dialogue offer testimony. When the Jew, rightly so, calls himself a "son of Abraham", he cannot forget—he can at most suppress it—that not only the first Christians in the distant past were sons of Abraham, but that also today nobody can be a Christian without acknowledging Abraham as the "father of all those who believe." Furthermore, the Jewish community is certain of the promise of a renewal of its covenant, as it is written: "Behold, the days are coming, says the Lord, when I will make a new covenant with the house of Israel and the house of Judah, not like the covenant which I made with their fathers when I took them by the hand to bring them out of the land of Egypt." (Jer 31.31 f.) The Jewish community, therefore, must not forget that there would never have been a community of the Christians if the latter had not known the call from the same God into his "New Covenant". That is why the Jew does not completely understand the manner in which Abraham became the "father of a multitude of nations" (Gen 17), if he does not take notice of, nor seek to understand the faith of today's Christian. But in order to do so, he needs to familiarize himself with the Christian faith and the Christian existence to which his Christian partners in the dialogue offer testimony.

4. Once the meaning of that which binds them together in history has entered their consciousness and has been acknowledged, there is a chance that both partners in the dialogue might let themselves be called to a responsibility for each other. Each becomes a witness for the other to those mighty acts of God which are the cause of his living as a Jew or as a Christian at the present time. The life out of faith, the life out of the center of existence, Christian as well as Jewish life has its being out of this testimony. And everywhere, where the life of a community becomes a testimony to God's act of salvation, this testimony is for the other believer, who lives from the same salvific acts of God, precious, indeed irreplaceable. Believers who live from the same origin incur guilt for one another if they do not give this testimony to one another.

III. CENTRAL THEMES OF THE DIALOGUE

1) Companionship of Jews and Christians

The common goal of God's saving rulership enables Jews and Christians to speak to one another from faith to faith. Both know themselves to have been addressed by God, both want to respond to the will of God,—graciously vouchsafed to them through an election by God,—in love, with all their heart, with all their soul, with all their mind, and with all their might. Such an agreement is important for common action in the world. But it is also important to evaluate not only the fact of agreement, but also the measure of agreement. This is all the more so because just there, where our consensus is most profound, the root of our disagreements is embedded.

For the Christian, the goal of God's saving rulership, promised in Israel's Bible, is mediated by the Jew Jesus. Already here, not only the dividing but also the uniting function of Jesus shows itself: Through the Jew Jesus, the Torah remains effective within Christianity. Through him, its realization becomes the task of the Christians—as God's promise and commandment. The Jew, on the other hand, does not first have to get to know Jesus in order to love the Torah. As a Jew, he has this love as his heritage. Of course, a dialogue of Jews and Christians can take place seriously only when the Jewish partner, too, begins with the assumption that God caused something to happen in Christianity, which concerns him "for God's sake"—even though he may not see in it a way on which he himself can or must go. That is why Christians ask whether the living presence of essential Jewish elements in the Christian divine service, in the Christian proclamation, in the Christian understanding of Scripture, and in Christian theology, does not make possible a Jewish interest in Christian faith and life—over and above a mere taking note from the distance. Conversely, Christians must grant the Jews that a Jewish interest in Christianity can be an interest "for the sake of the Kingdom of Heaven"—even though it does not lead to Jews becoming Christians. A possibility of understanding the Jewish interest in Christianity was expressed by the Jewish philosopher of religion, Franz Rosenzweig (1886-1929), when he said: "Whether Jesus was the Messiah will be shown when the Messiah comes." Such an ambiguous formulation does not, however, mean that Jews and Christians are free to postpone until "the Last Day" their conversation about the hope which unites them, and the question about the Messiah which divides them.

In the mutual questioning, some recognition of the salvific meaning of the other way can, therefore, most certainly be expressed. Jews can acknowledge that, for the Christians, Jesus has become the way on which they find Israel's God. But they will make their evaluation of the Christian way dependent upon this, that the faith of the Christians in the salvation granted to them through God's messiah who came from the Jews does not diminish, but rather demands their obligation to act in the service of righteousness and peace. Christians understand Jesus as the fulfilment of the Law and the promise only when they follow him "for the sake of the Kingdom of Heaven," and when doing so, they listen to his word: "Not every one who says to me 'Lord, Lord', shall enter the kingdom of heaven, but he who does the will of my Father who is in heaven." (Mtt 7.21).

The mutual evaluation of each other's way is thus indivisibly united with considerable divergencies in the approach to Jesus, and to the question whether he is God's messiah. But this compels neither Jews nor Christians to dissolve the fundamental bracket of contents of the one commanding will of God. That is why it is fundamentally prohibited to Jews and to Christians to seek to move the other to become disloyal to the call of God which he has received. It is not to be thought that this prohibition is based on tactical caluclations. Reasons of humane tolerance and respect for the freedom of religion, too, are not solely decisive in this. The deepest reason must rather be seen in this: that it is the same God by whom both Jews and Christians know themselves to have been called. Christians, on the basis of their own understanding of the faith, cannot forego to testify to Jesus as the Christ also vis-a-vis the Jews. Jews, on the basis of their self-understanding, cannot refrain from stressing the non-abrogation of the Torah also vis-a-vis the Christians. In either case, this includes the hope that, by means of this testimony, the other's loyalty to the call he has received from God might increase, and that mutual understanding might be deepened. On the other hand, the expectation should not be included that the other may renege on his "yes" to his call or weaken it.

Christians believe that the Messiah, who is promised in the Scriptures, has come in the person of Jesus. It is the nearness of Israel's God who familiarized them with Jesus as their brother and, at the same time, let them experience Jesus' love as God's turning towards them. That is why it seems to them not to be enough merely to regard Jesus as a shining example. Rather do they understand his life, death and return as a way on which God would lead all to salvation. That Jesus' love offers room for all, they see confirmed in the fact that God has exalted him and returned him alive. What differentiates him from everything in the past and from everything human is, therefore, not something in the line of mere quantitative magnification. Particularly the concept of a merely increased humanity in the case of Jesus could easily lead to the fatal confrontation: the Christians are the better Israelites, after all. A Christology which acknowledges in Jesus the Son of God having become man is in no need of such quantitative measurements. It has—perhaps only after its own painful experiences—the possibility to see the goal in a communion with Jesus, based upon the free "yes" of faith; but it must also know that there is the possibility of an open and growing companionship for all of those of whom God has taken hold. In this way Christians can give an acceptable sense to the words of Rosenzweig, quoted above.

The question of the Jews, whether the strict obligation to accept the one and unique God of Israel (cf. Deut 6.4-9) has not been given up by confessing the Son of God having become man, is answered by Christians with their faith and conviction that it was precisely Jesus who mediated and represented to them the one and unique God of Israel. For Christians, God's becoming man in Christ is by no means a negation of the unity and uniqueness of God but rather its confirmation. Indeed, God's becoming man presupposes that the one and unique God of Israel is not an isolated God without relationships, but a God who turns towards humankind and who is affected by human destiny. This characteristic of God, according to the testimony of the Talmudim and the Midrashim—albeit without reference to, or connection, with, Jesus—is likewise known to Rabbinic Judaism. Rabbinic Judaism, too, obviously knows that the one and unique God of Israel does not only "dwell" in transcendence, but also in the midst of His people, subjected to distress and persecution—as Lord, Father, Companion and Redeemer. The Christian-Jewish dialogue about the living God of Israel is, therefore, a great sign of hope.

2) The Common Commission

In spite of the disagreement in agreement, which has not been glossed over, Jews and Christians are united by their having received the commission to act and to testify jointly in the world. Examples of essential tasks which, for the sake of the future, they will jointly have to undertake, are the following:

• How, in the face of the mass murder which has been committed against the Jews and the attempted destruction of the Jewish people, is it still possible to believe in God. How is it possible to bear guilt and suffering in the presence of God, instead of suppressing or fixating them? What meaning is there for Jews and Christians, and for their mutual encounter, in the systematic extermination of large segments of European Jewry, and in the founding of the State of Israel? How, in the face of the founding of the State of Israel as a central event in recent Jewish history, is it possible to combine the millennial Jewish hope of God's salvation with concrete political action in the present, without advocating either a religiously grounded ideologizing of politics or a politization of religion?

- What is the meaning of the fact that, in a world which is as polytheistic as ever before (it is simply that the gods are given different names today), Jews and Christians believe in the One God? Is it not possible, indeed, is it not mandatory, for Jews and Christians, on the basis of their revelation, jointly to develop a critique of ideology—in a world which still fights wars which essentially are wars of religion (which becomes clear when we substitute the word "ideology" for the word "religion")?

- Do not Jews and Christians have the common obligation, in the face of world conditions which threaten the survival of humankind, to demonstrate and to show through personal example what the Bible understands by righteousness and liberty?

- The basic demands of biblical Revelation, common to Jews and Christians, is the absolute respect of the life of another human being. They should jointly specify the consequences which follow from this today for the maintenance of human dignity and human rights. In particular, they should, for example, together develop an ethics of the sciences, of technology, and of a concern for the future. (People who live after the year 2000 are also our "neighbors").

- What concrete consequences can be drawn from the conviction, common to Jews and Christians, that man has been created in God's image? What obligations follow from the commandment, common to Jews and Christians, of unrestricted love? (cf. Lev 19. 18 and Mark 12. 30 f.)

3) Reconsidering the Controversy about Law and Grace

The encounter of Jews and Christians will also lead both sides to a clearer perception of the questions put to one another.

Jews can convincingly reject the Christian reproach that they believe in "justification by works" only if they do not deny the danger which could follow from their position. All the more so since they know that a warning against "justification by works" is part of their own religious tradition. The fact that the Torah claims the whole life of man does not prevent his being dependent upon God's mercy. Liturgical texts, like those which characterize the celebration of the Day of Atonement, the most important High Holy Day in the Jewish year, could afford Christians an intimate view of this aspect of Jewish life.

Christians can convincingly reject the Jewish reproach that they suffer from a "loss of ethics" only if they do not deny the danger which could follow from the possibility that their hope for grace might seduce them from their responsibility in and for the world. All the more so since they know that a warning against this danger is included in their own religious tradition. Ecclesiastical texts concerning the relationship between faith and works (cf. the Council of Trent), and already the Pauline admonition about "faith working through love" (Gal 5.6) are eloquent examples of this.

Jewish and Christian criticism of "justification by works," and Jewish and Christian "rejoicing in the Law" (rejoicing is shared also by the Christian, as Paul expressly acknowledges in Rom 7. 12) have a common goal: to preserve the ability to pray and to praise God. That is why Jews and Christians find their way to the dialogue only when they together acknowledge what is said daily in the Jewish morning service: "We do not rely upon our own righteousness, but on Your great mercy." (Dan 9. 18.)

IV. POSTSCRIPT

The questions raised in this text seek to bring to awareness that the Jewish-Christian dialogue must no longer remain the monopoly of a few interested specialists, for the topics listed here hit the center of both the Jewish and the Christian self-understanding. Over and above their contribution to the encounter of Jews and Christians, they have something decisive to contribute to the understanding of all religions and to the problems of the human future. That is why the Workshop on "Jews and Christians" of the Central Committee of Roman Catholics in Germany appeals to all those who are responsible for the training and the continuing education of priests and other pastoral workers, to the organizers of adult education, to the media, and to the Jewish communities and institutions. It urges them to devote themselves increasingly to those central topics of the Jewish-Christian dialogue in the next few years, and to bring the importance of those topics to the attention of the public.

17
Pastoral Guidelines

For Priests, Religious
and Laypeople in England and Wales, 1980
[from Catholic Truth Society]

The Catholic Bishops of England and Wales declared:

We accept that the Second Vatican Council taught Catholics to look on the other great world Religions with respect and to recognize that God is also in them. The Church now encourages us to approach them in a spirit of dialogue, of listening and sharing with humility . . . We should try to become much better acquainted with the background and beliefs of non-Christians in our countries. In particular we should approach them in a spirit of openness and humility to learn, to understand, to appreciate and gain from their religious traditions. At the same time we should make known to them our own belief, the Good News of Jesus Christ . . . We wish to encourage personal contact, offers of hospitality and initiatives by parishes.

1. PRACTICAL APPLICATION OF SOME OF THE KEY PASSAGES CONTAINED IN THE VATICAN 'GUIDELINES AND SUGGESTIONS'

(i) 'Although Christianity sprang from Judaism . . . the gap dividing them has deepened more and more to such an extent that Christian and Jew hardly knew each other . . . Such relations as there have been between Jew and Christian have scarcely ever risen above the level of monologue. From now on, real dialogue must be established. Dialogue presupposes that each side wishes to know the other and wishes to increase and deepen its knowledge of the other.'

Clearly, personal contact is a priority. Catholics should take the initiative in promoting friendly relationships with their Jewish neighbours. An approach to a local Rabbi would seem to be the most fruitful means of discovering which of the Jews in the neighbourhood would welcome the opportunity of meeting a corresponding group of parishioners.

One of the parish confraternities, UCM, CWL, SVP, Knights of St Columba, etc., should be encouraged to form a housegroup for discussion of common problems, responsibilities and matters of civic concern. The scope of inter-religious dialogue is very wide. It can deal directly with religious experiences, beliefs and worships; it can also deal with social aspects of Christians and Jewish life.

(ii) 'In addition to friendly talks, competent people will be encouraged to meet and study together the problems deriving from the fundamental convictions of Judaism and Christianity.'

Catholic members of local Councils of Christians and Jews, and teachers who are preparing pupils for 'A' and 'O' Level examinations in Scripture may be willing to set up informal study groups, however modest their beginnings. Public and formal meetings, however, should have the approval of the Ordinary of the Diocese.

It is obvious that where Catholics and Jews meet for common study and careful reflection the principle of the equality of the participants must be respected and accepted.

(iii) 'Although we believe that the importance and meaning of the religious tradition of Judaism was deeply affected by the coming of Christ, it is nonetheless rich in religious values . . . The existing links between the Christian liturgy and the Jewish liturgy will be borne in mind.'

Dialogue at times includes extending and accepting invitations to visit each other's place of worship.

Young people of secondary-school age would be interested to see the resemblance between the synagogue and their own churches.

Children in primary schools take a pride in making models and wallcharts illustrating the Jewish background of Christ's everyday life. They are always delighted when these are put on display in the church porch.

(iv) 'Where possible, and mutually acceptable, one might encourage a common meeting in the presence of God in prayer and silent meditation.'

Working together, or visiting homes and places of worship will eventually raise the very difficult and important question of fuller sharing in common prayer and meditation. This demands a great sensitivity for one another's feelings. The order of the prayer meeting should always be prepared in consultation with the leader of the Jewish participants.

(v) 'The spiritual bonds and historical links binding the Church to Judaism condemn (as opposed to the very spirit of Christianity) all forms of anti-Semitism and discrimination . . . With respect to liturgical readings, care will be taken to see that homilies based on them do not distort their meaning, especially where passages seem to show the Jewish people in an unfavourable light.'

The pulpit offers a powerful platform for counteracting anti-Semitism in all its forms. In the course of the year there will be many opportunities for priests in the parishes and students at the seminaries to do this.

Holy Week is an opportune time to make clear that the term 'The Jews' as found in St John's Gospel refers not to the Jewish people as a whole but to the spiritual leaders of contemporary Judaism.

Priests who preach on the spiritual and historical links binding the Church to Judaism will find readings from St Paul's letter to the Romans, chs 10, 11 and 12 particularly appropriate.

(vi) 'In the spirit of the prophets, Jews and Christians will work willingly together, seeking social justice and peace at every level—local, national and international.'

Dialogue not only means praying together and sharing experiences and ideas; it also demands that we work together for the good of our fellow man so as to build up a more just, humane and peaceful society. Local Jewish leaders will welcome the opportunity of attending parochial action meetings at which important economic, social, cultural and political issues are discussed. We must always be conscious that we all belong to the same family, the family of the people of God and be aware that in God's designs that family is basically one.

2. ESSENTIAL REQUIREMENTS FOR FRUITFUL DIALOGUE

(i) *The practice of prayer*

Prayer is the very soul of religious dialogue. It is most important that those who take part in dialogue should prepare for it with a profound awareness and openness to the Word of God working in them. The realization of God's will in the world should therefore be the common programme of Catholics and Jews.

(ii) *A deep commitment to faith*

Dialogue is not undertaken from a position of doubt but with an open and clear faith that lives from the assurance of the truths revealed by God.

(iii) *Honesty and truthfulness*

Honesty in motivation is fundamental. But in expressing our convictions we should do so in all humility and in such a way as not to offend the susceptibilities of others.

(iv) *Love of God and love of others*

Like all Christian activity, dialogue can be genuine and fruitful only if it is an expression of love. 'Love is always patient and kind; it is never jealous; love is never boastful or conceited; it is never rude or selfish; it does not take offence and is not resentful . . . It is always ready to excuse, to trust, to hope and to endure whatever comes' (1 Cor. 13:4–6).

18
The Church and the Jews:
German Bishops' Conference, Bonn 1980

(English translation by Phil Jenkins) [from Catholic Truth Society] London

I. JESUS CHRIST—OUR APPROACH TO JUDAISM

He who encounters Jesus Christ encounters Judaism. According to the evidence of the New Testament he, as 'son of David' (Rom. 1:3) and 'son of Abraham' (Mt. 1:1; cf.Heb. 7:14) and 'of their flesh' (Rom. 9:5), was descended from the People of Israel. 'When the appointed time came, God sent his Son, born of a woman, born a subject of the Law' (Gal. 4:4). According to his human nature, Jesus of Nazareth was a Jew; he stemmed from Judaism. According to his ancestry, he has a place in the history of the people of Israel (cf. the genealogy of Jesus Mt. 1:1-17 and Lk. 3:23-38).

Today Jewish authors too, are discovering the 'Jewishness' of Jesus. Martin Buber saw in Jesus his 'big brother'.[1] Schalom Ben-Chorin acknowledges: 'Jesus is for me the eternal brother, not only a human brother, but also my Jewish brother. I feel his brotherly hand which grasps me, so that I should follow him . . . His faith, his unquestioning faith, absolute trust in God the Father, readiness to submit himself completely to the will of God, that is the attitude that we see in Jesus as an example, and which can bind us—Jews and Christians.[2]

II. ISRAEL'S SPIRITUAL HERITAGE

Jesus Christ, through his Jewish Origin, brought a rich spiritual heritage from the religious traditions of his people into the Christian faith, so that

Christ, is 'spiritually bound to the tribe of Abraham'[3] and perpetually draws on this heritage.

1. Holy Scriptures of the Old Testament

First, one points to the Scriptures of Israel, called by Christians the 'Old Testament' (that is, The Hebrew Bible). When the New Testament speaks of 'Scripture' or 'the Scriptures' or refers to that which is 'written' (cf., for example, Mt. 4:6; Mk 1:2; Lk. 24:44-46; Jn 19:36f.; 1 Cor. 15:3f; 2 Cor. 4:13; Gal. 3:10-13), it is referring to the Old Testament. The Second Vatican Council teaches: 'God, with loving concern contemplating and making preparation for the salvation of the whole human race, in a singular undertaking chose for himself a people to whom he would entrust his promises. . . . The story of salvation, foretold, recounted and explained by the sacred authors, is presented as the true Word of God in the books of the Old Testament.'[4] The Old Testament is a source of belief common to Jews and Christians, although for Christians the New Testment has become a special source of belief. In the Old Testament the God of Revelation speaks, the God of Abraham, Isaac and Jacob, who is also the God of Jesus. In addition, the Vatican 'Guidelines' on the implementation of *Nostra Aetate* (N.4), issued 1 December 1974 states: 'An effort will be made to acquire a better understanding of whatever in the Old Testament retains its own perpetual value, since that has not been cancelled by the later interpretation of the New Testament. Rather, there is a reciprocal elucidation and interpretation.'[5] One must not contrast the Old Testament and the Jewish tradition founded on it with the New Testament in such a way that the Old Testament appears to embody a religion of Justice, Fear and Law without the call to love God and one's neighbour (cf. Deut. 6:5; Lev. 19:18; Mt. 22:34-40).[6] The Church has rightly constantly refused all attempts aimed at removing the Old Testament from its scriptural canon and leave only the New Testament.

2. Belief in One God

The Hebrew Bible testifies above all to the one God: 'Hear, O Israel, the Lord our God the Lord is One!' (Deut. 6:4). This sentence is the 'credo' of the Jewish religion that is recited at family prayers, morning and evening as it is in the Synagogue service. To the question of the Scribes, 'Which is the first of all the commandments?' Jesus answered: 'The first is, ''Hear, O Israel: the Lord our God, the Lord is one; and you shall love the Lord your God with all your heart and with all your soul, and with all your mind and with all your strength'' '(Mk 12:29f.). The council teaches: God, 'did acquire a people for himself, and to them he revealed himself through word and deed as the one true living God, so that Israel might experience the ways of God with men, and that through the word of God out of the mouths of prophets they had to understand his ways more clearly and more fully, and make them known more widely among the nations (cf. Ps. 21:28f.; 95:1-3; Is 2:1-4; Jer. 3:17)'[7]

3. Belief in the Creation

This one God is also the Creator of the whole world. With classic precision, that is immediately expressed in the first verse of the Bible: 'In the beginning, God created the heavens and the earth' (Gen. 1:1). These words maintain the idea that the Creator and creation are not identical or interchangeable. They prevent a worldly idolatry, although Israel has, through her fascinating, thorough system, seen and extolled the world in her prayers. They protect the mind of man from the gnostic-neoplatonic interpretation of the world according to which the world was not created by God but emanates from Him, and guards it from that idealistic philosophy according to which the history of the universe is a self-development of God. Through Jesus and the Church the message of creation in the Old Testament came to the people of the world. It helps to acquire the right relationship to the world.

4. Man Is God's Image

Of particular significance today is the teaching of the Hebrew Bible that man is made 'in the image of God'. 'Then God said, ''Let us make man in our own image, in the likeness of ourselves and let them be masters of the fish of the sea, the birds of heaven, the cattle, all the wild beasts and all the reptiles that crawl upon earth.'' God created man in the image of himself, in the image of God he created him, male and female he created them' (Gen. 1:26f.). 'God made man imperishable and made him in the image of his own nature' (Wis. 2:23). The precept of man's image in God implies the incontestable dignity of man, and thereby also what man calls today 'human rights'. According to Jewish teaching, one who kills diminishes his likeness in the image of God.[8] One may not despise his neighbour, because he is made in the image of God.[9] The Lord created man with his own hands and made him in the likeness of his own countenance . . . He who despises the countenance of man, despises the countenance of the Lord!'[10] The letter of James, taken entirely from this belief of Judaism, puts it thus: 'We use it [the tongue] to bless the Lord, but we also use it to curse men who are made in God's image' (Js. 3:9).

5. Covenant

Israel knows that it has made a covenant with its God. This covenant is grace, and, at the same time, commitment. The demands of the covenant are aimed at the exclusive veneration of Yahweh through Israel. The 'rule of the covenant' reads: 'You will be my people, I will be your God.' The prophets warn their people about breaching the covenant.

The Hebrew Bible tells, too, of a former covenant with Abraham (cf. Gen. 15), where God gives to Abraham the sworn pledge of the fulfillment of the Promised Land; and, again, with Noah (cf. Gen. 9:9-17). The picture of salvation, in which the covenant with Noah is involved, is all-embracing, in that it refers to the whole 'earth' (Gen. 9:13), to 'all living creatures' (Gen. 9:10-12, 15, 16), to 'every living creature of every kind that is found on the earth' (Gen. 9:16f.) including the animal kingdom (Gen. 9:10). So it means that 'the history of nature and mankind is based on God's approval of his creation. God's approval of all life, so that neither through any catastrophe in the course of history, nor . . . through lapse, corruption or rebellion of man, can it be upset. God's promise will continue as strong as iron as long as earth exists'[11] God will save the world, even if the earth is once again 'defiled under its inhabitants' feet, for they have transgressed the law, violated the precept, broken the everlasting covenant' (Is. 24:5). God fulfils that which was promised in the covenant with Noah, which he concluded with the whole world, with all mankind.

The guarantor for the final fulfilment of the obligation of the covenant is the 'Divine Servant' whom God selects, in person, to be 'the covenant of my people' and at the same time 'the light of the nations' (Is. 42:6). According to Christian belief, he has appeared in Jesus Christ, whose blood, shed on the Cross, clearly refers to the 'blood of the covenant shed for many (Mk 14:24; Mt 26:28) as does the Chalice offered by him as the 'new covenant in my blood' (Lk. 22:20: 1 Cor. 11:25). Jesus makes use of this concept of Jewish tradition for the interpretation of his death. Salvation manifests itself as a covenant into which God has entered as a permanent act of faith with Israel and the whole world, a "covenant" that God will not forget his creation. The Creator is also the Redeemer (cf. Is. 54:5).

6. Commandments and Conscience

What the pious Jew holds particularly dear to this day is a life conforming to God's doctrine, called in Hebrew, 'Torah'. This 'doctrine' governs the everyday life of Jews before God. The core of the 'doctrine' is the Ten Commandments. Jesus, too, plainly accepted the commandments (cf. Mk 10:19). The 'Ten Words', as they are called in the Old Testament, mark the standard for the conscience of all mankind, not only the Jews. They are the embodiment of the ethical awareness of the human race. According to the Apostle Paul, they are 'by nature' 'written in the hearts [of all men]'—'they can call a witness, that is, their own conscience—they have accusation and defence' (Rom. 2:14f.). They are defined in positive phrases, and without their observation there is no true community life nor true relationship with God. The experience of history teaches that without a conscience based on God's precepts man becomes a beast. Opportunity for tyranny, dictatorship, loss of freedom and personal enmity is great. The commandments describe the spiritual order of man's behaviour; they are, therefore, indispensable for all time.

7. Messianic Hope

Messianic hope originates also in the Jewish religion. Its origins were already bound up in the Dynasty of David. Attention is drawn 2 Sam. 7:12–16: 'And when your days are ended and you are laid to rest with your ancestors, I will preserve the offspring of your body after you and make his sovereignty secure. It is he who shall build a house for my name, and I will make his royal throne for ever. I will be a father to him, and he a son to me . . . Your house and your sovereignty will always stand secure before me and your throne be established for ever.' The prophets of Israel established the Messianic hope time and again and bore witness to it in a distinct manner. If we ask what brought the Messianic tidings to mankind, three answers present themselves:

  i. The Messianic idea springs from man's cyclic thought. The history of the world does not move in a circle, is not the endless return to the same point; the Messianic promise allows history to be judged.
 ii. This movement of history towards a God-centred goal is a movement from disaster to salvation.
iii. The turning towards salvation will be brought by an ultimate Redeemer, who will be called the Messiah.

The Messianic hope came to the expectancies and hopes of the people, even if in a different form, through Jesus of Nazareth, whom the Church acknowledges and proclaims as the promised Messiah. In the first instance. Christian Messianism also wanted to be involved in a deep intensification of the relationship with God, so Jesus himself proclaimed his second coming at the end of time as an event that will concern the whole world: 'Then they will see the Son of Man coming in the clouds with great power and glory' (Mk 13:26). The Apocalypse, in particular, understands the second coming of the Lord as a world event in which the 'Antichrist' is destroyed by the returning Messiah Jesus, and a new heaven and earth will be raised.

Messianism is more influential than ever in the world today, even if frequently in a secularised form. The world no longer wants to go in circles, it looks to the future and towards a goal. The Messianic Belief testifies to the future, because it proclaims a coming saviour for Israel and all people. Moreover, Messianic hope unites with a longing for a just world and for total peace for all mankind, announced by the prophets of Israel as a future salvation, although they often link this proclamation with a censure of the social abuses of their time. The New Testament pursues this line. Christ is proclaimed in it as the one appointed to be the judge of the whole world (Acts 17:31) and who came to bring peace to those who were far away, and to those who were near at hand, that is, to all men (Eph. 2:17). The Church waits, with Israel 'for a new heaven and a new earth, the place where righteousness will be at home' (2 Pet. 3:13). Jesus certainly warned too, of false messiahs, who deceive the people with their ideologies (cf. Mk 13:22). Messianism can be perverted. The Church should know that; 'You, therefore, must be on your guard. I have forewarned you of everything' (Mk 13:23).

8. Prayer

Devout Jews are a praying people, glorifying God. From the great Hebrew treasury of prayer the Church has taken, above all, the psalms, which play a great role in public worship and, in particular, in the prayer of the hours. The Lord's Prayer, too, the 'Our Father', modelled on the Jewish prayers of petition, is, much as it bears the stamp of the spirit of Jesus, marked out as special by the salutation, 'Father'. The devout Jew, too, calls for the coming of God's kingdom, desires the hallowing of 'the Name' and concerns himself with the fulfillment of God's will; he prays for his daily bread, the forgiveness of sins and preservation from temptation. The two great hymns of praise form the time of Jesus's childhood, which are used in the Liturgy, the 'Benedictus' (Lk. 1:68–79) and the 'Magnificat' (Lk. 1:46–55), abound with words and phrases from the Old Testament.

9. Attitude to God

Israel's basic attitude before God, as shown in Awe of God, Obedience, Recognition of God, Conversion, 'Commemoration', Love, Trust, Holiness,

Praise of God and his holy deeds,[12] are also basic attitudes of the Christian community; they are not 'discoveries' of the Church, but belong to the spiritual dowry of Israel to the Church, which she in her mission passes on again to all people, established anew and conclusively in Christ.

10. Exodus, Passover, the Passion, Law, Resurrection

From the spiritual heritage of Israel one can quote those events in which the plan of God's salvation of man is an actual historical fact and can thus be shown. In particular, reference should be made to the following, which are linked: Exodus, Passover, the Passion, Judgement, Resurretion.

The Exodus is for Israel the crucial act of God's deliverance, time and again commemorated in the witness of the Scriptures.[13] 'Exodus' means the deliverance out of Egypt's 'house of bondage'. 'We were Pharaoh's bondsmen in Egypt, and the Lord our God brought us out therefrom with a mighty hand and an outstretched arm. Now if the Holy One, blessed be he, had not brought our fathers forth from Egypt, then we, and our children, and our children's children, would be servants to the Pharaoh in Egypt': so begins the answer in the communal Passover meal to the question of the youngest one present: 'Why is this night different from all others?'[14] Exodus means wandering through the desert in Israel's most intense encounter with God and with the experience of his help. Exodus is finally and conclusively the march depicted in the arrival in the land promised by God to Abraham and his descendants. The Exodus brought Israel the experience of life's bitterness, too: the experience (often self-imposed) of suffering and judgement, and, in this respect, the experience of suffering combined with the experience of salvation through God. For this reason Jewish tradition is aware of Exodus as a sign of hope and the final salvation through God in the Resurrection of the dead at the end of time.

The Exodus experience of his people is singularly mirrored in Jesus' departure from his native village of Nazareth and from his kin, in his travels, associated with suffering, through the land of Israel, in his way to Golgotha and the Cross, and also in his Resurrection from the dead and his glorification.

'In contrast with other people, the Jewish people do not commemorate the golden age of power, do not boast of a divine lineage, but recognise themselves as the people of bondage who experience God's redemption, and this brings the past into today's recompense and suffering.'[15] The Jewish religion is 'a religion of remembrance'; the concept of 'recollection'; 'remembrance' plays a central role in Hebrew Scriptures. The Jewish Festivals are festivals of remembrance: in its festivals Israel commemorates God's salvation of his people and recalls in them this divine salvation to each generation. In no festival is that more clear than at the Passover, when the Jews commemorate the night when they were freed, and when at the same time, hope is awakened for the time when they finally will be free. In the Jewish festivals the three dimensions of salvation, the Past, Present and Future, prevail.

Without recognition of this continuity, one cannot understand the great feasts of the Christian Church's year, especially the celebration of the Eucharist. Salvation in the past, present and future belongs substantially to them as well; they, too, are commemorations of his miracles. At the same time, although they do not run parallel to the feasts of Israel, they stand in a closely related association with them.[16]

Even though the Church is convinced that with the Resurrection of Jesus from the dead 'the coming aeon'—a phrase from early Judaism—is projected powerfully into this time, so is there also a lasting, common theme of Christian and Jewish eschatology, as, for instance, in the last clause of the Creed. 'With the prophets and the Apostle Paul, the Church anticipates the day when only God is recognised, when all people shall call the Lord with one voice and "serve him under the same yoke" (Zeph. 3:9).'[17] 'The Day of God plays as important a part in the Hebrew Bible as it does in the New Testament. This 'Day', according to the prophets and the New Testament, embraces the whole world; it plainly leads towards 'the conclusion'. This 'Day' is not a day reckoned by the calendar; only God knows it and directs it hither. This 'Day' fashions history and carries it to its conclusion. But this 'Day' is also a day of passing over into ultimate salvation and is thus a day of hope for Israel and the Church.

III. THE TESTIMONY OF THE SCRIPTURES AND THE CHURCH CONCERNING THE RELATIONSHIPS BETWEEN THE CHURCH AND JUDAISM

1. The Witness of the New Testament

a) The New Testament makes important statements on the Jewish people. The original missionaries themselves were descended, to a large extent, from the Jewish people; Jesus' life and death took place in the land of Israel; Jesus knows himself 'to be sent only to the lost sheep of the House of Israel' (Mt. 15:24). The Gospel, and, thereby, Christ's salvation, was 'first' proclaimed to the Jews (cf. Mk 7:27; Acts 2:39;3:26; 10:42;13:46; Rom. 1:16;2:10). The question of the salvation of the Jews was of profound concern, particularly to the Jews of the Primitive Church and to the former Pharisee, Paul.

b) It certainly cannot be denied that there are also to be found critical statements in the New Testament about the Jews at the time of Jesus. Jesus himself says: 'Jerusalem, Jerusalem, you that kill the prophets and stone those who are sent to you! How often have I longed to gather your children as a hen gathers her chicks under her wings, and you refused. So be it! Your house will be left to you desolate' (Mt. 23:37f.). Jesus calls the Pharisees 'blind men leading blind men' (Mt. 15:14) whose sin 'remains' (Jn. 9:41). 'The devil is your father, and you prefer to do what your father wants' (Jn 8:44). Jesus thus establishes responsible behaviour. Paul declares that 'not all those who descend from Israel are Israel' (Rom. 9:6); the Jews certainly have 'fervour in God, but their zeal is misguided' (Rom. 10:2). The Apostle asks reproachfully: 'Is it possible that Israel did not understand?' (Rom. 10:19); he speaks of a 'denial', a 'stubbornness' (Rom. 11:8), a 'stumbling' of Israel (Rom. 11:11) and of his 'rejection' (Rom. 11:15); the Jews are 'enemies of God . . . only with regard to the Good News' (Rom. 11:28). The Jews are the people who put the Lord Jesus to death, and the prophets, too. And now they have been persecuting us, and acting in a way that cannot please God and makes them the enemies of the whole human race, because they are hindering us from preaching to the pagans and trying to save them. They never stop trying to finish off the sins they have begun' (1 Thess. 2:15f.). Paul ends up, too, speaking of the persecution to which he was exposed through his fellow Jews (cf. 2 Cor. 11:24–26). The Acts of the Apostles tell, too, of the great difficulties which the Jews caused the Christian missionaries (cf. Acts 13:15;14:5–19;17:5–8;19:12 23:12).

These are facts that can throw an unfavourable light on Jews. At the same time, however, one must realise that one is dealing with facts from the past which do not warrant an overall judgement of Judaism, and that these negative declarations on the Jews must not be contemplated on their own, but must be seen in association with the many positive declarations in the New Testament.

c) In the first instance, one recalls the witness of John's Gospel: 'salvation comes from the Jews' (Jn. 4:22). The Saviour, Jesus Christ, stemmed from Judaism.

Important·positive declarations on the Jews are to be found in particular in the letter of St Paul to the Romans: 'Well then, is a Jew any better off? Is there any advantage in being circumcised? A great advantage in every way. First, the Jews are the people to whom God's message was entrusted' (Rom. 3: 1f.). This refers to the part of the Hebrew Scriptures that the Christians call the Old Testament. Later it says: 'My brothers of Israel . . . were adopted as sons, they were given the glory of the covenants; the Law and the ritual were drawn up for them . . . They were descended from the patriarchs and from their flesh and blood came Christ' (Rom. 9:4f.). Here the prerogative of Israel, as told by the Apostle, is also called its 'privileges', granted by God himself. God does not take these away from the Jews: 'God never takes back his gifts or revokes his choice.'[18]

In his letter to the Romans, 11:1f., 'the Apostle writes: 'Let me put a further question then: is it possible that God has rejected his people? Of course not . . . I could never agree that God had rejected his people, the people he chose specially long ago.' He asks, moreover, 'Have the Jews fallen for ever, or have they just stumbled? Obviously they have not fallen for ever' (Rom. 11:11). The Apostle speaks of the 'root' which supports the Church (Rom. 11:18). This refers to the whole people of Israel, not just the 'Fathers' (the Patriarchs). It is not just a question of the 'root', but also of the noble olive and its 'branches' (cf. Rom. 11:16-21).[19] That the Apostle stresses the 'root' so strongly—he refers to it four times in Rom. 11:16-18—is because it is the root from which the sap flows to the tree, and through which the tree receives its 'oiliness', that is, its fruitfulness. The (Gentile) Church is grafted on to the holy olive, and through the grace of God 'shares in the root' and the fruitfulness of the olive tree. Even if the Jews for the most part 'stumbled over the stumbling stone' (cf. Rom. 9:32) and, with regard to the Gospel, have become 'blind' (Rom. 11:7.25), according to the Apostle's prophetic announcement the Jews are, nevertheless, not excluded for ever from salvation for this reason: 'God is perfectly able to graft them back again; after all, if you were cut from your naturally wild olive to be grafted unnaturally on to a cultivated olive, it will be much easier for them, the natural branches, to be grafted back on the tree they came from' (Rom. 11:23f.). In addition to this Paul speaks of a mystery which refers to the final salvation of Israel, and which Paul makes known: 'One section of Israel has become blind, but this will last only until the whole pagan world has entered, and then after this the rest of Israel will be saved as well. As Scripture says ''the liberator will come from Zion, he will banish godlessness from Jacob'' (Rom. 11:25f.).

Paul compares the 'blindness' and 'discord' of Israel with regard to the Gospel with a singular, dialectic redemption of pagans: 'Let me put another question then: have the Jews fallen for ever, or have they just stumbled? Obviously they have not fallen for ever: their fall, though, has saved the pagans in a way the Jews may now well emulate. Think of the extent to which the world, the pagan world, has benefited from their fall and defection' (Rom.11:11f.). 'Since their rejection meant the reconciliation of the world, do you know what their admission will mean? Nothing less than resurrection from the dead! (Rom. 11:15) 'God has imprisoned all men in their own disobedience only to show mercy to all mankind' (Rom. 11:32). Only from that point of view is it possible to understand the Apostle's statement that the Jews became antagonistic to the Gospel and enemies only for your sake' (Rom. 11:28), that is, so that the pagans might be saved. There is no question in the letter to the Romans of settling debts with reprisals. We Christians must take seriously the prophetic statement of the Apostle Paul with regard to the final salvation of the Jews, even if we do not know more precisely the way in which God will save 'all Israel.' The Jews remain the 'chosen people, still loved by God' (Rom. 11:28).

In the Acts of the Apostles one sees the prophetic declaration of the eschatological 're-establishment' of Israel. Thus the Apostles ask of the Risen One: 'Has the time come? Are you going to restore the kingdom to Israel?' In his answer Jesus does not dismiss this question of the Apostles as an absurd one, he just alludes to the fact that the Father alone, in his authority, decided the appointed time for the 're-establishment' of the kingdom to Israel. The Apostles themselves, however, should proclaim the Gospel as Christ's witness 'indeed to the ends of the earth' (Acts 1:6-8). A re-establishment of the promised kingdom, as the prophets of the Hebrew Bible proclaimed, will also come, even if we do not know more precisely in what way. According to Acts 3:19-21 the Jews must turn to God, 'so that your sins may be wiped out, and so that the Lord may send the time of comfort. Then he will send you the Christ he has predestined, that is Jesus, whom heaven must keep till the universal restoration comes which God proclaimed, speaking through his holy prophets.' According to this text, the returning Christ is also the time of comfort for Israel ('for you'—the Jews). The Jews, too, will then be 'comforted' with all the redeemed ones and will be freed from their sufferings and sins. These positive declarations in the New Testament about the Jews and their salvation must be much more strongly considered than previously in Christian preaching and theology, particularly as the Second Vatican Council expressly undertook this task.

2. Declarations of the Catholic Church

a) In its Conciliar statement *Nostra Aetate* the Second Vatican Council expressed fundamental principles regarding the relationship of the Church to Judaism:

'Sounding the depths of the mystery which is the Church, this Sacred Council remembers the spiritual ties which link the people of the New Covenant to the stock of Abraham.

'The Church of Christ acknowledges that in God's plan of salvation the beginning of her faith and election is to be found in the patriarchs, Moses and the prophets. She professes that all Christ's faithful, who as men of faith are sons of Abraham, are included in the same patriarch's call and that the salvation of the Church is mystically prefigured in the exodus of God's chosen people from the land of bondage. On this account the Church cannot forget that she received the revelation of the Old Testament by way of that people with whom God in his inexpressible mercy established the ancient covenant. Nor can she forget that she draws nourishment from that good olive tree on to which the wild olive branches of the Gentiles have been grafted. The Church believes that Christ who is our peace has through his Cross reconciled Jews and Gentiles and made them one himself.

'Likewise the Church keeps ever before her mind the words of the Apostle Paul about his kinsmen: "They are Israelites, and to them belong the sonship, the glory, the covenants, the giving of the law, the worship, and the promises; to them belong the patriarchs, and of their race, according to the flesh, is the Christ" (Rom. 9:4-5), the son of the virgin Mary. She is mindful, moreover, that the apostles, the pillars on which the Church stands, are of Jewish descent, as are many of those early disciples who proclaimed the Gospel of Christ to the world.

'As holy Scripture testifies, Jerusalem did not recognise God's moment when it came. Jews for the most part did not accept the Gospel; on the contrary, many opposed the spreading of it. Even so, the apostle Paul maintains that the Jews remain very dear to God, for the sake of the patriarchs, since God does not take back the gifts he bestowed or the choice he made. Together with the prophets and that same apostle, the Church awaits the day, known to God alone, when all peoples will call on God with one voice and serve him "shoulder to shoulder" (Zeph. 3:9).

'Since Christians and Jews have such a common spiritual heritage, this sacred Council wishes to encourage and further mutual understanding and appreciation. This can be obtained, especially, by way of biblical and theological enquiry and through friendly discussions.

'Even though the Jewish authorities and those who followed their lead pressed for the death of Christ, neither all Jews indiscriminately at that time, nor Jews today, can be charged with the crimes committed during his Passion. It is true that the Church is the new people of God, yet the Jews should not be spoken of as rejected or accursed as if this followed from holy Scripture. Consequently, all must take care, lest in catechizing or in preaching the word of God, they teach anything which is not in accord with the truth of the Gospel message or the spirit of Christ.

'Indeed, the Church reproves every form of persecution against whomsoever it may be directed. Remembering, then, her common heritage with the Jews and moved not by any political consideration, but solely by the religious motivation of Christian charity, she deplores all hatred, persecutions, displays of anti-Semitism levelled at any time or from any source against the Jews.

'The Church always held and continues to hold that Christ out of infinite love freely underwent suffering and death because of the sins of all men, so that all might attain salvation. It is the duty of the Church, therefore, in her preaching to proclaim the cross of Christ as the sign of God's universal love and the source of all grace.'[20]

b) On 1 December 1974 the Vatican Guidelines for implementing *Nostra Aetate* (N.4) were issued.[21] They mark an important milestone in the history of Jewish-Christian relations. They speak of the gap which became deeper and wider 'to such an extent that Christian and Jew hardly knew each other.'[22] It is said that 'the spiritual bonds and the historical links binding the Church to Judaism condemn (as opposed to the very spirit of Christianity) all forms of anti-Semitism and discrimination'; furthermore, these 'links and relationships render obligatory a better mutual understanding and renewed mutual esteem.'[23] From the monologue which Jews and Christians have each directed to the other a 'dialogue' must come which demands a 'respect for the other as he is' and shuns all 'aggression'.[24] A great openness of spirit, an attitude of suspicion towards one's own prejudices, tact and caution are essential in order not to hurt (even involuntarily) those taking part.[25] The Liturgy is then referred to, with its common elements, and the perpetual value of the Old Testament and its later interpretation in Christian theology.[26] What began with the Council's change of thought must be continued in study and research.[27] The God of Israel and of Christians is the 'same God'. 'The history of Judaism did not end with the destruction of Jerusalem, and in its further growth evolved a religious tradition, whose development is rich in religious values, even if, as we believe, it has a profoundly different meaning with the coming of Christ.'[28]

c) On 22 October 1974 Pope Paul VI set up a Commission for Religious Relations with the Jews which is connected with the Secretariat for Christian Unity and whose members also include Jews.

In his address to the representatives of Jewish Organisations on 12 March 1979 Pope John Paul II drew attention to the Declaration in *Nostra Aetate* N. 4 where the Council made clear that 'while searching into the mystery of the Church' it recalled 'the spiritual bond linking the people of the New Covenant with Abraham's stock.' He underlined the value of the 'Guidelines' of 1 December 1974 and encouraged the Church to 'fraternal dialogue' and to 'fruitful working together' and to 'overcoming every kind of prejudice and discrimination' against the Jewish people.

On his visit to Auschwitz during his tour of Poland, the Holy Father observed: 'In particular I pause with you, dear partners in this meeting, before the tablet with the Hebrew inscription. It stirs memories of the nation whose sons and daughters were condemned to total extermination. This people stemmed from Abraham, our "father in faith" (cf. Rom 4:12), as Paul of Tarsus asserted. This very nation, which received from God the commandment, "Thou shalt not kill", has experienced to a pronounced degree what is meant by killing. No-one may pass by this memorial with indifference.'

d) The United Diocesan Synod of Bishops in the Federal Republic of Germany declared emphatically in its Resolution 'Our Hope' (V1, 2) 'for a new relationship with the history of the faith of the Jewish people.' The Statement by the French Bishops' Committee for Relations with Jews 16 April 1973 provides an important stimulus.[29] The Working Paper of the Workshop on 'Jews and Christians' of the Central Committee of German Catholics, 'Basic Theological Issues of Jewish-Christian Dialogue', 8 May 1979, is helpful, too.

3. Declarations of Other Churches

It is rewarding to refer to the evangelical reports issued on the theme of the Church and Judaism: 'People, Land and State'—an aid to a theological meditation issued by the Dutch Reformed Church,[30] 'Christians and Jews'— a study by the Council of the Evangelical Church in Germany 1975 with the appropriate working paper on the study by the Evangelical Church in Germany,[31] 'Reflections on the problem of the Church and Israel,' published by the Executive Committee of the Swiss Evangelical Church of the Confederation, May 1977,[32] and 'Towards the restoration of relations between Christians and Jews—suggestions for the members of Regional Synods, Circuit Synods and the Presbyteries of the Evangelical Church in the Rhineland.[33]

So, at the same time, Christians are thinking of their 'roots', 'Abraham's stock' in a thorough way, more keenly than before. They are reaching a new relationship with their older brethren, the Jewish people, certainly to the benefit of both. Respect and love for one another will come in place of contempt and disparagement. There must no longer be a place for anti-Semitism.

IV. DIFFERENCES OF BELIEF

In the dialogue between Jews and Christians the differences in Faith must be discussed frankly, even the distinctive, and if necessary, dividing differences; only then will a true and genuine dialogue succeed. The following should also be noted.

1. The Kingdom of God in Jesus the Messiah

In the first instance, the Christian belief is considered, that with Jesus of Nazareth the time has come and the Kingdom of God is close at hand (cf. Mk 1:15). For Christians, Jesus is the promised Messiah, the final era of history starts with him, the kingdom of God extends into 'this eternity'. Jesus' miracles are the 'prophetic sign' of the coming fulfilment, the strength of God's salvation is already effective, particularly in the Sacraments of the Church, the ultimate decisions are made. Christ is our peace, our reconciliation and our life. Indeed, a Christian knows, too, that not all the promises of the prophets of the Hebrew Bible will be fulfilled through Jesus of Nazareth: all-embracing justice is by no means established in the world yet, universal peace is yet to come, death still holds its devastating sway. A Christian must understand when Jews point to this still-outstanding 'balance of promise' and do not want to see Jesus of Nazareth as the promised one.

2. Belief in Jesus Christ

The most profound difference of belief manifests itself in the face of the strong connecting links between Christians and Jews. The Christian belief in Jesus Christ who as a consequence of his crucifixion and resurrection is affirmed and proclaimed, not only as the promised Messiah, but also as the consubstantial Son of God, appears to many Jews as something radically 'unjewish': they see him as an absolute contradiction, if not a blasphemy, to the strict monotheism as it is referred to every day, particularly by devout Jews, in the 'Shema Israel'. The Christian must understand this, even if he himself sees no contradiction to monotheism in the teaching of Jesus, Son of God. For him, the acknowledgement of a 'three-in-one' God is an intensification of the 'oneness' of God, a mystery in which he believes and before which he kneels in prayer.

3. The Problem of the Law

Jesus did not 'abolish the law' but fulfilled it (cf. Mt. 5:17), but to some extent he severely criticised the actual practice of the legal life of his people. He placed the dual commandment of love in the forefront (cf. Mk 12, 30–34). On to the commandment of love he focussed the many commandments and prohibitions of the Torah and the so-called 'traditions of the Fathers', which is the Pharisaic-rabbinic interpretation (called by the Jews 'Halacha'). With regard to the Cross and the Resurrection of Jesus, the Apostle Paul was positive, with the Primitive Church, that the way of man to redemption now leads exclusively through belief in the crucified and risen Christ and no longer through the 'keeping of the law' (Rom. 2:15; 3:20; Gal. 2:16; 3:2–5, 10). According to the Apostle's teaching and the Council of Apostles, the Christian was no longer pledged, like the Jew, to live a life directed by the Torah, which certainly did not mean that a Christian might live a 'lawless' life. He is even more bound to the 'law of Christ' which culminates in the commandment of love, in which the law is fulfilled (cf. Gal 5:14; Rom. 13:8–10).

In Christian-Jewish dialogue these differences of belief must be freely discussed.

V. CHANGE OF ATTITUDE TO JUDAISM

All too often Judaism was referred to in the Church in a false and distorted way, particularly in sermons and catechisms. False portrayal was the result. Wherever faults or misjudgement exist, rethinking and change of heart are necessary. The following should be particularly noted:

1. The Jews

The expression 'the Jews' which appears repeatedly in St. John's Gospel often leads to theological anti-Semitism insofar as it refers in an uncritical way to the whole Jewish nation in Jesus' time, whereas in reality the expression 'the Jews' meant, as a rule, the adversaries of Jesus who came from the leading groups of contemporary Jews, particularly the priestly caste.[34] In addition, one should consider the following: the Evangelist is considering, at the end of the first century, the event of Jesus and his crucifixion. He sets it all on a cosmic-universal plane. Thus the 'Jews', insofar as the notion has a negative emphasis, become the representatives of the 'cosmos' hostile to God. The Evangelist suggests, thereby, 'that world' which does not want to know anything of God and Christ. So St John's Gospel sees the trial of Jesus as a 'trial of the world', namely the darkness of the world in opposition to God's light. This has nothing to do with anti-Judaism.

2. The Pharisees

The same applies to the expression 'the Pharisees' often repeated in the Gospels. An examination of the statements about the Pharisees in the Gospels and in the aspects of tradition assimilated in them reveals unmistakably that the Pharisees were increasingly featured as the special enemies of Jesus, and certainly in connection with the process of separation, which was quite severe and difficult, that after Easter divided the Church from Israel. The Pharisees were, at the time of Jesus and later, a rigidly organised and influential group in contemporary Judaism with which Jesus came into conflict, above all because of the interpretation of the Law. They were men for whom the subject of God was of great importance. It is the task of present day exegesis, catechesis and homiletics to speak in a proper way about the Pharisees.

3. Observance of the Law

The devout Jew delights in the Torah. At the end of the Feast of Tabernacles he celebrates a special festival 'rejoicing of the law.' 'In the way of your decree lies my joy, a joy beyond all wealth' (Ps. 119, 14): 'I find my delight in your statutes. I do not forget your word' (Ps. 119:16); 'Your decrees are my delight, your statutes are my counsellors' (Ps. 119:24); 'Meditating all day on your law, how I have come to love it' (Ps. 119:97). The Jew is aware of the Torah as a pleasure, not as a burden.[35] He understands life according to the directions of the Torah, not as 'accumulating of gain' or as prominent 'achievement' to win glory before God, as many Christians suppose. A life according to the Torah, as appreciated by the Jew to this day, must be understood to have three basic elements which determine Jewish understanding of the Law: trust, realisation in deed, and sanctification of the mundane.[36] The devout Jew cannot envisage a belief in the One God without obedient realisation of God's instruction according to the Torah. Life conforming to the Torah sanctifies the mundane for this is the true sense of the instructions of the Torah in Jewish understanding. He who, daily and in all things, submits to the yoke of the law, "thereby frees the mundane from profanity and sanctifies his whole life in all his deeds and words. The Jew, Ernst Simon, formulated the facts thus: Jewish law moulds a way of life which is partly ascetic. No sphere of existence, no part of the world is excluded, everything is absolutely set free.[37] The distinguished teacher of early Judaism, Rabbi Jochanan ben Zakki (first century A.D.) said: 'If you have learnt much Torah, do not ascribe any merit to yourself, since it was for this you were created.'[38] The Christian must see this, if he wants to judge accurately the life of the devout Jew.

4. Deicide

The Jews must not be referred to as the 'killers of God'. The Council teaches: 'Even though the Jewish authorities and those who followed their lead pressed for the death of Christ, neither all Jews indiscriminately at that time, nor Jews today, can be charged with the crimes committed during his Passion.'[39]

Instead of putting the blame for Jesus' crucifixion on others we should think of our own sins, through which we are all implicated in the Cross of Jesus. The Roman Catechism teaches us that not only individuals, but all men are implicated. 'In us such guilt may indeed seem deeper than it was in the Jews, inasmuch as, according to the same Apostle [Paul] " if they had known it (God's wisdom) they would never had crucified the Lord of Glory" (1 Cor. 2:8): whereas we both profess to have known him, and yet, denying him by our "works" seem in a way to lay violent hands on him.'[40]

It was precisely that violent death of Jesus on the Cross that developed into something that made unusually heavy demands on the relationship between the Church and Judaism. This 'historical burden' must be removed by impartial discussions about Judaism. This can be obtained by thorough historical enquiry through Christian theology and the Jewish/Christian dialogue which the Church demands of us.[41]

Even though the Church had already separated from Israel in the first century A.D., the significance of Israel's redemption and God's pledge of redemption to Israel still continues. We are discouraged from making public statements in this connection, because the salvation of Israel is concealed in God's mystery, just as is the salvation of the whole non-Christian world (Rom. 11:25f).

5. Anti-Semitism

A serious dialogue of reciprocal love and understanding must replace the 'anti-Semitism' which, to some extent, still lives on in Christians. The 'spiritual bonds and historical statements that bind the Church and Judaism condemn any form of anti-Semitism as contradictory to the spirit of Christianity.'[42] Anti-Semitism is not only directed at the Good News of Jesus Christ, but ultimately against him himself.

Even though it must be emphasised that Auschwitz was an outcome of the decided defection from Jewish, as from the Christian, faith, so must the terrible happenings which are connected with Auschwitz and the other concentration camps shock us Christians, and stir us to rethinking and a change of outlook.

6. Prayer

Time and again we must comply with the demands of the Good Friday Liturgy: 'Let us pray for the Jewish people, the first to hear the word of God, that they may continue to grow in the love of his name and in faithfulness to his covenant.' Included also in the Christian duty towards the Jews is the perpetual prayer for the millions of Jews murdered in the course of history and the constant plea to God for forgiveness for the frequent failures and the numerous occasions of neglect which have made Christians guilty in their attitude to the Jews.

7. Guilt and Atonement

In Germany we have particular cause to ask forgiveness of God and of our Jewish brethren. Even though we thankfully remember that many Christians supported the Jews, often at great sacrifice, we may not, nor do we wish to, either forget or suppress what has been done by our nation to the Jews. We call to mind what the Fuldaer Bishops' Conference in 1945, their first meeting after the war, proclaimed: 'Many Germans, including Catholics, allowed themselves to be deluded by the false teachings of National Socialism, and remained indifferent to the crime against human freedom and human dignity; many abetted the crime through their behaviour, many became criminals themselves. A heavy responsibility rests on those, who by reason of their position, knew what was happening in our country, who through their influence could have prevented such crimes and did not do so, and so made these crimes possible, and by so doing, declared their solidarity with the criminals.'[43]

Once more we admit: 'Among us, countless human beings have been murdered because they belonged to the people from whose stock the Messiah took flesh.' We beg the Lord: 'Lead all to understanding and change of outlook, and those who among us were also guilty, through conduct, neglect or silence, lead them to understanding and change of outlook, that they may atone for their sins. For the sake of your Son, in your boundless mercy, forgive the immeasurable guilt which human atonement cannot expiate.'[44]

VI. COMMON GROUND

1. The devout Jew, in everyday life, is conscious of the realisation of God's precept as it is laid down in the Torah. He is preoccupied with 'conduct'. The word 'conduct' also plays a central role in the preaching of Jesus, as the Gospels show. The precepts of the Torah and Jesus' precepts are relevant to the will of God. The Psalmist prays: 'To do your will, my God, is my delight (Ps. 40:9). Jesus teaches: 'It is not those who say to me: Lord! Lord!, who will enter the kingdom of heaven, but the person who does the will of my Father in heaven' (Mt. 7:21). Of himself he acknowledges: 'My food is to do the will

of the one who sent me, and to complete his work' (Jn 4:34). Thus the realisation of God's will in the world should be the shared aim of Jews and Christians.

2. What is striking in the study of the prophets of Israel is the protest which they raised against existing injustice in economic and social fields and against all ideological oppression. Such protest is a permanent obligation for both the Church and Judaism. It is a protest against the many threats to freedom, a protest for the benefit of true humanity and of human rights, of love and of common interest: a protest against the ever-widening spread of lies in the world and in history: a protest against fascism, racism, communism and capitalism. The Judaic-Christian religion is therefore the anti-'opium' for all people.

3. Christians and Jews should, and can, mutually intercede for that which is known in the Hebrew language as 'Shalom'. This is an all-embracing conception which means Peace, Joy, Freedom, Reconciliation, Partnership, Harmony, Truth, Communication and Human Concern. 'Shalom' is, furthermore, a universal reality when all mutual relationships are finally settled, the relationships between God and man and between man and man. There must be no more racially-restricted concepts of peace. God does not want an 'Iron Curtain'! The precept of God's image in the Hebrew Scriptures as it applies to each individual, must, through the Gospels, become a universal reality: that all men know each other as brothers. For this reason, religions can no longer identify themselves with specific political doctrines. Judaism and Christianity must work together intensively and steadfastly for unrestricted peace in the whole world.

4. Man, by himself, is not in a position to lead the world to ultimate salvation. That power is God's alone; that is the conviction of believing Jews and Christians. At the same time, the experience of history helps them. Neither through evolution, nor through revolution, will the world reach ultimate redemption. Evolution produces 'Nature' but not 'Redemption'. Only God leads the world to final salvation. He creates and grants 'the new heaven and the new earth' for which both Jews and Christians are waiting (Is. 65:17; 66:22; Rev. 21:1).

5. With classic conciseness the Apostle Paul formulated the final goal of all history, and the history of salvation, in 1 Cor. 15:28—'God all in all.' Both Jews and Christians can agree with this idea, 'God all in all.' It signifies: Ultimately God and the essence of God will take effect in the universal salvation of mankind. 'The last enemy to be destroyed is death' (1 Cor. 15:26). That God, whom Israel, Jesus and the Church proclaim, will then be revealed. He will awaken the dead and thus show his invincible might. We wait for the res-

urrection of the dead and the life in the world to come. To bear witness to that in the eyes of the whole world is the mutual task of Jews and Christians.

NOTES

1. M. Buber, *Werke* I, (Munich/Heidelberg, 1962), p. 657.
2. Sch. Ben-Chorin, *Bruder Jesus, der Nazarener in jüdischer Sicht* (Munich, 1967), p. 12.
3. Vatican II on the Jews, *Nostra Aetate* (n. 4). Cf. H. Croner, ed., *Stepping Stones to Further Jewish-Christian Relations* (London/New York: Stimulus Books, 1977), pp. 1f.
4. Vatican II Dogmatic Constitution on Divine Revelation, *Dei Verbum* (n. 14). Cf. A. Flannery, ed., *Vatican Council II Documents* (Dublin, 1975). An American edition appeared at Wm. B. Eerdmans, Grand Rapids, 1975.
5. *Ibid*. Cf. also H. Croner, *op. cit.*, pp. 11ff.
6. *Ibid.*
7. *Dei Verbum* (n. 14).
8. *Mekhilta Bahodesh* 8, 72f.
9. *Ibid.* 20, 26.
10. 2 Enoch 44, 1.
11. C. Westermann, *Genesis I* (Neukirchen, 1974), pp. 633f.
12. Cf. F. Mussner, *Traktat über die Juden* (Munich, 1979), pp. 103–120.
13. Cf. A.H. Friedlander, "Die Exodus Tradition. Geschichte und Heilsgeschichte aus jüdischer Sicht", in H.H. Henrix/M. Stohr, eds., *Exodus und Kreuz im ökumenischen Dialog zwischen Juden und Christen* (Aachen, 1978), pp. 30–44.
14. *Ibid.*, p. 35.
15. *Ibid.*, p. 40.
16. Cf. N. Fuglister, *Die Heilsbedeutung des Pascha* (Munich, 1963).
17. Cf. *Guidelines*, in H. Croner, *op. cit.*, pp. 11ff.
18. *Nostra Aetate* (n. 4), with reference to Rom 11:28f; cf. also the Dogmatic Constitution on the Church *Lumen Gentium* (n. 16), in A. Flannery, *op. cit.*, pp. 350ff.
19. Mussner, *op. cit.*, pp. 68–70.
20. *Nostra Aetate* (n. 4).
21. Cf. H. Croner, *op. cit.*, pp. 11ff.
22. *Ibid.*
23. *Ibid.*
24. *Ibid.*
25. *Ibid.*
26. *Ibid.*
27. *Ibid.*
28. *Ibid.*
29. *Ibid.*, p. 60.
30. *Ibid.*, p. 91.

31. *Ibid.*, pp. 133 ff.

32. See pp. 198ff, this volume.

33. See pp. 207ff, this volume.

34. Cf. Mussner, *op. cit.*, pp. 281–291.

35. Cf. H. Gross, "Tora und Gnade im Alten Testament", in *Kairos,* NF 14 (1972), pp. 220–231; R.J.Z. Werblowsky, "Tora als Gnade", in *ibid.* 15 (1973), pp. 156–163; E.L. Ehrlich, "Tora im Judentum", in *Evang. Theologie* 37 (1977), pp. 536–549.

36. Cf. N. Oswald, "Grundgedanken zu einer pharisäisch-rabbinischen Theologie", in *Kairos* 6 (1963), pp. 40–58.

37. E. Simon, *Brücken, Gesammelte Aufsätze* (Heidelberg, 1965) p. 468.

38. Abot II. 8b.

39. *Nostra Aetate* (n. 4).

40. *Catechismus Romanus ex Decreto Concilii Tridentini* I, cap. V qu. 11.

41. *Nostra Aetate* (n. 4).

42. Cf. *Guidelines,* in H. Croner, *op. cit.*, pp. 11ff.

43. Pastoral Statement of the German Bishops, August 23, 1945.

44. From the Prayer for the murdered Jews and their persecutors, which on the instructions of the German Bishops' Conference was offered in all German Catholic Churches on June 11, 1961.

19
Ecumenical Guidelines: Diocese of Rome
January 1983
[from SIDIC]

This document was published during the Week of Prayer for Christian Unity (January 25, 1983). The emphasis is put on different ways of developing an ecumenical mentality *in the faithful. It is interesting to see that the diocesan Ecumenical Commission has judged it opportune to devote a whole section to relations with the Jews, in the* context of a search for a wider reconciliation which embraces the whole People of God, of both Old and New Testaments.

RELATIONS WITH THE JEWS

The diocesan Ecumenical Commission has been mandated to promote contact and dialogue with the Jewish community of Rome. Ecumenical experience has shown that the search for Christian unity leads to a search for a wider reconciliation which embraces the whole People of God, of both Old and New Testaments.

From a doctrinal point of view, this dimension has already been emphasized by the Second Vatican Council which recalled the words of the Apostle Paul with regard to his own people: *to them belong the sonship, the glory, the covenants, the giving of the law, the worship, and the promises; to them belong the patriarchs, and of their race, according to the flesh, is the Christ* (Rom. 9:4–5) the son of the virgin Mary. (Nostra Aetate 4)

Moreover, the Council spoke of the *spiritual ties which link the people of the New Covenant to the stock of Abraham* and specified the various ways in which the Christian people is linked with the Jewish people. The Church of Christ recognizes herself as sharing a common belief in one God and the call of Abraham in faith, and she also relives the salvation *mysteriously prefigured in the exodus of God's chosen people from the land of bondage.* (Nostra Aetate 4)

In fact *the history of Judaism did not end with the destruction of Jerusalem, but rather went on to develop a religious tradition. And although we believe that the importance and meaning of that tradition were deeply affected by the coming of Christ, it is still nonetheless rich in religious values.* (Guidelines and Suggestions for implementing *Nostra Aetate* 4, III)

It also emphasized the common eschatological destiny of both Jews and Christians, even if seen from different points of view. (Nostra Aetate 4)

The Jews wait for the Messiah as he who is to come; for Christians he has already come, he comes and he will come again in glory. This eschatological expectation, motivated in different ways, is a gift from God, which creates for both Jews and Christians a common tension and a special way of being and acting in the day-to-day commitment to history. Consequently the awaited Messiah is not only the subject of divergent opinions, but is also the one who in some way unites both together in a common expectation.

Furthermore, the Diocese of Rome recognizes alongside this general bond the particular and more immediate link it has with the Jewish community in Rome. The Church in Rome was actually founded by the Apostles Peter and Paul, who were of Jewish stock. Moreover, there is in Rome two thousand years of history shared by both Jews and Christians, history which—while unhappily interwoven with too many negative events—has nevertheless created in our diocese a social and cultural pattern which has, and must have in the future, repercussions in the religious context.

With these brief directives the Diocese of Rome hopes to encourage and promote relations inspired by what has been written here.

a) In the first place, the necessary condition for dialogue *is to strive to learn by what essential traits the Jews define themselves in the light of their own religious experience.* (Guidelines and Suggestions . . . I)

b) Particular attention must be paid to the content and language used in different pastoral situations; preaching, catechesis, liturgy, teaching of religion, publication etc., giving special care to the celebration of Holy Week, in order to avoid both explicit and implicit antisemitism and to rediscover and give value in the liturgy to our Jewish roots.

c) To develop any initiatives (meetings, conferences, publications etc.) likely to make the faith and religious traditions of the Jews better known, both in their historical development and the way in which they are lived today.

d) Reading the Old Testament together is particularly recommended, so that the light shed by Jewish tradition in its different modes (normative, narrative and mystical) may help to develop an approach to the sacred text which can be especially helpful in plumbing the depths of the Word of God.

e) Once mutual respect has been established, to initiate and encourage knowledge of and familiarity with both synagogue and family worship, in which are to be found the roots of our own Christian liturgy.

f) To encourage a common commitment to a more humane and brotherly lifestyle in the city of Rome, upholding *the dignity of man, made in the divine image and likeness . . . the right to life . . . the values of the family . . . human rights . . . religious liberty . . . young people in trouble . . . the fight against drugs . . .* (Discourse by the Chief Rabbi of Rome, Dr. Elio Toaff, on the occasion of a papal visit to the parish of S. Carlo ai Catinari)

g) To propose an objective collaboration between the Jewish community and the parish community.

h) Marriages between a Catholic and a non-baptised person are to be found in our diocese. Where there is just cause, the competent office of the Roman Vicariate can dispense from the diriment impediment. This dispensation is necessary for the *validity* of the marriage.

These marriages require a different kind of pastoral care. The unity of the couple must be based on a search for human and religious values other than Christian ones; the Catholic partner will be invited to deepen his or her own faith along the lines laid down by Saint Paul: *the non-believing husband will be sanctified by his wife, and the non-believing wife will be sanctified by her believing husband* (I Cor. 4:14).

Pastoral action need not present a difficulty if in such marriages the human and religious values common to both Judaism and Christianity are brought out and emphasised so that the conscience and liberty of both partners is respected.

D) LATIN AMERICA

20
Orientations for Catholic-Jewish Dialogue

National Commission for Catholic-Jewish Religious Dialogue: C.N.B.B. (National Conference of Brazilian Bishops) 1984

1. After twenty centuries of co-existence which lately were marked by the events in Europe preceding and accompanying the Second World War, a new awareness of the origins and history of both Judaism and Christianity demonstrates the need for reconciliation between Jews and Christians. This reconciliation must take the form of dialogue, inspired by a healthy desire for knowledge of one another, together with mutual understanding.

2. It is indispensable for dialogue that Catholics should strive to learn by what essential traits the Jews define themselves, that is to say, as a people clearly defined by religious and ethnic elements.

3. The first constitutive element of the Jewish people is its religion, which in no way authorizes Catholics to envisage them as if they were simply one of the many religions in the world today. It was in fact through the Jewish people that faith in the one true God, that is to say, monotheism, has entered human history.

4. It should be noted, on the other hand, that according to biblical revelation, God Himself constituted the Hebrews as a people. The Lord did this after having made a covenant with them (cf. Gen. 17:7; Ex. 24:1–8). We are indebted to the Jewish people for the five books of the Law, the Prophets and

the other sacred books which make up the Hebrew Scriptures that have been adopted by Christians as an integral part of the Bible.

5. Judaism cannot be considered a purely social and historical entity or a leftover from a past which no longer exists. We must take into account the vitality of the Jewish people which has continued throughout the centuries to the present. St. Paul bears witness that the Jews have a zeal for God (Rom. 10:2); that God has not rejected His people (Rom. 11:1ff); He has not withdrawn the blessing given to the chosen people (Rom. 9:8). St. Paul teaches also that the Gentiles, like a wild olive shoot, have been grafted onto the true olive tree which is Israel (Rom. 11:16–19); Israel continues to play an important role in the history of salvation, a role which will end only in the fulfillment of the plan of God (Rom. 11:11, 15, 23).

6. It is thus possible for us to state that all forms of antisemitism must be condemned. Every unfavorable word and expression must be erased from Christian speech. All campaigns of physical or moral violence must cease. The Jews must not be considered a deicide people. The fact that a small number of Jews asked Pilate for Jesus' death does not implicate the Jewish people as such. In the final analysis, Christ died for the sins of all humanity. Christian love, moreover, which embraces all persons without distinction, in imitation of the Father's love (Mt. 5:44–48), should likewise embrace the Jewish people and seek to understand their history and aspirations.

7. Unfavorable judgments with regard to Jews must be avoided, particularly in catechetical teaching and in the liturgy. It is desirable that courses in Catholic doctrinal formation, in addition to liturgical celebrations, should emphasize those elements common to Jews and Christians. It should be pointed out, for example, that the New Testament cannot be understood without the Old Testament. The Christian feasts of Easter and Pentecost, as well as liturgical prayers, the Psalms especially, originated in Jewish tradition.

8. A contrast must not be made between Judaism and Christianity, claiming, for example, that Judaism is a religion of fear while Christianity is one of love. We find, in fact, in the holy books of Israel the origins of that expression of great love which exists between God and humanity (Dt. 6:4, 7:6–9; Pss. 73–139; Hos. 11; Jer. 31:2ff, 19–22; 33:6–9).

9. It is fitting to recall as well that the Lord Jesus, his holy Mother, the apostles and the first Christian communities were of the race of Abraham. The roots of Christianity are in the people of Israel.

10. In regard to the land of Israel, it is well to remember that, as the fruit of His promise, God gave the ancient land of Canaan in which the Jews lived to Abraham and his descendants. The Roman occupation and successive invasions of the land of Israel resulted in harsh trials for the people who were dispersed among foreign nations. We must recognize the rights of Jews to a calm political existence in their country of origin, without letting that create injustice or violence for other peoples. For the Jewish people these rights became a reality in the State of Israel.

11. Finally, we should emphasize the eschatological expectation which is the hope of Jews and Christians, despite their different ways of interpretation. Both are awaiting the fulfillment of the Kingdom of God; for Christians this has already begun with the coming of Jesus Christ, while Jews are still awaiting the coming of the Messiah. At all events, this eschatological perspective awakens as much in Jews as in Christians the awareness that we are walking on a road, like the people who came out of Egypt, searching for a land "flowing with milk and honey" (Ex. 3:8).

II. PROTESTANT DOCUMENTS

A) WORLD COUNCIL OF CHURCHES

21
Dialogue in Community: Statement and Reports of a Theological Consultation, Chiang Mai, Thailand, April 1977, to the World Council of Churches. (From *Oikoumene*, Geneva)

CHRISTIAN-JEWISH RELATIONS

1. The present situation

While there are Jewish communities in all continents, formal dialogue between Christians and Jews has taken place primarily in North America, Western Europe and Israel. Often these dialogues were initiated by the Jews, and the Jewish participants are selected by organizations of our Jewish partners (e.g. International Jewish Committee for Inter-Religious Consultations (IJCIC)). The choice of topics requires mutual acceptance. Through the Dialogue with People of Living Faiths and Ideologies (DFI) there has also been Jewish participation in multilateral dialogues (Colombo), and our Jewish partners have expressed great interest in broadening the contact with Christians beyond the western orbit.

2. On the specific nature of relationship

(a) The historic relationship between Jews and Christians is unquestionably unique as Christianity emerged from within Judaism. The Jewishness of Jesus and the Apostles is a historical fact, and the Bible of the Jews became the Old Testament of the Christian Bible. Christian liturgy and theology have historic roots in the Jewish community. We thus have much in common.

(b) This unique historic relationship has marked the history of Jewish-Christian relations. At times it has expressed itself in mutual respect and even calling, as in the Jewish medieval scholar Maimonides' vision of Christianity (and Islam) as the bearer of Torah (Instruction) to the Gentiles, and in peaceful co-existence of Jewish and Christian communities, especially during long periods of Muslim rule and also, for example, in India and now in secular societies.

(c) The position of majority rule of one of the two parties lead, however, more often than not to various forms of suppression. The pre-Christian phenomenon of anti-semitism (in the sense of anti-Judaism) became part of church history, especially in Europe, and found intensified forms in cultural and national histories, culminating in events like the Crusades, the Inquisition (spiritual genocide), and the Nazi Holocaust (physical genocide).

(d) To many western Christians this record makes it the first priority for Jewish-Christian relations to seek ways of eradicating once and for all the anti-semitism that has plagued the churches and the cultures in which they witness, and to warn other churches lest they fall prey to the sin of anti-semitism. This calling of western Christians has intensified their need for dialogue, and lead some of them to forms of identifying with Israel that may be questioned by other Christians, who should seek to give their own answers to the relationship between Jews and Christians.

(e) We noted that oppressed people have found much strength by identifying with the experience of Israel as a chosen people. For example, in Africa, among American Blacks, and in contemporary liberation theologies the Exodus is central to the faith, and suppressed people have so found in the very Bible brought by their oppressors the Word of God which gave them dignity and identity. Such an appropriation through Jesus Christ of Israel's experience is at the same time an affirmation of God's history with Israel.

(f) We want to consider in more depth how Jews and Christians are jointly, yet distinctly, participating in God's mission to his creation toward the "Hallowed be Thy Name" (missio dei/qiddush ha-Shem) (see 3, b, ii).

3. Recommendations for issues in further Christian-Jewish dialogue

(a) In all dialogues with Jews the following unavoidable questions will be present. Christians may give different answers to them, but the questions must be faced and recognized as valid in any dialogue

(i) What assurances can Christians give as to the eradication of the anti-semitism known in Christian history?

(ii) In what sense can Christians identify with the right of the Jewish People to statehood?

(iii) What assurances can Christians give against proselytising of Jews?

(b) Three issues may be recommended for future Christian-Jewish dialogue.

(i) In what sense are the Christian Old Testament and the Bible of the Jews "the same Scripture"?
(ii) Is there a mission and are there concerns that Jews and Christians have in common?
(iii) How can our two communities contribute to world-wide community through dialogue?

22
Third Revised Text
of British Working Group
for World Council of Churches Consultation
on the Church and the Jewish People:
Guidelines/Recommendations on Jewish-
Christian Relations, 1977

I INTRODUCTION

1. Christian motivation of relating to Persons of Other Faiths

In the past when Christians have related to persons of Other Faiths and Ideologies, their tendency has been to emphasize their Christian stance from which they approach Other Faiths. This has changed, for in a shrunken world the very nearness and accessibility of one to the other has thrown into relief our common humanity. This situation should make us feel concerned about and involved with each other. Further, this makes us aware of primary human concerns such as Knowledge of God, a Way of Salvation and the Problem of Good and Evil, all of them approached in varied ways by world religions.

2. The Phenomenon of Antisemitism

Most Christians are aware that there has been a special relationship between the Jewish People and the Church and are conscious that something has gone radically wrong in that relationship. The fact that Judaism is the matrix of Christianity would be sufficient to explain some tension but is hardly able to account for the terrible relationship of two thousand years. It was the caricaturing of Jews and Judaism in what has come to be known as the *'Teaching of Contempt'* which considered Judaism as both legalistic and an anachronism, at best a preparation for the Church, that explains the Church's involvement in theological anti-Judaism.

3. Resurgence of the Jewish People

Christians should be aware of the vibrant and continuing development of Judaism in post-Biblical times. Between the First century and the present day there was—and is—an enormous output of Jewish religious and philosophical literature and commentary. In modern times Jewish religious movements have made major contributions to European religious thought. European Jewry was virtually destroyed by the Nazis—and it is nothing short of a miracle that the destruction of six million Jews should have been followed by the reconstruction of Jewish life with its special centres in Israel, America and, to a certain extent, Britain. By centres we mean places and institutions of higher Jewish learning that act as a renewal of religious life the world over. The most remarkable of all such resurgence is the emergence of the State of Israel which by restoring the *'Land'* to its relationship with *'People'* and *'Religion'* has made it possible for Judaism to regain its wholeness.

4. Moving Forward to Dialogue

Historical developments, as outlined above, would by themselves suggest the necessity for a review on the part of the Church of its traditional attitude of proselytism. Christians, however, have been facing the challenge and demands of religious pluralism by a new way of relating to Other Faiths epitomized by dialogue. Meeting in dialogue is more radical than renewing academic interest in comparative religions or merely updating traditional attitudes and approaches. It demands respect at a deeper level and acceptance of the integrity of the faith of the other. We allow others to define their religious identity in terms of their own self-understanding and expect that our own Christian commitment and identity is similarly respected.

II GUIDELINES OF THE NEW RELATIONSHIP

1. About the Bible

Jews, Christians and Muslims share some part of their Bible. A small part of the Old Testament and some traces of the story of Jesus are shared by Christians and Muslims but the most direct sharing is between Jews and Christians.

Christians share the whole of the Jewish Bible, i.e., the Old Testament, with Jews but have interpreted it crucially by the New Testament. However, Judaism reads the text of the Hebrew Bible, and particularly the Five Books of Moses, through the dynamic interpretations of Jewish tradition contained in later Rabbinic literature (e.g., *Midrash, Talmud,* and commentaries). This tradition and exposition by Rabbis and teachers is, for Jews, part of a continual and authoritative revelation. Jesus' exposition of the Old Testament was largely within the framework of this Jewish tradition. At present, Christian scholars are rediscovering the Jewish background and roots of New Testament teaching, increasing our awareness of a common Biblical heritage.

2. The Israel of God

Although we talk of Jewish-Christian relationships as though both communities were monolithic, in fact those communities and the ways in which they define themselves are complex. Their self-definition and self-understanding are neither parallel to nor symmetrical with each other. The complex interrelationship of people, land, religion and nation has no similar or comparable pattern in Christian thought. Again, traditionally, Christianity has often defined itself over against the Judaism from which it sprang. The Jewish revelation, however, does not need Christianity at all for its self-definition.

It was because of the need to define itself against Judaism that Christianity ultimately began to affirm itself by totally negating Judaism. There is, nevertheless, nothing in the New Testament which describes the Jewish People as deprived of their election by God nor, for that matter, anything which affirms that the first covenant became invalid because of the newer one. Far from giving the impression that an *'Old Israel'* had been superseded by a *'New Israel'*, substituted as the new People of God, the picture is that of a (gentile) Christian community being included within the People of God ("Once you were no people, now you are God's people." 1 Peter 2:10). The Jewish People, far from being repudiated, continues to be the People of God—*'populus secundum electionem carissimus'*.

As long as Christians regard Judaism as a mere preparation for Christianity, as long as Christians can only affirm the validity of God's revelation to them by negating the validity of God's revelation to the Jewish People, then respect for Judaism as a revelation in its own right, acknowledgment of the continued election of the Jewish People, even stress upon the common hope and common ground of Christians and Jews are almost impossible because Judaism is denied its theological validity. Is it too much to hope that the people of the two covenants, the Church and Jewry—*together the continuing People of God*—may still stand in creative tension, enriching and encouraging each other, despite the appalling record of the relationship between the two communities over the centuries?

3. Jewish Self-understanding and Identity

Traditionally the Church has thought of other religions as not agreeing with the fundamental Christian assertion that *'Jesus is Lord'*. Another Christian tradition has more positively reviewed the insight of other religions as partly revealing Jesus. Both these approaches hide the fact that other religions do not merely negate or support Christianity for they have a distinctive nature of their own, indeed, their own structure of identity. The emphasis in Judaism is on worship by action; observing the commandments of God in daily life, taking Biblical revelation as its authority. Judaism believes that there is a positive spiritual purpose in fulfilling as many of God's commandments as possible; the opportunity for this is at its highest in the Holy Land, where the commandments concerning the Holy Land and its produce may be observed, and where the sanctity to Judaism of worship in previous times is keenly felt. Thus the yearning of the Jewish People to be able to practise their religion in their land is, for them, a yearning of the highest degree of holiness and spirituality. In modern times, many Jews have therefore seen a strong, religious purpose in the strengthening of Jewish settlement in Israel. Understandably this is a point difficult for Christians to take. But the first stage must be that of understanding before a critical appraisal can be attempted.

III CHRISTIAN TEACHING, PREACHING AND LITURGY

Much of the traditional Christian view of Jews and Judaism persists in the liturgy, hymns and services of the Church. Perhaps the most persistent of these is the conviction that Judaism has been superseded by Christianity. This needs to be reviewed to bring it into line with the contemporary understanding of Judaism. Most difficult of all are certain aspects of the New Testament, written at the time when the controversy between those Jews who had accepted Jesus and those who had not found sharp expression. This is particularly true of the frequent use of the particular designation of *'the Jews'* in St. John's Gospel. Another point of difficulty is the Passion narrative when all too easily the enemies of Jesus are identified with *'all Jews'* and *'all Jews'* are seen as the cause of the Crucifixion rather than the deeper strain of New Testament teaching that has always insisted on seeing the death of Jesus as being caused by our common sin. On this point we should like to draw special attention to the ICCJ's *'Ten Points of Seelisberg'* (see pp. 32f of this volume).

IV PRACTICAL PROGRAMMES

1. Correcting points of theology in the past Christian-Jewish relationship is important but it is no substitute for being a good neighbour to Jews. Apart from a good human relationship it is necessary to have some understanding of the Jewish religion not only as it is expressed in the Jewish Festivals and observance of, for example, the Sabbath (*'Shabbat'*) and the Jewish food laws; but *also other aspects* of Jewish practice, the laws of charity, hospitality, study, parent-child relationships and so on.

2. In these days of discussion groups which are part of most Parishes and congregations, much profit can be derived from the formation of a joint Jewish-Christian discussion group at a parish and congregational level with a synagogue congregation.

3. A special opportunity at the present is Pilgrimage to the Holy Land. Group Travel is able to bring this within the reach of most people. Such Pilgrimages today are not only an opportunity of revitalising the Christian faith by direct contact with the places associated with the ministry of Jesus, but are also opportunities for witnessing the unique Jewish presence in the Land of Israel, as well as Arab Christian communities which form a link with the historic Eastern Churches.

4. Further to discussion groups at the parish level, some special dialogue groups have been arranged at leadership level, both nationally and internationally. Perhaps the best known are the *'Rainbow Groups'* of Jerusalem and London which consist of groups of 20 to 30 participants equally divided between Jews and Christians. At this level some of the more difficult aspects of theology are being discussed.

The World Council of Churches and the corresponding Jewish organisation (The International Jewish Committee for Inter-religious Consultations) have arranged several international colloquia in which scholars from both communities are invited to discuss specific themes. Although some of these official dialogues may seem far removed from the grass roots, they have a world significance both for the confidence they give to the dialogue movement as a whole and also by their providing a platform for the discussion of mutual concerns and anxieties. The contemporary movement of dialogue needs the stimulus and the interaction of local, national and global groups.

23
WCC on Authentic Christian Witness [from SIDIC]

The following extract is taken from the conference paper on Christian-Jewish relations adopted by the Jerusalem Conference of the World Council of Churches Consultation on the Church and the Jewish People which met in Jerusalem June 20 to 23, 1977

1. Proselytism, as distinct from Mission or Witness, is rejected in the strongest terms by the WCC: "Proselytism embraces whatever violates the right of the human person, Christian or non-Christian, to be free from external coercion in religious matters, or whatever, in the proclamation of the Gospel, does not conform to the ways God draws free men to himself in response to his calls to serve in spirit and in truth" (*Ecumenical Review* 1/1971, p. 11).

We now realize more than ever before that the world in which we live is a world of religious pluralism. This demands from us that we treat those who differ from us with respect and that we strongly support the religious liberty of all.

2. This rejection of proselytism and our advocacy of respect for the integrity and the identity of all peoples and faith-communities is the more urgent where Jews are concerned. For our relationship to the Jews is of a unique and very close character. Moreover, the history of "Christian" anti-Semitism and forced baptisms of Jews in the past makes it understandable that Jews are rightly sensitive towards all religious pressures from outside and all attempts at proselytizing.

3. We reject proselytism both in its gross and more refined forms. This implies that all triumphalism and every kind of manipulation are to be abro-

gated. We are called upon to minimize the power dimension in our encounter with the Jews and to speak at every level from equal to equal. We have to be conscious of the pain and the perception of the others and have to respect their right to define themselves.

4. We are called upon to witness to God's love for and claim upon the whole of humankind. Our witness to Christ as Lord and Savior, however, is challenged in a special way where Jews are concerned. It has become discredited as a result of past behavior on the part of Christians. We therefore are seeking authentic and proper forms of Christian witness in our relations with the Jews. Some of us believe that we have to bear witness also to the Jews; some among us are convinced, however, that Jews are faithful and obedient to God even though they do not accept Jesus Christ as Lord and Savior. Many maintain that as a separate and specific people the Jews are an instrument of God with a specific God-given task and, as such, a sign of God's faithfulness to all humankind on the way towards ultimate redemption.

24
Ecumenical Considerations on Jewish-Christian Dialogue
World Council of Churches, 1982
[from SIDIC]

DIALOGUE WITH PEOPLE OF LIVING FAITHS AND IDEOLOGIES

Historical Note

In 1975 the Consultation on the Church and the Jewish People (CCJP) voted to begin the process that has borne fruit in these Ecumenical Considerations on Jewish-Christian Dialogue. The first step was to request preparatory papers from the various regions with experience in Jewish-Christian dialogue. When the Central Committee adopted "Guidelines on Dialogue" in 1979, work on developing specific suggestions for Jewish-Christian dialogue began and, after a period of drafting and revisions, a draft was presented for comments to the International Jewish Committee on Interreligious Consultations (IJCIC), the CCJP's primary Jewish dialogue partner. After discussion in the DFI Working Group in 1980, a revised draft was circulated among interested persons in the churches and comments solicited. Many and substantial comments and suggestions were received.

When it met in London Colney, England, in June 1981, the CCJP adopted its final revisions and submitted them to the DFI Working Group, which adopted them at its meeting in Bali, Indonesia, 2 January 1982, having made its own revisions at a few points. On the advice of the February 1982 WCC Executive Committee, various concerned member churches and various members of the CCJP were further consulted in order to revise and re-order the text. The result, "Ecumenical Considerations on Jewish-Christian Dialogue" was "received and commended to the churches for study and action" by the Executive Committee of the World Council of Churches at Geneva on 16 July 1982.

Preface

> 1.1 One of the functions of dialogue is to allow participants to describe and witness to their faith in their own terms. This is of primary importance since self-serving descriptions of other peoples' faith are one of the roots of prejudice, stereotyping, and condescension. Listening carefully to the neighbours' self-understanding enables Christians better to obey the commandment not to bear false witness against their neighbours, whether those neighbours be of long-established religious, cultural or ideological traditions or members of new religious groups. It should be recognized by partners in dialogue that any religion or ideology claiming universality, apart from having an understanding of itself, will also have its own interpretations of other religions and ideologies as part of its own self-understanding. Dialogue gives an opportunity for a mutual questioning of the understanding partners have about themselves and others. It is out of a reciprocal willingness to listen and learn that significant dialogue grows. (WCC Guidelines on Dialogue, III.4)

1.2 In giving such guidelines applicable to all dialogues, the World Council of Churches speaks primarily to its member churches as it defines the need for and gifts to be received by dialogue. People of other faiths may choose to define their understanding of dialogue, and their expectations as to how dialogue with Christians may affect their own traditions and attitudes and may lead to a better understanding of Christianity. Fruitful "mutual questioning of the understanding partners have about themselves and others" requires the spirit of dialogue. But the WCC Guidelines do not predict what partners in dialogue may come to learn about themselves, their history, and their problems. Rather they speak within the churches about faith, attitudes, actions, and problems of Christians.

1.3 In all dialogues distinct asymmetry between any two communities of faith becomes an important fact. Already terms like faith, theology, religion, Scripture, people, etc. are not innocent or neutral. Partners in dialogue may rightly question the very language in which each thinks about religious matters.

1.4 In the case of Jewish-Christian dialogue a specific historical and theological asymmetry is obvious. While an understanding of Judaism in New Testament times becomes an integral and indispensable part of any Christian theology, for Jews, a "theological" understanding of Christianity is of a less than essential or integral significance. Yet, neither community of faith has developed without awareness of the other.

1.5 The relations between Jews and Christians have unique characteristics because of the ways in which Christianity historically emerged out of Judaism. Christian understandings of that process constitute a necessary part of the dialogue and give urgency to the enterprise. As Christianity came to define its own identity over against Judaism, the Church developed its own understandings, definitions and terms for what it had inherited from Jewish traditions, and for what it read in the Scriptures common to Jews and Christians. In the process of defining its own identity the Church defined Judaism, and assigned to the Jews definite roles in its understanding of God's acts of salvation. It should not be surprising that Jews resent those Christian theologies in which they as a people are assigned to play a negative role. Tragically, such patterns of thought in Christianity have often led to overt acts of condescension, persecutions, and worse.

1.6 Bible-reading and worshipping Christians often believe that they "know Judaism" since they have the Old Testament, the records of Jesus' debates with Jewish teachers and the early Christian reflections on the Judaism of their times. Furthermore, no other religious tradition has been so thoroughly "defined" by preachers and teachers in the Church as has Judaism. This attitude is often enforced by lack of knowledge about the history of Jewish life and thought through the 1,900 years since the parting of the ways of Judaism and Christianity.

1.7 For these reasons there is special urgency for Christians to listen, through study and dialogue, to ways in which Jews understand their history and their traditions, their faith and their obedience "in their own terms". Furthermore, a mutual listening to how each is perceived by the other may be a step towards understanding the hurts, overcoming the fears, and correcting the misunderstandings that have thrived on isolation.

1.8 Both Judaism and Christianity comprise a wide spectrum of opinions, options, theologies, and styles of life and service. Since generalizations often produce stereotyping, Jewish-Christian dialogue becomes the more significant by aiming at as full as possible a representation of views within the two communities of faith.

2. *Towards a Christian Understanding of Jews and Judaism*

2.1 Through dialogue with Jews many Christians have come to appreciate the richness and vitality of Jewish faith and life in the covenant and have been enriched in their own understandings of God and the divine will for all creatures.

2.2 In dialogue with Jews, Christians have learned that the actual history of Jewish faith and experiences does not match the images of Judaism that have dominated a long history of Christian teaching and writing, images that have been spread by Western culture and literature into other parts of the world.

2.3 A classical Christian tradition sees the Church replacing Israel as God's people, and the destruction of the second temple of Jerusalem as a warrant for this claim. The covenant of God with the people of Israel was only a preparation for the coming of Christ, after which it was abrogated.

2.4 Such a theological perspective has had fateful consequences. As the Church replaced the Jews as God's people, the Judaism that survived was seen as a fossilized religion of legalism—a view now perpetuated by scholarship which claims no theological interests. Judaism of the first centuries before and after the birth of Jesus was therefore called "Late Judaism". The Pharisees were considered to represent the acme of legalism, Jews and Jewish groups were portrayed as negative models, and the truth and beauty of Christianity were thought to be enhanced by setting up Judaism as false and ugly.

2.5 Through a renewed study of Judaism and in dialogue with Jews, Christians have become aware that Judaism in the time of Christ was in an early stage of its long life. Under the leadership of the Pharisees the Jewish people began a spiritual revival of remarkable power, which gave them the vitality capable of surviving the catastrophe of the loss of the temple. It gave birth to Rabbinic Judaism which produced the Mishnah and Talmud and built the structures for a strong and creative life through the centuries.

2.6 As a Jew, Jesus was born into this tradition. In that setting he was nurtured by the Hebrew Scriptures, which he accepted as authoritative and to which he gave a new interpretation in his life and teaching. In this context Jesus announced that the Kingdom of God was at hand, and in his resurrection his followers found the confirmation of his being both Lord and Messiah.

2.7 Christians should remember that some of the controversies reported in the New Testament between Jesus and the "scribes and Pharisees" find parallels within Pharisaism itself and its heir, Rabbinic Judaism. These controversies took place in a Jewish context, but when the words of Jesus came to be used by Christians who did not identify with the Jewish people as Jesus did, such sayings often became weapons in anti-Jewish polemics and thereby their original intention was tragically distorted. An internal Christian debate is now taking place on the question of how to understand passages in the New Testament that seem to contain anti-Jewish references.

2.8 Judaism, with its rich history of spiritual life, produced the Talmud as the normative guide for Jewish life in thankful response to the grace of God's covenant with the people of Israel. Over the centuries important commentaries, profound philosophical works and poetry of spiritual depth have been added. For Judaism the Talmud is central and authoritative. Judaism is more than the religion of the Scriptures of Israel. What Christians call the Old Testament has received in the Talmud and later writings interpretations that for Jewish tradition share in the authority of Moses.

2.9 For Christians the Bible with the two Testaments is also followed by traditions of interpretation, from the Church Fathers to the present time. Both Jews and Christians live in the continuity of their Scripture and Tradition.

2.10 Christians as well as Jews look to the Hebrew Bible as the story recording Israel's sacred memory of God's election and covenant with this people. For Jews, it is their own story in historical continuity with the present. Christians, mostly of gentile background since early in the life of the Church, believe themselves to be heirs to this same story by grace in Jesus Christ. The relationship between the two communities, both worshipping the God of Abraham, Isaac and Jacob, is a given historical fact, but how it is to be understood theologically is a matter of internal discussion among Christians, a discussion that can be enriched by dialogue with Jews.

2.11 Both commonalities and differences between the two faiths need to be examined carefully. Finding in the Scriptures of the Old and New Testaments the authority sufficient for salvation, the Christian Church shares Israel's faith in the One God, whom it knows in the Spirit as the God and Father of the Lord Jesus Christ. For Christians, Jesus Christ is the only begotten Son of the Father, through whom millions have come to share in the love of, and to adore, the God who first made covenant with the people of Israel. Knowing the One God in Jesus Christ through the Spirit, therefore, Christians worship that God with a Trinitarian confession to the One God, the God of Creation, Incarnation and Pentecost. In so doing, the Church worships in a language foreign to Jewish worship and sensitivities, yet full of meaning to Christians.

2.12 Christians and Jews both believe that God has created men and women as the crown of creation and has called them to be holy and to exercise stewardship over the creation in accountability to God. Jews and Christians are taught by their Scriptures and Traditions to know themselves responsible to their neighbours especially to those who are weak, poor and oppressed. In various and distinct ways they look for the day in which God will redeem the creation. In dialogue with Jews many Christians come to a more profound appreciation of the Exodus hope of liberation, and pray and work for the coming of righteousness and peace on earth.

2.13 Christians learn through dialogue with Jews that for Judaism the survival of the Jewish people is inseparable from its obedience to God and God's covenant.

2.14 During long periods, both before and after the emergence of Christianity, Jews found ways of living in obedience to Torah, maintaining and deepening their calling as a peculiar people in the midst of the nations. Through history there are times and places in which Jews were allowed to live, respected and accepted by the cultures in which they resided, and where their own culture thrived and made a distinct and sought after contribution to their Christian and Muslim neighbours. Often lands not dominated by Christians proved most favourable for Jewish diaspora living. There were even times when Jewish thinkers came to "make a virtue out of necessity" and considered diaspora living to be the distinct genius of Jewish existence.

2.15 Yet, there was no time in which the memory of the Land of Israel and of Zion, the city of Jerusalem, was not central in the worship and hope of the Jewish people. "Next year in Jerusalem" was always part of Jewish worship in the diaspora. And the continued presence of Jews in the Land and in Jerusalem was always more than just one place of residence among all the others.

2.16 Jews differ in their interpretations of the State of Israel, as to its religious and secular meaning. It constitutes for them part of the long search for that survival which has always been central to Judaism through the ages. Now the quest for statehood by Palestinians—Christian and Muslim—as part of their search for survival as a people in the Land—also calls for full attention.

2.17 Jews, Christians and Muslims have all maintained a presence in the Land from their beginnings. While "the Holy Land" is primarily a Christian designation, the Land is holy to all three. Although they may understand its holiness in different ways, it cannot be said to be "more holy" to one than to another.

2.18 The need for dialogue is the more urgent when under strain the dialogue is tested. Is it mere debate and negotiation or is it grounded in faith that God's will for the world is secure peace with justice and compassion?

3. Hatred and Persecution of Jews—A Continuing Concern

3.1 Christians cannot enter into dialogue with Jews without the awareness that hatred and persecution of Jews have a long persistent history, especially in countries where Jews constitute a minority among Christians. The tragic history of the persecution of Jews includes massacres in Europe and the Middle East by the Crusaders, the Inquisition, pogroms, and the Holocaust. The World Council of Churches Assembly at its first meeting in Amsterdam,

1948, declared: "We call upon the churches we represent to denounce anti-semitism, no matter what its origin, as absolutely irreconcilable with the profession and practice of the Christian faith. Antisemitism is sin against God and man". This appeal has been reiterated many times. Those who live where there is a record of acts of hatred against Jews can serve the whole Church by unmasking the ever-present danger they have come to recognize.

3.2 Teachings of contempt for Jews and Judaism in certain Christian traditions proved a spawning ground for the evil of the Nazi Holocaust. The Church must learn so to preach and teach the Gospel as to make sure that it cannot be used towards contempt for Judaism and against the Jewish people. A further response to the Holocaust by Christians, and one which is shared by their Jewish partners, is a resolve that it will never happen again to the Jews or to any other people.

3.3 Discrimination against and persecution of Jews have deep-rooted socio-economic and political aspects. Religious differences are magnified to justify ethnic hatred in support of vested interests. Similar phenomena are also evident in many interracial conflicts. Christians should oppose all such religious prejudices, whereby people are made scapegoats for the failures and problems of societies and political regimes.

3.4 Christians in parts of the world with a history of little or no persecution of Jews do not wish to be conditioned by the specific experiences of justified guilt among other Christians. Rather, they explore in their own ways the significance of Jewish-Christian relations, from the earliest times to the present, for their life and witness.

4. Authentic Christian Witness

4.1 Christians are called to witness to their faith in word and deed. The Church has a mission and it cannot be otherwise. This mission is not one of choice.

4.2 Christians have often distorted their witness by coercive proselytism—conscious and unconscious, overt and subtle. Referring to proselytism between Christian churches, the Joint Working Group of the Roman Catholic Church and the World Council of Churches stated: "Proselytism embraces whatever violates the right of the human person, Christian or non-Christians, to be free from external coercion in religious matters". (*Ecumenical Review*, 1/1971, p. 11)

4.3 Such rejection of proselytism, and such advocacy of respect for the integrity and the identity of all persons and all communities of faith are urgent in relation to Jews, especially those who live as minorities among Christians.

Steps towards assuring non-coercive practices are of highest importance. In dialogue ways should be found for the exchange of concerns, perceptions, and safeguards in these matters.

4.4 While Christians agree that there can be no place for coercion of any kind, they do disagree—on the basis of their understandings of the Scriptures—as to what constitutes authentic forms of mission. There is a wide spectrum, from those who see the very presence of the Church in the world as the witness called for, to those who see mission as the explicit and organized proclamation of the gospel to all who have not accepted Jesus as their Saviour.

4.5 This spectrum as to mission in general is represented in the different views of what is authentic mission to Jews. Here some of the specifics are as follows: There are Christians who view a mission to the Jews as having a very special salvific significance, and those who believe the conversion of the Jews to be the eschatological event that will climax the history of the world. There are those who would place no special emphasis on a mission to the Jews, but would include them in the one mission to all those who have not accepted Christ as their Saviour. There are those who believe that a mission to the Jews is not part of an authentic Christian witness, since the Jewish people finds its fulfilment in faithfulness to God's covenant of old.

4.6 Dialogue can rightly be described as a mutual witness, but only when the intention is to hear the others in order better to understand their faith, hopes, insights, and concerns, and to give, to the best of one's ability one's own understanding of one's own faith. The spirit of dialogue is to be fully present to one another in full openness and human vulnerability.

4.7 According to rabbinic law, Jews who confess Jesus as the Messiah are considered apostate Jews. But for many Christians of Jewish origin, their identification with the Jewish people is a deep spiritual reality to which they seek to give expression in various ways, some by observing parts of Jewish tradition in worship and life style, many by a special commitment to the well-being of the Jewish people and to a peaceful and secure future for the State of Israel. Among Christians of Jewish origin there is the same wide spectrum of attitudes towards mission as among other Christians, and the same criteria for dialogue and against coercion apply.

4.8 As Christians of different traditions enter into dialogue with Jews in local, national, and international situations, they will come to express their understanding of Judaism in other language, style, and ways than has been done in these Ecumenical Considerations. Such understandings are to be shared among the churches for enrichment of all.

B) U.S. CHURCH GROUPS

25
The American Lutheran Church and the Jewish Community, 1979

PREAMBLE

In response to the request of the 1972 General Convention that a special committee prepare a statement about the relationship of American Lutherans to Jews, we wish to place this result of our deliberations in the hands of the Church Council.

There are many cogent reasons which urge us to reconsider the relationship of Lutherans, and indeed of all Christians, to Jews. Christians are not as aware as they should be of the common roots and origin of the church and the Jewish tradition of faith and life. Both Judaism and Christianity regard the Hebrew Bible—the Old Testament—as the document which bears witness to the beginning of God's saving work in history. They worship the same God and hold many ethical concerns in common, even though they are divided with respect to faith in Jesus of Nazareth as the Messiah.

Christians must also become aware of that history in which they have deeply alienated the Jews. It is undeniable that Christian people have both initiated and acquiesced in persecution. Whole generations of Christians have looked with contempt upon this people who were condemned to remain wanderers on the earth on the false charge of deicide. Christians ought to acknowledge with repentance and sorrow their part in this tragic history of estrangement. Since anti-Jewish prejudice is still alive in many parts of the world, Christains need to develop a sympathetic understanding of the renewal among Jews of the terror of the Holocaust. It is as if the numbness of the injury has worn off, old wounds have been reopened, and Jews live in dread of another disaster. Christians must join with Jews in the effort to understand the theological and moral significance of what happened in the Holocaust.

We need also to look to the future to see if there are things Christians and Jews can do together in service to the community. Better communication between Christians and Jews can lead to more adequate joint-efforts on behalf of a humane society. The new atmosphere in theological research and interfaith encounter which has developed within recent years summons us to undertake serious conversations with Jewish people. Some Christians feel a special concern to explore the contribution which American churches might make in and through contacts with their Jewish neighbors and others to a resolution of the conflict in the Middle East that will be to the benefit of all those living in that region.

The urgency of the foregoing considerations is heightened by the fact that about fifty percent of all Jews live in North America. As Lutherans we ought, therefore, to regard our Jewish neighbors as major partners in the common life.

We urge that Lutherans should understand that their relationship to the Jewish community is one of solidarity, of confrontation, and of respect and cooperation.

I. SOLIDARITY

Our Common Humanity

Lutherans and Jews, indeed all mankind, are united by virtue of their humanity. Lutherans and Jews agree that all people, regardless of race, religion, or nationality are equally God's children, and equally precious in his sight. This conviction is based on a concept of God as Creator of the universe, who continues to care for his creation, whose mercies are over all his creatures.

Our Common Heritage

The existence of Jewish congregations today shows that a religious traditon which traces it ancestry back to the time of Abraham is still living and growing. It is a tradition that gave rise to Christianity: a tradition from which Christianity has borrowed much. But modern Judaism has grown, changed, and developed considerably beyond the Judaism of biblical times, just as the modern church has grown, changed, and developed considerably beyond its New Testament beginnings.

It is unfortunate that so few Christians have studied Judaism as it grew and flowered in the centuries since the New Testament era. The first step for Lutherans, therefore, is to devote themselves to completing this long-neglected homework. It is strongly recommended that Lutherans ask the Jews themselves to teach them about this long and critically important period in Jewish history.

Our Spiritual Solidarity

Our solidarity is based on those ideas and themes held in common, most of which were inherited by Christianity from the Jewish tradition. It is important to note that the ministry of Jesus and the life of the early Christian community were thoroughly rooted in the Judaism of their day. To emphasize the Jewishness of Jesus and his disciples, and to stress all that binds Jews and Christians together in their mutual history, is also to attack one of the sources of anti-Jewish prejudice. We are, after all, brothers one to another. Judaism and Christianity both worship the one God. We both call Abraham father. We both view ourselves as communities covenanted to God. We both feel called to serve in the world as God's witnesses and to be a blessing to mankind.

This emphasis on solidarity is not meant to ignore the many differences that exist between Lutherans and Jews. Rather it is through an understanding and appreciation of what we have in common that we can best discuss our differences. But for the moment, Lutherans have an obligation to fulfill— namely, to understand adequately and fairly the Jews and Judaism. This is the immediate purpose of Lutheran conversations with Jews.

It is hoped that as Lutherans better understand this similar, yet different religious tradition, the wounds of the past will be healed, and Lutherans and Jews together will be able to face the future receptive to the direction of the Holy Spirit as he seeks to accomplish the will of the One in whom all men live and move and have their being.

II. CONFRONTATION

The History of Separation and Persecution

American Lutherans are the heirs of a long history of prejudicial discrimination against Jews, going back to pre-Christian times. The beginnings of this history of hate are obscure, but gross superstition and the desire for a scapegoat were prominent aspects. The separation between church and synagogue became final by the end of the first century. When Christianity was made the official religion of the Roman empire, a systematic degradation of Jews began in which both church and empire played their parts. Jews were regarded as enemies who were to be eliminated by defamation, extermination, prohibition of their writings, destruction of their synagogues, and exclusion into ghettos and despised occupations. During these nineteen centuries, Judaism and Christianity never talked as equals. Disputation and polemics were the media of expression. More recent developments reflect the continuation of patterns of ethnic behavior growing out of this heritage, by which Jews have been excluded by non-Jews, and have, in turn, themselves drawn together in separate communities.

No Christian can exempt himself from involvement in the guilt of Christendom. But Lutherans bear a special responsibility for this tragic history of persecution because the Nazi movement found a climate of hatred already in existence. The kindness of Scandinavian Lutherans toward Jews cannot alter the ugly facts of forced labor and concentration camps in Hitler's Germany. That the Nazi period fostered a revival of Luther's own medieval hostility toward Jews, as expressed in pugnacious writings, is a special cause of regret. Those who study and admire Luther should acknowledge unequivocally that his anti-Jewish writings are beyond any defense.

In America, Lutherans have been late and lethargic in the struggle for minority rights in the face of inherited patterns of prejudice. We have also been characterized by an inadequate level of ethical sensitivity and action in social and political areas.

Distinctive Ideas, Doctrines, Practices

Customarily American Lutherans have increased misunderstanding by trying to picture Jews as a "denomination" or "faith-community" like themselves. Actually, Jewishness is both a religious phenomenon and a cultural phenomenon which is exceedingly hard to define. While for most Jews, ancient and modern, it is seen as a matter of physical descent, the aspects of religion and nationhood have at times occupied decisive positions, as is currently true in regard to Zionism. We create misunderstanding when we persist in speaking of "Jewish" creeds and "Jewish" theology, for not all Jews necessarily believe in Judaism, although that religion is their heritage.

Judaism, while it does indeed have teachings, differs markedly from Christian denominations in that its essence is best summed up not in a set of beliefs or creeds, but in a way of life. The distinctive characteristics of the words "Jew" and "Judaism" should neither be ignored nor should they be revised to fit better with Christian presuppositions. We must rather allow Jewishness to be defined by Jews, and content ourselves with the already tremendous difficulties of trying to keep aware of the complexities of this shifting and not uncontradictory self-understanding.

To the extent that both religious practices and theological reflection manifest themselves among Jews, some basic guidelines can be attempted. There is no reason why Jewish practices or beliefs should be understood or judged differently from those of any minority group. They ought, indeed, to be respected especially by Christians, since they flow from a tradition which served as the "mother" of Christianity. But even where they are in disagreement with the practices and beliefs of Christians, they still deserve the same full protection and support which are given to the religious convictions of any American citizen. While modern interest in ethnicity has furthered the appreciation of diversity of heritages, American Lutherans still need warnings against bigotry and urgings to work toward minority rights.

The unique situation of the sharing of the books of the Hebrew Scriptures by Lutherans and Jews is the source of great problems as well as the potential for significant dialogue. Because Jews are not a "denomination" with a unity shaped by a theological consensus, these Scriptures do not have the same role for them as they do for us. For both Jews and Lutherans the Old Testament has a kind of mediate authority. For Jews this authority is mediated by millenia of tradition and by the individual's choice as to whether or not he will be "religious." For Lutherans as well, the Hebrew Scriptures do not have independent authority. They gain their significance from their role as *Old* Testament and are subordinated to the New Testament Christ, in whom they find a complex fulfillment, involving cancellation as well as acceptance, and reinterpretation as well as reaffirmation. Lutherans must affirm what Jews are free to accept or reject, namely, that it is the same God who reveals himself in both Scriptures. The consequence of this is that Lutherans must view Judaism as a religion with which we in part agree wholeheartedly and yet in part disagree emphatically. Judaism worships the same God as we do (the God of Abraham is our God), yet it disavows the Christ in whom, according to Christian faith, all God's promises have their fulfillment and through whom God has revealed the fulness of his grace.

In view of these divergences, Lutherans and Jews will differ, sometimes drastically, about questions of biblical interpretation, especially in regard to Christian claims about the fulfillment of the Old Testament. Such disagreements should not be the cause of either anger or despair, but rather should be seen as the doorway to a dialogue in which there can occur the discovery of both the real sources of the divergences and their appropriate degree of importance. Out of such learning there can come a mutuality of understanding which can make witness far more meaningful.

III. RESPECT AND COOPERATION

In recognition of the solidarity that unites us and of the tensions and disagreements which have divided us, we affirm the desire of the American Lutheran Church to foster a relationship of respect and cooperation with our Jewish neighbors.

Cooperation in Social Concern

Jews and Lutherans live together in the same society. They have common problems and obligations. The bonds of common citizenship ought to impel Lutherans to take the initiative in promoting friendly relationships and in making common cause with Jews in matters of civic and social concern. It is of special importance that Lutherans demonstrate their commitment to the intrinsic worth of Jewish people by giving them all possible assistance in the struggle against prejudice, discrimination, and persecution. Jews and Lutherans need not share a common creed in order to cooperate to the fullest extent in fostering human rights.

A Mutual Sharing of Faith

Within a context of respect and cooperation, Lutherans should invite Jews to engage in a mutual sharing of convictions. Lutherans who are aware of the Jewish roots of their faith will be moved by both a sense of indebtedness and a desire for deeper understanding to share on the level of religious commitment. Many Lutherans wish to engage in mutual sharing of convictions not only for the sake of greater maturity but also because Christian faith is marked by the impulse to bear witness through word and deed to the grace of God in Jesus Christ.

It is unrealistic to expect that Lutherans will think alike or speak with one voice on the motive and method of bearing witness to their Jewish neighbors. *Some Lutherans find in Scripture* clear directives to bear missionary witness in which conversion is hoped for. *Others hold that when Scripture* speaks about the relation between Jews and Christians its central theme is that God's promises to Israel have not been abrogated. The one approach desires to bring Jews into the Body of Christ, while the other tends to see the church and the Jewish people as together forming the one People of God, separated from one another for the time being, yet with the promise that they will ultimately become one.

It would be too simple to apply the labels "mission" and "dialogue" to these points of view, although in practice some will want to bear explicit *witness* through individuals, special societies or ecclesiastical channels, while others will want to explore the new possibilities of interfaith dialogue. Witness, whether it be called "mission" or "dialogue," includes a desire both to know and to be known more fully. Such witness is intended as a positive, not a negative act. When we speak of a mutual sharing of faith, we are not endorsing a religious syncretism. But we understand that when Lutherans and Jews speak to each other about matters of faith, there will be an exchange which calls for openness, honesty, and mutual respect. One cannot reveal his faith to another without recognizing the real differences that exist and being willing to take the risk of confronting these differences.

We wish to stress the importance of interfaith dialogue as a rich opportunity for growth in mutual understanding and for a new grasp of our common potentiality for service to humanity. We commend to the American Lutheran Church the LCUSA document, "Some Observations and Guidelines for Conversations between Lutherans and Jews," as a helpful means toward realizing the goals of interfaith dialogue. It should be understood that the LCUSA document limits itself to the aims and methods of dialogue and does not attempt to cover the entire field of Lutheran-Jewish relationships. Consequently, its comment that "neither polemics nor conversions are the aim of such conversations" does not rule out mission.

The State of Israel

The LCUSA "Guidelines" wisely suggests that "the State of Israel" be one of the topics for Jewish-Lutheran conversations. The tragic encounter of two peoples in the Middle East places a heavy responsibility upon Lutherans to be concerned about the legitimacy of the Jewish state, the rights of the Palestinians, and the problems of all refugees.

The history and circumstances of the Israeli-Arab conflict are very complicated. It is understandable that Lutherans should be deeply divided in their evaluation of the situation in the Middle East. In Jewish opinion, Israel is more than another nation. It is a symbol of resurrection following upon the near extinction of the Jewish people within living memory. There are also some Lutherans who find a religious significance in the State of Israel, seeing in recent events a fulfillment of biblical promises. Other Lutherans espouse not a "theology of the land," but a "theology of the poor," with special reference to the plight of the Palestinian refugees. Still other Lutherans endorse what might be called a "theology of human survival," believing that the validity of the State of Israel rests on juridical and moral grounds.

It seems clear that there is no consensus among Lutherans with respect to the relation between the "chosen people" and the territory comprising the present State of Israel. But there should be a consensus with respect to our obligation to appreciate, in a spirit of repentance for past misdeeds and silences, the factors which gave birth to the State of Israel and to give prayerful attention to the circumstances that bear on the search for Jewish and Arab security and dignity in the Middle East.

26
Dialogue: A Contemporary Alternative to Proselytization— A Statement of the Texas Conference of Churches: Jewish-Christian Relations [from SIDIC] 1982

The Texas (U.S.A.) Conference of Churches approved by unanimous vote the following statement on Jewish-Christian Relations

PREAMBLE: A NEW AWARENESS

From the very beginning God's Spirit has moved over the waters of creation, bringing order out of chaos, light out of darkness, life out of death.

It was indeed this same Spirit of God which inspired the ecumenical movement among the Churches of Jesus Christ. In our time we have seen the effects of this movement. Today Christians of diverse traditions enjoy increased understanding among themselves because they have responded to this gift of God's Holy Spirit. Through dialogue we have eliminated much ignorance and prejudice. We share a common mission of witness and service to the world. We have rejected proselytism as unworthy of our relationship to each other.

There is little doubt that the Spirit of God is once again moving over the waters. From every direction there are reports of a new awareness, a new consciousness, a new understanding between Jews and Christians. In this statement we wish to respond to this newest movement of the Spirit of God and even claim it as our own.

The task of ecumenism is far from completed. The movement toward greater unity is still a task of the Christian churches. We believe, however, that today the interfaith movement is summoning us into a renewed relationship with the Jewish people.

The Spirit of God moves among us through the events of our day. The Holocaust, the systematic and deliberate killing of six million Jews by the Third Reich, is the most singular event of our time summoning the Christian churches to reexamine (and reform) their traditional understanding of Judaism and the Jewish people. Biblical scholars and theologians of both Jewish and Christian traditions are affording us new insights into our common origins. Vatican Council II in its 1965 document, "Nostra Aetate", encouraged and called for "mutual understanding and appreciation" between Christians and Jews (paragraph 4).

In issuing this statement, it is the hope of the Texas Conference of Churches to encourage and promote this latest movement of the Spirit of God in our times. This statement is intended as a basis of discussion between Christians and Jews. We hope, too, that it will lead us into a renewed relationship with the Jews, one characterized by both dialogue and shared witness to the world.

I. Judaism as a Living Faith

A) We acknowledge with both respect and reverence that Judaism is a living faith and that Israel's call and covenant are still valid and operative today. We reject the position that the covenant between the Jews and God was dissolved with the coming of Christ. Our conviction is grounded in the teaching of Paul in Romans, chapters 9–11, that God's gift and call are irrevocable.

B) The Jewish people today possess their own unique call and mission before God and their covenant. They are called to faithfulness in fulfilling the command to witness to the world of the holiness of God's Name (Exodus 3:15, 9:16).

II. Relationship between the Two Covenants

A) The Christian covenant grew out of and is an extension of the Hebrew covenant. We Christians cannot understand ourselves or our relationship to God without a thorough knowledge of Judaism. "Thou bearest not the root, but the root thee" (Romans II:18).

B) Jews and Christians share a common calling as God's covenanted people. While we differ as to the precise nature of the covenant, we share a common history and experience of God's redemptive presence in history. Both Jews and Christians are called to faithfulness to the covenant as they understand it.

C) We believe that the interfaith movement is one toward greater understanding and unity among all major religions of the world, especially among Judaism, Christianity and Islam. The kinship of Jews and Christians, however, is unique because of the special relationship between the two covenants.

D) We confess thankfully the Scriptures of the Jewish people, the Old Testament of our Bible, to be the common foundation for the faith and work of Jews and Christians. By referring to the Hebrew Scriptures as the "Old Testament" it is not our intention to imply that these Scriptures are not timelessly new for both Jew and Christian today.

III. Dialogue, the Road to Understanding

A) In response to the movement of the Holy Spirit today, we believe that the desired and most appropriate posture between Christians and Jews today is one of dialogue.

B) Dialogue is the road to understanding between the two faiths and leads us to enlightenment and enrichment. We believe that dialogue will reduce misunderstanding and prejudice (on both sides).

C) In a dialogical relationship we dedicate ourselves to the observance of the following principles:

1) The strictest respect for religious liberty.

2) Respect for others as they define themselves in light of their own experience and tradition.

3) Avoidance of any conversionary intent or proselytism in the relationship. This does not exclude Jews and Christians from affirming to each other their respective beliefs and values.

4) An assumption of good will on both sides and a willingness to listen and learn from each other.

IV. Witnesses before Each Other and to the World

A) In the face of the growing secularizing and profaning of human life today, we believe that in their calling Jews and Christians are always witnesses of God in the presence of the world and before each other.

B) We acknowledge the universal nature of the mission[1] of Christian churches, and the need to witness,[2] to all nations. However, because of our unique relationship to Jews and Judaism, we believe that a posture of dialogue and shared mission is the one appropriate to the singular relationship.

C) In particular, it is our belief that Jews and Christians share a common mission to work together in the accomplishment of these tasks:

1) The hallowing of God's Name in the world.

2) Respect for the dignity and importance of the individual person as created in the image and likeness of God.

3) The active pursuit of justice and peace among and within the nations of the world.

4) To be a sign of hope in the future as promised by God.

D) In view of this shared mission, we eschew all forms of unwarranted proselytism[3] between Christians and Jews. In particular, we as Christian leaders, reject the following:

---

1. This part of the statement is intended to acknowledge the universal scope of the mission of the Christian churches. The Church must evangelize all nations, in keeping with the command of Christ. While acknowledging this, the statement then goes on to address the special relationship between Christians and Jews and how this special relationship calls for dialogue and shared witness, rather than "unwarranted proselytism".

It is of interest that Professor Tommaso Federici, in a paper presented at a meeting in Venice of Catholic-Jewish Liaison Committee, expressed the Church's mission, in reference to the Jews, in these words:

". . . renewed examination of Paul's text (in Romans) allows the conclusion . . . that the church's mission to Israel consists rather in living a Christian life in total fidelity to the one God and his revealed word." (See p. 44, this volume.)

2. The word "witness" is an important one in defining the desired relationship between Jews and Christians. The word itself can mean many things. In this statement we, as Christians, use the word to mean the permanent activity whereby the Christian or the Christian community proclaims God's actions in history and seeks to show how in Christ has come "the light that enlightens every man" (May 1970 report of the Joint Working Group between the Roman Catholic Church and the World Council of Churches). Witnessing in this sense can take three forms:

a) The witness of a life lived in justice, love and peace.

b) The witness of a more formal proclamation of God's Word to the world, to society (includes liturgical gatherings of the community).

c) The witness of social action on behalf of justice.

This statement recommends that such witnessing by Christians be done with due consideration of the rights of human persons to religious liberty. It also recommends that, in view of the special relationship between Christians and Jews, a common or shared witness is most appropriate.

3. "Unwarranted proselytism" is a deliberately chosen expression, which defines proselytism in its pejorative sense, i.e., zeal for converting others to faith which infringes upon the rights of human beings.

1) Anything which infringes upon or violates the right of every human person or community not to be subjected to external or internal constraints in religious matters.

2) Ways of preaching the gospel which are not in harmony with the ways of God, who invites us to respond freely to his call and serve him in spirit and truth.

3) Any kind of witness or preaching which in any way constitutes a physical, moral, psychological or cultural constraint on Jews.

4) Every sort of judgment expressive of discrimination, contempt, or restriction against individual Jews or against their faith, worship or culture.

5) Untrue and hateful forms of comparison which exalt the religion of Christianity by throwing discredit on the religion of Judaism.

6) Actions which, on educational, social or other pretexts, aim to change the religious faith of Jews by offering more or less overt protection and legal, material, cultural, political and other advantages.

7) Attempts to set up organization of any sort for the conversion of Jews.

V. Conclusion: A Messianic Hope

Jews and Christians share a great common hope in a future and final coming of God's reign in the world, a messianic age. While we differ in our understanding of whether and to what extent that promised age arrived in the person of Jesus Christ, we stand on common ground in hoping that one day there will be "a new heaven and a new earth" (Revelation, Isaiah). We believe that God's Spirit is moving over the waters once again. This statement is offered by the Texas Conference of Churches with the hope that it will facilitate the coming of that great day of righteousness and peace.

C) EUROPEAN CHURCH GROUPS

27
Declaration of the Belgian Protestant Council on Relations Between Judaism and Christianity, 1967

Translated from the original French
by Helga Croner

When we study the mystery of the church, it becomes evident that the church as community of the disciples of Jesus Christ is intimately linked to the Jewish people who are of Abraham's stock.[1] The church confesses that all those who have faith in Christ are Abraham's sons by faith. In fact, the apostle Paul teaches that those previously separated from Israel by the Torah have obtained full citizenship through Christ (Eph 2:12–13). They have been incorporated with the people of God and have become co-citizens with the saints and members of the family of God (Eph 2:19–20).[2] Therefore, both are now heirs to the promise, the sons who received the Torah[3] and those who received the faith of Abraham, who for that reason may be called the father of both.[4] That is how the church, linked to Israel, has become a part of the single people of God.

God namely has chosen the people Israel from among all the nations of the earth, that it may be to Him a precious people (Dt 7:6; 10:15; 14:2; 1 Kgs 3:8; Is 41:8; 44:1; [49:7]; Pss 32:12; 134:4).

Several times in the course of their history, however, the Hebrews abandoned the Eternal-One and followed other gods. But God has always manifested His fidelity toward His people by keeping a remnant of them for life (Is 37:4; 2 Kgs 19:4; etc.) He preserved a remnant that did not bend a knee before idols (1 Kgs 19:18; etc.) and that remained true to God or that returned (Is 10:21–22; etc.). This remnant had, and still has, to fulfill a special task in

193

God's plan of salvation and must proclaim the glory of God among the nations (Is 66:18–19; Mi 5:6), so that these will come to adore the God of Israel together with Israel (1 Kgs 8:41–43; Is 2:2–4; Mi 4:1–5; Zech 2:10–12; 8:20–23; 14:16).

The church confesses that in Jesus Christ the Promise is fulfilled and that it must be realized in the world.[5] The apostle Paul designates as remnant those Jews who came to believe in Jesus Christ and through whose mediation salvation is actually given to the nations, without however denying Israel the right to call itself Israel or, just as acceptably, to remain the unique people of God (Rom 9:27; 11:5), without transferring the name of Israel to the nations. In fact, God has not rejected His people; Israel remains the people of God, the Beloved (or those beloved) on account of the fathers (Rom 11:1, 28–29; 9:4–5).

There is only one people of God, the holy people of Israel. The "remnant" represents Israel; and so Israel in its totality continues to be the people of God, precisely because a remnant has converted.[6] It is the part for the whole. We must not lose sight of the fact that in the word of God the meaning of the term "remnant" is more nuanced than Christian theology often teaches. It may also mean those who escaped catastrophes and wars as well as those who kept the faith; and in different periods it may be applied to still other groups.

Thus the apostle Paul applies the term to the Jewish disciples of Jesus of Nazareth.[7] We ourselves can apply it to those who escaped the Nazi terror and to those who remained true to the faith of the fathers, as well as, with Paul, to those Jews who accepted faith in Jesus as the Messiah. In their own way, all of these represent Israel and manifest the inviolable fidelity of God toward all of Israel.

The church's claim to be the sole, new Israel of God can in no way be based on the Bible.[8] In this respect, too, we must express ourselves in carefully nuanced terms. It is Christ who has made the two, Jew and non-Jew, one single person by breaking down the wall of separation and destroying the enmity that had arisen between them because Israel was separated from the nations as by a girdle through the Torah and the precepts (Eph 2:14–16).

Christians from among the gentiles may now consider themselves co-heirs in Christ, forming one single body with Israel and taking part in the promise through the Gospel (Eph 3:6), to constitute one single body with Israel, one people of God, just as there is only one God who is the father of all of us (Mal 2:10; 1 Cor 8:4–6). That means the church must give up all pretentiousness and recognize humbly and gratefully that, in conformity with hope in the promise according to which the gentiles will participate in salvation and in the glorification of God, she represents all those who *in* Christ and *with* Israel (the "remnant" in all its nuances) are the revelation of the one people of God.

The words "The kingdom of God will be taken from you and given to a people who will produce its fruit" (Mt 21:43) must never be interpreted in a heavy-handed and simplistic manner as if they expressed an historical law or an inevitable fate of the Jewish people. Rather, these words must be left in their parenetic and warning context, as a call to this unique people as a whole, that is, addressed also to the church as a part of the single people, and not exclusively to Jews.

Within this single people of God parenesis must function with a feeling of unity that is truly ecumenical; it must manifest itelf in reciprocal responsibility: not only the church vis à vis Israel, and Israel vis à vis the church, but also the responsibility of the Christian who lives in the certainty of Jesus' messiahship[9] vis à vis the Christian who, by his life or his theology, dishonors this messiahship. In its totality as this single people of God, the Jewish people and the church march together toward fulfillment, when God will be all in all (Rom 11:25; 1 Cor 15:28), and they must put into practice their joint responsibility to manifest the kingdom of God in the world.[10]

Neither in the scriptures nor in the apostolic writings[11] is there a break between "old" and "new."

"New" means the "accomplishment," "fulfillment," "flourishing," "actualization" of that which already is in existence. What is new is this: a single people of God, Israel and the church, begins to walk toward realization of the promises of the word of God (Torah, Prophets, Writings, Apostolic Writings) in regard to Israel and the nations.[12]

In sorrow, Christians must therefore repent of any hostility on their part, of any enmity between Christians and Jews, between the church and Israel. By his death on the cross, Christ wanted to bring to an end the hostility between Israel and the nations, between Jews and non-Jews (Eph 2:14–16). That is why the church must imitate her Lord, must begin her battle against such enmity, and do all she can to reveal the authentic links between the church and Israel. Only in this way can Jews really understand the meaning of the words, "Christ is our peace and has made the two into one" (Eph 2:14). That indicates the church's full solidarity with Israel. The church confesses with all her heart that the deliverance of the people of God from slavery in Egypt is fulfilled in the redemption by the Messiah on the cross.[13] The church must therefore put into practice this confession of faith by condemning and actually fighting any kind of persecution, oppression and violence. This will be not only in respect to Israel but also in regard to any other group, community or nation—all antisemitism inside or outside the church—by defending the peace with and for Israel, and for the world. In this way the link between the church and Israel will have ecumenical character and will manifest itself in the joint study of God's revelations and in true communion between Jews and Christians, with charity and understanding.

NOTES

1. In rabbinic literature, Gen 2:24 is quoted in regard to the incorporation of proselytes. In Eph 2:14–16 *passim,* Paul probably alludes to this when speaking of the unity between Jews and non-Jews in the messianic era.

2. Before the messianic time, pagans had a right to citizenship in Israel only when they accepted the prescriptions for proselytes in the Torah.

3. Torah—teaching. The translation "law" often leads to wrong interpretations. The term "Torah" has the meaning of covenant in rabbinic literature, that is, the covenant of Abraham and of Moses.

4. "Of both": that means the two complementary parts of the single people of God. "For union between identicals is impossible . . . similarity is the cause of separation" (A. Néher, *"Le Puits de l'Exile. La théologie dialectique du Maharal de Prague,* series "Présence du Judaïsme," ed. Albin Michel, Paris, 1966), p. 175, where he speaks of the ties between Israel and the nations.

5. The accomplished promise obliges the church to identify herself with that which she already is in Jesus Christ. That is the paradox in the life of the church, the tension between the "already" and the "not yet"; in Christ, the promise is accomplished, but the single people of God (Israel and the church) must make it manifest.

6. Premise: Rom 11:16.

7. Paul does not intend to determine once and for all the theological meaning of the term "remnant" and its function in salvation history. He employs it only in one aspect of a much larger idea. One does not find, then, all of the Old Testament in the New. The Old Testament contains many values that have their place in the theology and life of the church, which are not found again in the New Testament, and which are the word of God just as much as the New Testament.

8. There is a great difference between appropriating the name "Israel" and participating in the claim to the title "Israel." Through Christ, the church is incorporated in Israel. The name "Israel" is part of the Covenant; in that sense it refers to the mission and vocation to be a light to the nations (Is 49:1–7). That mission was never taken from Judaism; in Christ, we now participate in the mission of the Jewish people.

9. That is, in whom Christ (= Messiah) is formed (Gal 4:19).

10. In the apostolic writings as well as in rabbinic literature, "kingdom of heaven" always means "kingdom of God."

11. It is not correct to designate the Torah, Prophets and Writings (in abbreviated form the three together are called Scriptures) as "Old Testament," and the Apostolic Writings as "New Testament." This terminology suggests an opposition or contrast

that does not exist. In Jewish-Christian dialogue exactitude should be taken into account.

12. Cf. note 1 above.

13. Luke 9:31 speaks literally of his ''exodus'' which he will accomplish in Jerusalem, according to the old Jewish tradition that in Messianic times one will no longer read primarily the exodus from Egypt at Easter because the great Messianic deliverance has been acomplished (TB Ber 12B–13A). That probably is the reason why the Apostolic Writings are so full of reminiscences of the Exodus and of Easter.

28
Reflections on the Problem 'Church-Israel', issued by the Central Board of the Union of Evangelical Churches in Switzerland, 1977

[English translation from **Encounter Today]**

FOREWORD

The Central Board of the **Schweizerische Evangelische Kirchenbund** (Union of Evangelical Churches in Switzerland) is deeply interested in the destiny of the Jewish people as the Covenant People of God in the Old Testament, the people from whose ranks were descended Jesus of Nazareth, the early Apostles and the oldest Christian community. The history of the Church as well as the history of the Jews down to the present time question us about the relationship of Church and Israel and about the stand taken by Christians to Jews.

The ingathering of many Jews in parts of the Land promised them in the Old Testament causes the Church in her thought and action to share with burning concern in the problems of the Near East in which Jews and Arabs confront each other.

Through these problems and through the religious-historical links with Judaism and also through the options made inside the Church, which range from solidarity with the State of Israel, over theological dialogue, to a call for missions to the Jews, the Board is being asked questions which claim the attention of all Christians.

The Board therefore commissioned a working-group consisting of Professor Robert Martin-Achard of Geneva, Martin Klopfenstein of Berne and the

President of the Council of Christians and Jews, Pastor Heinrich Oskar Kuehner of Basle, in whose work Dr. Walter Sigrist, President of the **Kirchenbund** has also taken part. The texts submitted by this working-group were discussed by the Board itself and are herewith offerd to the public as "Reflections on the Problem Church-Israel" in view of stimulating personal thinking.

I. THE PEOPLE OF GOD'S COVENANT

"Has God rejected his people? By no means" (Rom. 1:11).

The people of the Old Testament of which present day Judaism considers itself the heir, is still in existence and lives partly again in the Land of its Fathers—this in spite of many attempts at its destruction and in spite of its own aspirations at assimilation. This fact earnestly reminds the Church of its duty to be concerned with this people. This duty, which is based upon what Paul calls "the mystery of Israel" is independent of the existence of the State, it confronts the Church permanently.

We state the following points:

1. According to the witness of the Old and New Testaments God called the People of Israel to be his covenanted people. This election is but a free choice of grace, i.e. is not based upon any quality which Israel might possess in advantage over other peoples. The object of the election is to bear witness to the God of Abraham, Isaac and Jacob in the face of the world and to serve him. According to Gen. 12:3, God will thereby let his blessing come upon all nations. This alone constitutes the specific character of the people of Israel. There is no biological explanation for this specificity.

2. This covenant relationship should become manifest in the whole life of this people. This intention conforms to the will of God "to become flesh and dwell among us", and "to let his kingdom come to us", and "to let his will be done in heaven and on earth." This intention has finally become fully realized in Christ Jesus—a Jew.

3. Indeed the Jewish people all through its history has often broken the covenant and failed to fulfil God's will. Yet this does not annul God's fidelity to the covenant. Nor does the non-recognition of Jesus of Nazareth as the Christ by the majority of the Jews repeal the covenant promise given to the Jewish people according to Rom. 9–11.

4. Because God has not rejected his people, there is no question that the Church has taken the place of Israel as "the new people of God". Although the Church, already in the New Testament, applied to herself several promises

made to the Jewish people she does not supersede the covenant people, Israel. Much rather do Israel and the Church stand side by side and belong together in several ways, while being at the same time separate on essentials. It should be important for us, Christians, to recognize what links us to the Jews and what separates us from them. We are conscious that there are deliberately different views on this point within the Church.

II. CHRISTIANS AND JEWS BELONG TOGETHER

"The faith of Christ links us together" . . . (Shalom Ben Chorin.)

1. Jesus was a Jew, "born of a Jewish mother". He was sent to the Jews first (Matth. 15:24). His message is of value for "the Jew first and then also for the Greek" (Rom. 1:16 and elsewhere in Rom.).
2. The teaching of Jesus is rooted in Jewish thinking, in Jewish teaching and in Jewish life.
3. The Church has included the Old Testament into her canon. The New Testament cannot be fully understood without the help of the Old.
4. Historically the Christian Church has grown out of Judaism. This existing relationship must be respected at all times.
5. The early Christians were Jews and understood themselves as members of the Jewish people who believed in Christ Jesus.
6. The Christian Church has taken over many customs from Judaism, e.g. the celebration of the Seventh Day, Passover, Pentecost, the pattern of public worship with readings and prayers from the Bible, singing and praying of psalms i.a.

III. CHRISTIANS AND JEWS HAVE BEEN SEPARATED FROM ONE ANOTHER

. . . "Faith in Jesus separates us. . ." (Shalom Ben Chorin).

1. The attitude to Jesus is the central moment of parting between Judaism, and the Church. This was manifest already in the New Testament and is so still today.
The rift has grown deeper through the following facts:

—that on the part of Christians, the crucifixion of Jesus is often ascribed to the Jews as a collective guilt;

—that on the part of Christians, the Jews are often blamed for choosing their own righteousness as the way to God instead of the grace of God.

2. Added to this comes the fact that in the eyes of the Jews it is unthinkable to belong to the people of God unless one observes their own religious prescriptions (e.g. circumcision, dietary laws, sabbath, etc.).

From the Jewish point of view the bedevilment of Jews by Christians (cf. 3:1), their defamation and outlawing down to physical extermination over 1700 years have weighed heavily upon every attempt at a rapprochement on the part of Christians.

The silence of many Churches on the persecutions of Jews in the 20th century and on the threat to the State of Israel in our days has been a bitter disillusion to them.

3. The persecutions have caused theologians and lay people in Christian Churches to re-discover the link between Judaism and Christianity, and led to a new understanding of their belonging together.

IV. WHO ARE THE JEWS AND WHO ARE THE CHRISTIANS?

We, Christians, have often had no idea at all of Judaism, or else a false one. It is an urgent task for Christian communities to correct our partial knowledge or ignorance of Judaism.

1. (a) This particularly concerns the proclamation of the Gospel and the teaching of both young and adult. It is urgent to amend the defamatory concept of the collective guilt of the Jews for the death of Jesus on the cross.

(b) The real cause of the separation of Jews and Christians in the 1st century should be correctly investigated.

(c) It is part of the programme of Christian communities to learn about Judaism through reading and personal contacts.

2. (a) Such efforts lead also to the self-knowledge of Christian Churches. Many things which are commonly regarded as typically Christian (e.g. neighbourly love) are recognized as just as typically Jewish, as taken over from Judaism and therefore as common good. On the other hand, what is really essential in the Christian faith will become clearer.

(b) The meeting with Judaism helps Christians better to understand Jesus and his message.

V. MISSION ALSO TO THE JEWS?

1. "A church which is not missionary has resigned" **(demissioniert)** (Emil Brunner). Without a mission Christianity would have remained a sect within Judaism.

2. Mission means proclamation of Jesus Christ, just as the Jews on their part have borne witness to us of the unity and holiness of God and still do so. Mission is not conversion to Christian culture and customs.

3. Christians have to bear witness of their faith in Christ also to the Jews. We regard the Jews as men whom "God so loved that he gave his only Son for them" (John 3:16).

4. The New Testament gives Christians unequivocal directions as to how they have to bear witness to their faith: "In your hearts reverence Christ as Lord! Always be prepared to make a defence to any one who calls you to account for the hope that is in you. Yet do it with gentleness and reverence". (I Petr. 3:15–16a). We have also to consider that God alone can make converts, not we, men. This attitude as witnesses is also binding for Christians in their dialogue with Jews.

5. The phrase "mission to the Jews" puts Jews on a par with heathens and undervalues the specific position of the Jewish people among the nations (cf. 1:1), as well as the fact that Judaism has known the God of the Bible and believed in him long before the birth of the Church.

6. The Christian witness cannot be exhausted by dialogue alone nor by proclamation of the Word. It is credible only if every one, including the Jews, is convinced through deeds.

VI. ZIONISM—STATE OF ISRAEL

Zionism is a movement rooted in biblical as well as post-biblical traditions. The Jewish tradition has always included and still includes in various forms, the hope that the Jewish people would return to the Land of its Fathers (e.g. festivals, prayers, worship, etc.). The hope of Zion has been handed down and remains alive in the Jewish people to the present day.

Ever since the second half of the 19th century the political movement founded by Theodor Herzl has been able to inspire the Jews because, among other things, this modern Zionism was related to the traditional Jewish self-awareness. It strove to obtain a legally established home in the land of the Fathers in order to guarantee an existence worthy of men in their own State to the Jews who were ever and again being threatened and persecuted. It was also intended to facilitate to the Jewish people the realization of their right to self-determination.

1. The outcome of this movement was the foundation of the State of Israel, decided upon by UNO in Resolution 181 (II) on 29 November 1947, and proclaimed on 14 May 1948.

2. Some Christians and many Jews see in the foundation of the State of Israel the fulfilment of the biblical promises. Others, among both Christians and Jews, regard it merely as a political deed which like every historical change entails political and human problems. The appreciation and the preservation of the Jewish people should determine our reflections between two standpoints.

3. This new State has become a homeland not only for many victims of West-European persecutions, but also for emigrants under the pressure of East European, North-African and Oriental States.

When considering these problems we must take into account all these root causes which have led to the formation of the State of Israel and its present situation.

4. As often happens in world history, in this political growth of the new State the good fortune of some has become the misfortune of others. Together with the anxiety for the Jewish people we feel painfully concerned for the Palestinian Arabs who live inside and outside Israel.

5. We are conscious that antisemitic elements of European politics past and present are partially responsible for the present situation and that extreme hate propaganda, terror and the cold calculation of the Great Powers threaten the life of the Jews in the State of Israel, while in spite of all the lot of Palestinian Arabs is not being improved.

6. We consider it the duty of the Christian Churches and all Christians to intervene in defence of the right to existence of the Jewish people, which is especially linked with us (cf. 1:4; 2:1–6) and to stand by Israel in her growing isolation.

7. We regard it also as a duty for Christian Churches and all Christians to intervene so that the right to live and the conditions of life of Palestinian Arabs be appreciated. In this connection we regard it as an urgent task to work out a clarification of the concept "Palestinian" and to examine their possibility of self-determination.

8. Above all it is our duty to break down hate, to keep ourselves from the influence of one-sided propaganda and to serve reconciliation and peace. We reject every form of anti-Judaism, but also every form of anti-Arab feeling.

VII. JERUSALEM

1. Various Christians, including Evangelicals, identify the historically and topographically located city of Jerusalem with ''the new Jerusalem'', described in Apoc. 21, and ''the heavenly Jerusalem'' in so many songs.

2. Most Christians have a special feeling of belonging to Jerusalem because she is the city of the beginnings and the place of the great events of salvation.

3. According to the Churches of the Reformation neither the fulfilment of the promise nor the reality of faith in the events of salvation are linked to geographically and historically located ''holy places''.

4. The Reformed Churches also are longing for the dignified and respectful preservation of the places where the events of salvation took place.

5. We are conscious that Jerusalem represents a complex cultural, political, religious and emotional problem. At the same time we recognize that the Israeli government is making great efforts to deal fairly with this situation, although these efforts cannot lead to the satisfaction of all parties concerned.

We establish:

a) that in Jerusalem today under Israeli administration the monuments connected with historical events are as much as possible maintained and kept in repair with respect and care.

b) that the Christian denominations as well as the Islamic and Jewish communities practise today their religions freely undcr Israeli administration and are able to fulfil their rites, as well as marriages, children's rights, burials and religious instruction, each according to their own religiously determined legislations.

c) that freedom of religion is granted more extensively today than in Mandate times and also better than under Jordanian rule. (In the latter phase of the Mandate the Israelis were barred access to the Western Wall. Under Jordanian rule Christians living in Israel could visit the Holy Sepulchre only on definite festivals; Jews were not permitted at all to go to the Western Wall; Muslims from the Gaza strip could not travel to Jerusalem).

CONCLUSION

We consider that it is an urgent duty for the Christian Church to pray for Israel, for her neighbours and for peace in the Near East as well as the whole world. This prayer of intercession however does not absolve us of the above mentioned tasks. It renders them all the more binding.

29

We, the Mennonites, and the Jewish People: A Call for Taking a Stand in our Days. Distributed to the participants at the Mennonite European Regional Conference, Elspeet, The Netherlands, May 1977

1. The 16th-century founders of our small but now world-wide Brotherhood understood correctly, that Christian baptism by water—like that of John the Baptist among the Jews of his century—may only be administered in response to the stated desire of the person who himself wants to be baptized.

2. Equally correctly, they understood that Jesus came not to destroy the Covenant of God with the Jews, but only to affirm it in a manner that would bring the blessing of God's people to non-Jews, also.

3. Unfortunately, they never came to a distinct definition of their own, and our, position with Israel as co-heirs of God's promises concerning the independent and continuously existing Jewish people living along side them and us, however,—any more than did later Mennonites and other advocates of adult-baptism, such as the Baptists, have yet done so.

4. Such a declaration of Position has become an absolute requirement for our Brotherhood in this century—now that persecution of Jews by so-called Christian peoples has grown without precedent in extent and intensity—and now that the successful restoration of Jewish national independence has been achieved for the first time in 18 centuries.

5. It is precisely we, as Mennonites, who unlike almost all other Christians have emphatically rejected the union of Christ's work with that of the Roman Empire, asserted by the Emperor Constantine and maintained as normal by his successors in East and West, who should have shown understanding for the right of the Jews to independent existence of their people.

6. That during the most abhorrent persecution of Jews in human history and during the attempts to rebuild the state of Israel we, as Brotherhood, stood by in silence and inactivity was, therefore, an offence and omission which we must confess before God and for which to the Jews we must acknowledge our guilt.

7. On us rests the duty to support the Jews in word and deed and faithful friendship in their fight for renewal of the existence of their people; for we, too, as Mennonites in diverse areas of the world have attempted under constantly difficult circumstances to construct a community inspired by the biblical witness—and thus their concern is also our own.

8. Because to our distress we have seen that by no means all Mennonites are willing to acknowledge the seriousness of the offense of our Brotherhood to the Jewish people, we desire, if given the opportunity, to place this definition of standpoint and the enclosed Call for Freedom for Israel on the agenda of the World Conference next year in the United States of America in direct relation to the chosen theme: The Rule of God in this World;

9. And because we desire to make it clear to the Jews how much we want our relation with their people to become entirely different. In the end, we know God—specifically in the Messiah—as No One other than the God of Israel.

10. We desire that this may be made known also by the choice of Jerusalem as the location for the Mennonite World Conference to be held in 1984.

30
Toward Renovation of the Relationship of Christians and Jews: The Synod of the Protestant Church of the Rheinland, 1980 [from SIDIC]

Thou bearest not the root, but the root thee. Romans 11:18b.

1. In agreement with the "Message to the Congregations concerning the Dialogue between Christians and Jews" from the provincial Synod of the Protestant Church in the Rheinland (12 January 1978), the provincial Synod accepts the historical necessity of attaining a new relationship of the church to the Jewish people.

2. The church is brought to this by four factors:

(1) The recognition of Christian co-responsibility and guilt for the Holocaust—the defamation, persecution and murder of Jews in the Third Reich.

(2) The new biblical insights concerning the continuing significance of the Jewish people for salvation history (e.g., Romans 9–11), which have been attained in connection with the Church struggle.

(3) The insight that the continuing existence of the Jewish people, its return to the Land of Promise, and also the creation of the State of Israel, are signs of the faithfulness of God toward His people.

(4) The readiness of Jews, in spite of the Holocaust, to (engage in) encounter, common study and cooperation.

3. The provincial Synod welcomes the study "Christians and Jews" by the Council of the Protestant Church in Germany (E.K.D.).[1]

The provincial Synod recommends to all congregations that the Study be

---

1. Cf. *Stepping Stones to Further Jewish-Christian Relations*, Helga Croner, ed., Stimulus Books (London, New York, 1977) pp. 133–149.

made the starting point of an intensive work on Judaism and the foundation of a new consciousness of the relationship of the church to the Jewish people.

4. In consequence the provincial Synod declares:

(1) Stricken, we confess the co-responsibility and guilt of German Christendom for the Holocaust.

(2) We confess thankfully the "Scriptures" of the Jewish people (Lk. 24:27; I Cor, 15:3f), our Old Testament, to be the common foundation for the faith and work of Jews and Christians.

(3) We confess Jesus Christ the Jew, who as the Messiah of the Jews is the Saviour of the world and binds the peoples of the world to the people of God.

(4) We believe in the permanent election of the Jewish people as the people of God and realize that through Jesus Christ the church is taken into the covenant of God with His people.

(5) We believe with the Jews that the unity of righteousness and love characterizes the saving work of God in history. We believe with the Jews that righteousness and love are the admonitions of God for our whole life. As Christians we see both rooted and grounded in the work of God with the Jewish people and in the work of God through Jesus Christ.

(6) We believe that in their calling Jews and Christians are always witnesses of God in the presence of the world and before each other. Therefore, we are convinced that the church may not express its witness toward the Jewish people as it does its mission to the peoples of the world.

(7) Therefore, we declare:

Throughout centuries the word "new" has been used against the Jewish people in biblical exegesis: the new covenant was understood as contrast to the old covenant, the new people of God as replacement of the old people of God. This obliviousness to the permanent election of the Jewish people and its relegation to non-existence marked Christian theology, church preaching and church work ever and again right to the present day. Thereby we have also made ourselves guilty of the physical elimination of the Jewish people.

Therefore, we want to perceive the unbreakable connection of the New Testament with the Old Testament in a new way, and learn to understand the relationship of the "old" and "new" from the standpoint of the promise: as a result of the promise, as fulfilment of the promise, as confirmation of the promise. "New" means therefore no replacement of the "old". Hence we deny that the people Israel has been rejected by God or that it has been superseded by the church.

(8) As we are turning around we begin to discover what Christians and Jews both give witness to:

We both confess God as the creator of heaven and earth, and know that we are singled out in the ordinary life of the world by the same God by means of the blessing of Aaron.

We confess the common hope in a new heaven and a new earth and the power of this messianic hope for the witness and work of Christians and Jews for justice and peace in the world.

5. The provincial Synod recommends to the district synods the calling of a special officer of the Synod for Christian-Jewish dialogue.

The provincial Synod commissions the church leadership to constitute anew a committee ''Christians and Jews'' and to invite Jews to work with this committee. It is to advise the church leadership in all questions concerning the relationship of the church and Jewry and to assist the congregations and church circles toward a deeper understanding of the new standpoint in the relationship of Jews and Christians.

The provincial Synod makes the church leadership responsible to consider in what form the Protestant Church of the Rheinland can undertake a special responsibility for the Christian settlement Nes Ammim in Israel, as other churches (e.g., in the Netherlands and in the German Federal Republic) have already done.

The provincial Synod makes the church leadership responsible to see to it that in church instructions, continuing education and advanced education the matter of ''Christians and Jews'' shall be appropriately paid attention to.

The provincial Synod considers it desirable that a regular teaching post with the thematic ''Theology, Philosophy and History of Jewry'' shall be established in the Wuppertal seminary and the Wuppertal general college, and requests the church leadership to consult with the Wuppertal seminary, the Wuppertal general college, and with the state of Nordrhein-Westfalen to this end.

Note: This statement of the Rheinland Synod has aroused discussion and comment among Jews and Christians alike. On both sides reactions have been positive and negative.

Two facts emerge from this discussion:

  i) the importance for Jewish-Christian relations of such a statement issued by the governing body of a Christian Church with a view to correcting negative teachings about the Jewish people;

  ii) the urgency for theologians of all denominations to initiate or continue to formulate a basic theology of Jewish-Christian relations which will result in full recognition of the unity of God's plan for salvation.

31
Declaration of the Council of Churches in The Netherlands, on Persistent Antisemitism, intended for Dutch Christians and Churches. Amersfoort, 1981

1. INTRODUCTION

Antisemitism is an age-old phenomenon that time and again raises its head in many different forms: it seems to be ineradicable. Whoever had imagined that after the horrors of the Second World War it would have disappeared forever from our society has been sorely deceived.

Since the War, expressions of Jew-hatred have been heard many times. True, in most cases it was not a mass phenomenon, but even so it is of alarming persistence. Small fanatical groups may be responsible for desecrations of cemeteries, for abusive words on the street or over the telephone, and for painting anti-Jewish slogans and swastikas on synagogues and Jewish shops. But the incidental eruptions of Jew-hatred occasion great alarm and uncertainty among Jews. By such events, many are violently reminded of the Jewish persecutions before and during the Second World War; anxiously they ask themselves: Is it all starting again?

We should not forget that in the 1920's antisemitism began in Germany with small splinter groups, which originally nobody took seriously. Yet, as time went by, antisemitism—and other expressions of discrimination—ultimately found a fertile soil within wide strata of the population, due to disastrous economic regression. It is understandable, therefore, that Jewish fellow-citizens—and not only they—draw parallels between then and now. Today we also live in a time of economic regression and growing unemployment. Feelings of fear and hatred against "the other" are being fed moreover by the growing number of aliens in our country.

The Church cannot leave in doubt that she watches attentively and opposes any form of discrimination against minorities. That she calls special attention to the ever recurrent flaring up of antisemitism is due to the fact that a special tie exists between the Jewish people and the Church. Therefore she can and should speak about antisemitism in a special way.

It is imperative, for a correct understanding, first to deal with the particular relation between the Church and the Jewish people, i.e., Jews within and outside the State of Israel.

2. OUR TIE WITH THE JEWISH PEOPLE

(a) God's unfailing faithfulness to the Jewish people

The promises which the God of Abraham, Isaac, and Jacob has made to the Jewish people have never been revoked by their God, who is our God, too. Nor did God ever recall the covenant which He, through Moses, had made with them. We Christians call this covenant—by a term which has occasioned much misunderstanding—the "old covenant." This covenant was not abolished or replaced by the "new covenant" in and through the coming of Jesus Christ. Jesus himself states emphatically the fulfillment of the Law and the Prophets (Mt 5:17). Paul wrote about those Jews who did not recognize the Messiah in Jesus: "As regards election they are beloved for the sake of their forefathers. For the gifts and the call of God are irrevocable" (Rom 11:28f). The apostle even emphasizes the advantage of Jews, for they "are entrusted with the oracles of God" (Rom 3:2).

Unfortunately, this enduring love of God for the Jewish people has often been forgotten or even denied by Christians in the past. Wrongly, Jews were spoken about as if God had rejected them as His own people. Wrongly, too, time and again the great suffering which this people has experienced during the centuries has been interpreted by Christian tradition as deserved punishment from the hand of God, instead of as culpable work by men. Wrongly, the evil done to members of this people has been covered up, even excused.

Through the shock of the dreadful persecution and destruction during the Second World War many Christians in various churches have again become aware of and have rediscovered, the central biblical thought of God's unfailing faithfulness to the Jewish people.

It is of great importance for Christians to realize that by such awareness they make a choice. In the New Testament, texts are to be found violently criticizing the doings of Jews; but the issue is always a dispute and conflict between those Jews who did and those Jews who did not believe in Jesus. We Christians of the twentieth century, who have seen the evil such texts have brought about, cannot and must not simply fall back on them and use them, as if during two thousand years of church history nothing had happened.

(b) The calling of the Gentiles

Gentile Christians are grafted onto the already existing Jewish trunk (Rom 11:17). We have received a share in the promises which God gave to the people of the Jews. We would therefore cut off ourselves from the life-giving root—both individually and as churches—if carelessly and indifferently we would pass by the fate of those who originated from that root and are still the ones first called.

(c) Guilt of Christians toward Jews

Not only must Christians not carelessly and indifferently pass by the fate of Jews. To our shame, we have to admit that in the past even worse things have happened. By wrongly applying certain biblical texts, by discrimination, Jew-hatred, and pogroms, Christians helped to prepare the way which ultimately resulted in the annihilation camps in Nazi Germany. We are not permitted to forget this dismal history between Christians and Jews. If openly and thoroughly we admit that guilt of the past, we will not minimize even the hidden forms of antisemitism in the present time. What happened is not to happen again.

3. INCREASING CRITICISM OF THE STATE OF ISRAEL

(a) Tie of the Jews to the land

In the dispersion, the Jewish people has preserved all through the centuries its longing for its country at the eastern end of the Mediterranean and for the city of Jerusalem. This tie, retained through the ages, is an historical datum giving the Jews a right in this land—a right which since 1948 has been internationally affirmed by the recognition of the State of Israel.

That is not to say that others have not also an historical right to the same region as their dwelling place. The difficulty and tragedy is that here right does not stand opposite wrong, but the right of Jews opposite the right of Palestinians. It will be extremely difficult to reconcile these two rights without detracting from either. In this connection we want to recall the declaration of the

Council of Churches in 1979 regarding the conflict in the Middle East, which deals with these problems and states among others: ''Israel's right to political existence and safety has to be recognized without reservation. The right of Palestinians to self-determination and to political existence has to be recognized without reservation, too.''

(b) From sympathy toward criticism

The founding of the State of Israel in 1948 was of great significance to large groups in the churches, too. It seemed that old prophecies were being fulfilled, and high hopes resulted. The young state could rejoice in the sympathy of many. The fight of a small group of Jews against manifestly superior forces caught the imagination.

This often uncritical attitude toward the State of Israel had also its questionable aspects. Much of the sympathy for Israel was nourished from a dubious source, namely an undigested and not openly admitted feeling of guilt. That became evident, for instance, when an uncritical option in favor of that state went together with a lack of understanding for the rights of Palestinians and sympathy with their fate.

Since the 1970's the State of Israel has lost many friends and much sympathy in the entire Western world, including the Netherlands. It is no exaggeration to speak of an increasingly negative attitude toward the State of Israel.

(c) Disturbed relations

Criticism of the doings of the State of Israel—as of any state—is of course permitted and even necessary, provided, as a matter of principle, the right of existence of the state is not negated and the above described tie between the Jewish people and the land is not forgotten. On the basis of such solidarity, criticism is possible, for instance, of the settlement policies and the expropriation of Arab land in Galilee.

Nevertheless, caution remains necessary; furthermore, in criticizing, some particular considerations have to be taken into account. For many Jews the Second World War has not yet become past history. Remembrance of the annihilation of six million Jews gives a unique significance to the existence of a country of their own where Jews are at home. Is it surprising, then, that criticism of their state is easily experienced by them as a threat to their last refuge and, thus, a form of antisemitism?

A second consideration: Through the role which the church and theology have played in creating a breeding ground for antisemitic outbursts, Jews have become suspicious of Christians. Conscious of this guilt, Christians should take it into account in criticizing the actions and policies of the State of Israel.

Third, it should not be forgotten that many Christians had excessive expectations regarding the State of Israel. When those expectations were not fulfilled, harsh criticism replaced positive attitudes. The Jewish people, which according to its own tradition was called to be "a light to the nations" (Is 42:6), should be an example to others—so it was now said—especially in the actions of its state. As far as these expectations are based on faith in the lasting election of the Jewish people, they cannot simply be rejected. Such expectations become dangerous and unfair, however, if they are divorced from the understanding that the special call of the Jews is the reserve of God's gift and grace. If that is forgotten, the expectations take the menacing form of a pityless demand and easily turn into unmerciful criticism and disappointment.

(d) Additional causes for disturbed relations

One can doubltessly point to yet other causes for a decline in sympathy. Present policies of the Israeli government might well be one of its main causes—though we should never forget that these policies are also induced by the traumatic remembrance of the past. In our country, the justified claims of Palestinians are better recognized in recent years. And who would deny that economic interests also play an increasing part? Ties with Israel are severely tested by the fact that a number of oil producing countries use the awarding of economically attractive orders as a weapon against support of Israel and normal business relations with that country. Many people cannot help feeling that criticism of the State of Israel contributes to the fact that little protest is heard against these ignoble practices. Thus, Israel is increasingly being threatened and isolated and for that reason feels the necessity to act in a way for which it then is criticized.

(e) Criticism and antisemitism

Criticism founded on a deep and lasting solidarity with Jews cannot possibly be interpreted as antisemitism. Still, whoever criticizes the State of Israel should be deeply aware of the above-mentioned aspects. Therefore, here more than anywhere else, utmost care is demanded toward anything which willingly or not could again fuel former antisemitism. Well-intentioned and justified criticism can easily be misused.

4. WHAT CHRISTIANS CAN DO

It is not possible within this framework to offer an elaborate and precise outline for Christian action, but we do want to suggest some possibilities for further consideration.

In the first place, we can and must fight antisemitism here in our country. To do that it will be necessary to study the background of this phenomenon in order to recognize it even in its hidden forms. Moreover, we must eradicate all causes of antisemitism which still exist in our Christian tradition. We owe that not only to the Jewish people; it also is a liberating experience for ourselves. We can leave behind our guilty past only when we are able to stop its effects on the present.

Yet, we are not only involved in the fate of Jews in our own country but also in the fate of the State of Israel and of the Palestinian people. Whether we like it or not, we are in the midst of that conflict. Adopting an attitude of aloofness is hypocritical and untrue; we are not neutral spectators or well-meaning outsiders.

We are involved as Christians, though we cannot change the situation there. Ultimately, the solution of the conflict will have to be found by Jews and Palestinians through political, diplomatic means. But Christians of Western Europe can act as bridge builders because they have access both to Jews and to Palestinian Christians. We have in mind the part which Christian politicians can play internationally to create a climate in which such a solution becomes possible. Churches and individual Christians should do all they can so that Jews here and in Israel can feel secure. In regard to Israel, the feeling of insecurity leads the state to strive for self-protection, for which especially the Palestinians have to pay the bill. The Palestinian people, threatened and despairing, react in their turn with fear and violence. That violence, in turn, evokes understandable emotions among Jews within and outside of Israel. If Christians in their attitudes and actions show their ties with Jews, the Jewish people can feel more secure in the community of men and nations. Thereby the spiral of violence—so we hope—can be broken and talks between Jews and Palestinians come to be an actual possibility.

32
The Relationship of the Church with the People of Israel: Document on Ecumenism: Synod of the Waldensian and Methodist Churches of Italy, August 1982 [from SIDIC]

After having discussed Ecumenism in general and Unity in Christ, the document of the Synod turned its attention to the Church's relationship with the Jewish People, seeing in this relationship an integral part of the ecumenical question.

Apostolic Christianity also had its "ecumenical" problem. This did not, however, consist in more or less harmonious relationships between different kinds of Christian communities which have existed since the first century; according to the New Testament, co-existence was not always peaceful, but it was genuine and profound. The "ecumenical" problem in the first century concerned the relationship of the Church as a whole with the people of Israel. The fundamental "division" which New Testament Christian awareness had to face up to was the internal rupture (the "hardening" of "part of Israel") of which the apostle Paul speaks in Romans 11:25; he explains it as a "mystery" produced in Israel when confronted by the person of Christ and in particular by his cross and resurrection, a rupture within the people of God which was both painful and dramatic, ("I have great sorrow and unceasing anguish in my heart . . ."; ". . . I could wish that I myself were accursed and cut off from Christ . . ." Rom. 9:2–3) yet at the same time tremendously fruitful (". . . now if their trespass means riches for the world, and if their failure means riches for the Gentiles, how much more will their full inclusion mean"; . . . and so all Israel will be saved"—Rm. 11:12,26).

Very early on the Church lost the awareness of unity between church and synagogue as an essential element in the unity of the People of God. The history of Jewish-Christian relations over the 2,000 years which are behind us is a painful one, with great guilt on the part of Christians, who perhaps have sinned against no one as much as against the Jews.

It will necessitate no small change in contemporary Christian awareness to recognize that Israel, as a community of faith, is an integral part of the ecumenical question. Our churches must become sensitized to the message, disregarded until now, which is found in Romans 9, 10 and 11, that of recovering this ''lost dimension'' of their life and witness: the relationship with the Jewish community.

33

A Declaration on the Relationship between Christians and Jews by the Baden Provincial Synod of the German Evangelical Church, May 1984. [From *Christian Jewish Relations*]

1. The Evangelical Synod of Baden obeys the command of history to gain, in conformity with biblical teaching, a new relationship of the Church towards the Jewish people. Throughout the centuries, Christian theology, Church preaching, instruction and Church action were vitiated by the idea that the Jewish people were rejected by God. This Christian anti-Judaism became one of the roots of antisemitism. Accordingly we, being concerned, confess that Christendom in Germany bears a joint responsibility for and guilt at the Holocaust.

2. In our endeavor for a new understanding, we greatefully acknowledge the inseparable link between the New and the Old Testament. We are realizing this relationship on the basis of God's promise: God gives, fulfills and re-affirms it anew. The 'New' does not replace the 'Old.'

3. We believe in God's faithfulness. He has chosen his people Israel and he stands by the election. Therefore we must contradict when it is said that Israel has been rejected by God. Nor is the election of Israel cancelled by the election of the Church out of Jews and Gentiles. We Christians acknowledge our allegiance to Jesus who was a Jew, believing that he is the Lord who was crucified for all, resurrected and is certain to return, the savior of the world. It pains and saddens us to think that this confession separates us from the faith of the Jewish people. In the belief in Jesus Christ and obedient to him, we want to understand anew our relationship to the Jews, cherishing our ties with them.

4. We acknowledge, with the Jews, God as the creator of heaven and earth. We believe, with the Jews, that justice and love are God's guidance for the whole of our lives. We hope, with the Jews, for a new heaven and a new earth and with them we want the power of this hope for justice and peace to be a living force in this world.

34
Commission for Religious Relations with the Jews: Notes on the Correct Way To Present the Jews and Judaism in Preaching and Catechesis in the Roman Catholic Church, June 1985

Johannes Cardinal Willebrands (President)
Pierre Duprey (Vice-President)
Jorge Mejia (Secretary)

PRELIMINARY CONSIDERATIONS

On March 6, 1982, Pope John Paul II told delegates of episcopal conferences and other experts, meeting in Rome to study relations between the Church and Judaism:

> You yourselves were concerned, during your sessions, with Catholic teaching and catechesis regarding Jews and Judaism. . . . We should aim, in this field, that Catholic teaching at its different levels, in catechesis to children and young people, presents Jews and Judaism, not only in an honest and objective manner, free from prejudices and without any offenses, but also with full awareness of the heritage common to Jews and Christians.

In this passage, so charged with meaning, the Holy Father plainly drew inspiration from the Council Declaration *Nostra Aetate*, 4, which says:

> All should take pains, then, lest in catechetical instruction and in the preaching of God's Word they teach anything out of harmony with the truth of the

Gospel and the spirit of Christ. . . . Since the spiritual patrimony common to Christians and Jews is thus so great, this sacred Synod wishes to foster and recommend mutual understanding and respect.

In the same way, the *Guidelines and Suggestions for Implementing the Conciliar Declaration Nostra Aetate (§ 4)* ends its chapter III, entitled ''Teaching and Education,'' which lists a number of practical things to be done, with this recommendation:

Information concerning these questions is important at all levels of Christian instruction and education. Among sources of information, special attention should be paid to the following:

—catechisms and religious textbooks;
—history books;
—the mass media (press, radio, cinema, television).

The effective use of these means presupposes the thorough formation of instructors and educators in training schools, seminaries and universities (*AAS* 77, 1975, p. 73).

The paragraphs which follow are intended to serve this purpose.

I. RELIGIOUS TEACHING AND JUDAISM

1. In *Nostra Aetate* 4, the Council speaks of the ''spiritual bonds linking'' Jews and Christians and of the ''great spiritual patrimony'' common to both, and it further asserts that ''the Church of Christ acknowledges that, according to the mystery of God's saving design, the beginning of her faith and her election are already found among the patriarchs, Moses and the prophets.''

2. Because of the unique relations that exist between Christianity and Judaism—''linked together at the very level of their identity'' (John Paul II, March 6, 1982)—relations ''founded on the design of the God of the Covenant'' (*ibid.*)—the Jews and Judaism should not occupy an occasional and marginal place in catechesis: their presence there is essential and should be organically integrated.

3. This concern for Judaism in Catholic teaching has not merely historical or archeological foundation. As the Holy Father said in the speech already quoted, after he had again mentioned the ''common patrimony'' of the Church and Judaism as ''considerable'': ''To assess it carefully in itself

and with due awareness of the faith and religious life of the Jewish people *as they are professed and practiced still today* can greatly help us to understand better certain aspects of the life of the Church'' (italics added). It is a question then of *pastoral* concern for a still living reality closely related to the Church. The Holy Father has stated this permanent reality of the Jewish people in a remarkable theological formula, in his allocution to the Jewish community of West Germany at Mainz, on November 17, 1980: ". . . the people of God of the Old Covenant, which has never been revoked. . . ."

4. Here we should recall the passage in which the *Guidelines and Suggestions* (I) tried to define the fundamental condition of dialogue: "respect for the other as he is," knowledge of the "basic components of the religious tradition of Judaism," and again learning "by what essential traits the Jews define themselves in the light of their own religious experience" (Introd.).

5. The singular character and the difficulty of Christian teaching about Jews and Judaism lies in this, that it needs to balance a number of pairs of ideas which express the relation between the two economies of the Old and New Testament:

> Promise and Fulfillment;
> Continuity and Newness;
> Singularity and Universality;
> Uniqueness and Exemplary Nature.

This means that the theologian or the catechist who deals with the subject needs to show in his practice of teaching that:

- promise and fulfillment throw light on each other;
- newness lies in a metamorphosis of what was there before;
- the singularity of the people of the Old Testament is not exclusive and is open, in the divine vision, to a universal extension;
- the uniqueness of the Jewish people is meant to have the force of an example.

6. Finally, "work that is of poor quality and lacking in precision would be extremely detrimental" to Judaeo-Christian dialogue (John Paul II, speech of March 6, 1982). But it would be above all detrimental—since we are talking of teaching and education—to Christian identity (*ibid.*).

7. "In virtue of her divine mission, the Church," which is to be "the all-embracing means of salvation" in which alone "the fullness of the means of salvation can be obtained" (*Unit. Red.* 3), "must of her nature proclaim Jesus Christ to the world" (cf. *Guidelines and Suggestions,* I). Indeed we believe that it is through him that we go to the Father (cf. Jn 14:6) "and this is eternal life, that they know thee the only true God and Jesus Christ whom thou hast sent" (Jn 17:3).

   Jesus affirms (Jn 10:16) that "there shall be one flock and one shepherd." Church and Judaism cannot then be seen as two parallel ways of salvation and the Church must witness to Christ as the Redeemer for all, "while maintaining the strictest respect for religious liberty in line with the teaching of the Second Vatican Council (Declaration *Dignitatis Humanae*)" (*Guidelines and Suggestions,* I).

8. The urgency and importance of precise, objective and rigorously accurate teaching on Judaism for our faithful follows too from the danger of anti-Semitism which is always ready to reappear under different guises. The question is not merely to uproot from among the faithful the remains of anti-Semitism still to be found here and there, but much rather to arouse in them, through educational work, an exact knowledge of the wholly unique "bond" (*Nostra Aetate,* 4) which joins us as a Church to the Jews and to Judaism. In this way, they would learn to appreciate and love the latter, who have been chosen by God to prepare the coming of Christ and have preserved everything that was progressively revealed and given in the course of that preparation, notwithstanding their difficulty in recognizing in him their Messiah.

II. RELATIONS BETWEEN THE OLD* AND NEW TESTAMENT

1. Our aim should be to show the unity of biblical revelation (O.T. and N.T.) and of the divine plan, before speaking of each historical event, so as to stress that particular events have meaning when seen in history as a whole—from creation to fulfillment. This history concerns the whole human race and especially believers. Thus the definitive meaning of the election of Israel does not become clear except in the light of the complete fulfillment (Rom 9–11) and election in Jesus Christ is still better under-

---

*We continue to use the expression *Old Testament* because it is traditional (cf. already 2 Cor 3:14) but also because "Old" does not mean "out of date" or "outworn." In any case, it is the *permanent* value of the O.T. as a source of Christian revelation that is emphasised here (cf. *Dei Verbum,* 3).

stood with reference to the announcement and the promise (cf. Heb 4:1–11).

2. We are dealing with singular happenings which concern a singular nation but are destined, in the sight of God who reveals his purpose, to take on universal and exemplary significance.

   The aim is moreover to present the events of the Old Testament not as concerning only the Jews but also as touching us personally. Abraham is truly the father of our faith (cf. Rom 4:11–12; Roman Canon: *patriarchae nostri Abrahae*). And it is said (1 Cor 10:1): "*Our* fathers were all under the cloud, and all passed through the sea." The patriarchs, prophets and other personalities of the Old Testament have been venerated and always will be venerated as saints in the liturgical tradition of the Oriental Church as also of the Latin Church.

3. From the unity of the divine plan derives the problem of the relation between the Old and New Testaments. The Church already from apostolic times (cf. 1 Cor 10:11; Heb 10:1) and then constantly in tradition resolved this problem by means of typology, which emphasizes the primordial value that the Old Testament must have in the Christian view. Typology however makes many people uneasy and is perhaps the sign of a problem unresolved.

4. Hence in using typology, the teaching and practice of which we have received from the liturgy and from the Fathers of the Church, we should be careful to avoid any transition from the Old to the New Testament which might seem merely a rupture. The Church, in the spontaneity of the Spirit which animates her, has vigorously condemned the attitude of Marcion** and always opposed his dualism.

5. It should also be emphasized that typological interpretation consists in reading the Old Testament as preparation and, in certain aspects, outline and foreshadowing of the New (cf., e.g., Heb 5:5–10, etc.). Christ is henceforth the key and point of reference to the Scriptures: "the rock *was* Christ" (1 Cor 10:4).

6. It is true then, and should be stressed, that the Church and Christians read the Old Testament in the light of the event of the dead and risen Christ and that on these grounds there is a Christian reading of the Old Testament which does not necessarily coincide with the Jewish reading. Thus Christian identity and Jewish identity should be carefully distinguished in their

---

**A man of gnostic tendency who in the second century rejected the Old Testament and part of the New as the work of an evil god, a demiurge. The Church reacted strongly against this heresy (cf. Irenaeus).

respective reading of the Bible. But this detracts nothing from the value of the Old Testament in the Church and does nothing to hinder Christians from profiting discerningly from the traditions of Jewish reading.

7. Typological reading only manifests the unfathomable riches of the Old Testament, its inexhaustible content and the mystery of which it is full, and should not lead us to forget that it retains its own value as revelation that the New Testament often does no more than resume (cf. Mk 12:29–31). Moreover, the New Testament itself demands to be read in the light of the Old. Primitive Christian catechesis constantly had recourse to this (cf., e.g., 1 Cor 5:6–8; 10:1–11).

8. Typology further signifies reaching toward the accomplishment of the divine plan, when "God will be all in all" (1 Cor 15:28). This holds true also for the Church which, realized already in Christ, yet awaits its definitive perfecting as the body of Christ. The fact that the body of Christ is still tending toward its full stature (cf. Eph 4:12–19) takes nothing from the value of being a Christian. So also the calling of the patriarchs and the exodus from Egypt do not lose their importance and value in God's design from being at the same time intermediate stages (cf., e.g., *Nostra Aetate,* 4).

9. The exodus, for example, represents an experience of salvation and liberation that is not complete in itself, but has in it, over and above its own meaning, the capacity to be developed further. Salvation and liberation are already accomplished in Christ and gradually realized by the sacraments in the Church. This makes way for the fulfillment of God's design, which awaits its final consummation with the return of Jesus as Messiah, for which we pray each day. The kingdom, for the coming of which we also pray each day, will be finally established. With salvation and liberation the elect and the whole of creation will be transformed in Christ (Rom 8:19–23).

10. Furthermore, in underlining the eschatological dimension of Christianity we shall reach a greater awareness that the people of God of the Old and the New Testament are tending toward a like end in the future: the coming or return of the Messiah—even if they start from two different points of view. It is more clearly understood that the person of the Messiah is not only a point of division for the people of God but also a point of convergence (cf. *Sussidi per l'ecumenismo* of the diocese of Rome, n. 140). Thus it can be said that Jews and Christians meet in a comparable hope, founded on the same promise made to Abraham (cf. Gen 12:1–3; Heb 6:13–18).

11. Attentive to the same God who has spoken, hanging on the same word, we have to witness to one same memory and one common hope in him

who is the master of history. We must also accept our responsibility to prepare the world for the coming of the Messiah by working together for social justice, respect for the rights of persons and nations and for social and international reconciliation. To this we are driven, Jews and Christians, by the command to love our neighbor, by a common hope for the kingdom of God and by the great heritage of the prophets. Transmitted soon enough by catechesis, such a conception would teach young Christians in a practical way to cooperate with Jews, going beyond simple dialogue (cf. *Guidelines,* IV).

III. JEWISH ROOTS OF CHRISTIANITY

12. Jesus was and always remained a Jew; his ministry was deliberately limited "to the lost sheep of the house of Israel" (Mt 15:24). Jesus is fully a man of his time, and of his environment—the Jewish Palestinian one of the first century, the anxieties and hopes of which he shared. This cannot but underline both the reality of the incarnation and the very meaning of the history of salvation, as it has been revealed in the Bible (cf. Rom 1:3–4; Gal 4:4–5).

13. Jesus' relations with biblical law and its more or less traditional interpretations are undoubtedly complex, and he showed great liberty toward it (cf. the "antitheses" of the Sermon on the Mount: Mt 5:21–48, bearing in mind the exegetical difficulties—his attitude to rigorous observance of the sabbath: Mk 3:1–6, etc.).

But there is no doubt that he wished to submit himself to the law (cf. Gal 4:4), that he was circumcised and presented in the temple like any Jew of his time (cf. Lk 2:21, 22–24), that he was trained in the law's observance. He extolled respect for it (cf. Mt 5:17–20) and invited obedience to it (cf. Mt 8:4). The rhythm of his life was marked by observance of pilgrimages on great feasts, even from his infancy (cf. Lk 2:41–50; Jn 2:13; 7:10 etc.). The importance of the cycle of the Jewish feasts has been frequently underlined in the Gospel of John (cf. 2:13; 5:1; 7:2.10.37; 10:22; 12:1; 13:1; 18:28; 19:42 etc.).

14. It should be noted also that Jesus often taught in the synagogues (cf. Mt 4:23; 9:35; Lk 4:15–18; Jn 18:20, etc.) and in the temple (cf. Jn 18:20, etc.), which he frequented as did the disciples even after the resurrection (cf., e.g., Acts 2:46; 3:1; 21:26 etc.) He wished to put in the context of synagogue worship the proclamation of his Messiahship (cf. Lk 4:16–21). But above all he wished to achieve the supreme act of the gift of himself in the setting of the domestic liturgy of the Passover, or at least of the

paschal festivity (cf. Mk 14:1, 12 and parallels; Jn 18:28). This also allows of a better understanding of the "memorial" character of the Eucharist.

15. Thus the Son of God is incarnate in a people and a human family (cf. Gal 4:4; Rom 9:5). This takes away nothing, quite the contrary, from the fact that he was born for all men (Jewish shepherds and pagan wise men are found at his crib: Lk 2:8–20; Mt 2:1–12) and died for all men (at the foot of the cross there are Jews, among them Mary and John: Jn 19:25–27, and pagans like the centurion: Mk 15:39 and parallels). Thus he made two peoples one in his flesh (cf. Eph 2:14–17). This explains why with the *Ecclesia ex gentibus* we have, in Palestine and elsewhere, an *Ecclesia ex circumcisione,* of which *Eusebius* for example speaks (H.E. IV,5).

16. His relations with the Pharisees were not always or wholly polemical. Of this there are many proofs:

   • It is Pharisees who warn Jesus of the risks he is running (Lk 13:31);
   • Some Pharisees are praised—e.g., "the scribe" of Mk 12:34;
   • Jesus eats with Pharisees (Lk 7:36; 14:1).

17. Jesus shares, with the majority of Palestinian Jews of that time, some pharisaic doctrines: the resurrection of the body; forms of piety, like almsgiving, prayer, fasting (cf. Mt 6:1–18) and the liturgical practice of addressing God as Father; the priority of the commandment to love God and our neighbor (cf. Mk 12:28–34). This is so also with Paul (cf. Acts 23:8), who always considered his membership of the Pharisees as a title of honor (cf. Acts 23:6; 26:5; Phil 3:5).

18. Paul also, like Jesus himself, used methods of reading and interpreting Scripture and of teaching his disciples which were common to the Pharisees of their time. This applies to the use of parables in Jesus' ministry, as also to the method of Jesus and Paul of supporting a conclusion with a quotation from Scripture.

19. It is noteworthy too that the Pharisees are not mentioned in accounts of the Passion. Gamaliel (Acts 5:34–39) defends the apostles in a meeting of the sanhedrin. An exclusively negative picture of the Pharisees is likely to be inaccurate and unjust (cf. *Guidelines,* Note 1; cf. *AAS, loc. cit.* p. 76). If in the Gospels and elsewhere in the New Testament there are all sorts of unfavorable references to the Pharisees, they should be seen against the background of a complex and diversified movement. Criticisms of various types of Pharisees are moreover not lacking in rabbinical sources (cf. the *Babylon Talmud,* the *Sotah* treatise 22b, etc.). "Phari-

seeism'' in the pejorative sense can be rife in any religion. It may also be stressed that, if Jesus shows himself severe toward the Pharisees, it is because he is closer to them than to other contemporary Jewish groups (cf. *supra*, n. 17).

20. All this should help us to understand better what St. Paul says (Rom 11:16ff) about the ''root'' and the ''branches.'' The Church and Christianity, for all their novelty, find their origin in the Jewish milieu of the first century of our era, and more deeply still in the ''design of God'' (*Nostra Aetate*, 4), realized in the patriarchs, Moses and the prophets (*ibid.*), down to its consummation in Christ Jesus.

IV. THE JEWS IN THE NEW TESTAMENT

21. The *Guidelines* already say (note 1) that ''the formula 'the Jews' sometimes, according to the context, means 'the leaders of the Jews' or 'the adversaries of Jesus', terms which express better the thought of the evangelist and avoid appearing to arraign the Jewish people as such.''

     An objective presentation of the role of the Jewish people in the New Testament should take account of these various facts:

A. The Gospels are the outcome of long and complicated editorial work. The dogmatic constitution *Dei Verbum,* following the Pontifical Biblical Commission's Instruction *Sancta Mater Ecclesia,* distinguishes three stages: ''The sacred authors wrote the four Gospels, selecting some things from the many which had been handed on by word of mouth or in writing, reducing some of them to a synthesis, explicating some things in view of the situation of their Churches, and preserving the form of proclamation, but always in such fashion that they told us the honest truth about Jesus'' (n. 19).

     Hence it cannot be ruled out that some references hostile or less than favorable to the Jews have their historical context in conflicts between the nascent Church and the Jewish community. Certain controversies reflect Christian-Jewish relations long after the time of Jesus.

     To establish this is of capital importance if we wish to bring out the meaning of certain Gospel texts for the Christians of today.

     All this should be taken into account when preparing catechesis and homilies for the last weeks of Lent and Holy Week (cf. already *Guidelines* II, and now also *Sussidi per l'ecumenismo nella diocesi di Roma,* 1982, 144b).

B. It is clear on the other hand that there were conflicts between Jesus and certain categories of Jews of his time, among them Pharisees, from the beginning of his ministry (cf. Mk 2:1–11, 24; 3:6 etc.).

C. There is moreover the sad fact that the majority of the Jewish people and its authorities did not believe Jesus—a fact not merely of history but of theological bearing, of which St. Paul tries hard to plumb the meaning (Rom 9–11).

D. This fact, accentuated as the Christian mission developed, especially among the pagans, led inevitably to a rupture between Judaism and the young Church, now irreducibly separated and divergent in faith, and this state of affairs is reflected in the texts of the New Testament and particularly in the Gospels. There is no question of playing down or glossing over this rupture; that could only prejudice the identity of either side. Nevertheless it certainly does not cancel the spiritual ''bond'' of which the Council speaks (*Nostra Aetate,* 4) and which we propose to dwell on here.

E. Reflecting on this in the light of Scripture, notably of the chapters cited from the epistle to the Romans, Christians should never forget that the faith is a free gift of God (cf. Rom 9:12) and that we should never judge the consciences of others. St. Paul's exhortation ''do not boast'' in your attitude to ''the root'' (Rom 11:18) has its full point here.

F. There is no putting the Jews who knew Jesus and did not believe in him, or those who opposed the preaching of the apostles, on the same plane with Jews who came after or those of today. If the responsibility of the former remains a mystery hidden with God (cf. Rom 11:25), the latter are in an entirely different situation. Vatican II in the declaration on *Religious Liberty* teaches that ''all men are to be immune from coercion . . . in such wise that in matters religious no one is to be forced to act in a manner contrary to his own beliefs, nor . . . restrained from acting in accordance with his own beliefs'' (n. 2). This is one of the bases—proclaimed by the Council—on which Judaeo-Christian dialogue rests.

22. The delicate question of responsibility for the death of Christ must be looked at from the standpoint of the conciliar declaration *Nostra Aetate,* 4 and of *Guidelines and Suggestions* (III): ''What happened in (Christ's) passion cannot be blamed upon all the Jews then living without distinction nor upon the Jews of today,'' especially since ''authorities of the Jews and those who followed their lead pressed for the death of Christ.'' Again, further on: ''Christ in his boundless love freely underwent his passion and death because of the sins of all men, so that all might attain salvation'' (*Nostra Aetate,* 4). The *Catechism* of the Council of Trent teaches that Christian sinners are more to blame for the death of Christ than those few Jews who brought it about—they indeed ''knew not what they did'' (cf.

Lk 23:34) and we know it only too well (Pars I, caput V, Quaest. XI). In the same way and for the same reason, "the Jews should not be presented as repudiated or cursed by God, as if such views followed from the holy Scriptures" (*Nostra Aetate,* 4), even though it is true that "the Church is the new people of God" (*ibid.*).

V. THE LITURGY

23. Jews and Christians find in the Bible the very substance of their liturgy: for the proclamation of God's word, response to it, prayer of praise and intercession for the living and the dead, recourse to the divine mercy. The liturgy of the word in its own structure originates in Judaism. The prayer of Hours and other liturgical texts and formularies have their parallels in Judaism as do the very formulas of our most venerable prayers, among them the Our Father. The eucharistic prayers also draw inspiration from models in the Jewish tradition. As John Paul II said (Allocution of March 6, 1982): ". . . the faith and religious life of the Jewish people, as they are professed and practiced still today, can greatly help us to understand better certain aspects of the life of the Church. Such is the case of liturgy. . . ."

24. This is particularly evident in the great feasts of the liturgical year, like the Passover. Christians and Jews celebrate the Passover: the Jews, the historic Passover looking toward the future; the Christians, the Passover accomplished in the death and resurrection of Christ, although still in expectation of the final consummation (cf. *supra,* n. 9). It is still the "memorial" which comes to us from the Jewish tradition, with a specific content different in each case. On either side, however, there is a like dynamism: for Christians it gives meaning to the eucharistic celebration (cf. the antiphon *O sacrum convivium*), a paschal celebration and as such a making present of the past, but experienced in the expectation of what is to come.

VI. JUDAISM AND CHRISTIANITY IN HISTORY

25. The history of Israel did not end in 70 A.D. (cf. *Guidelines,* II). It continued, especially in a numerous diaspora which allowed Israel to carry to the whole world a witness—often heroic—of its fidelity to the one God and to "exalt him in the presence of all the living" (Tobit 13:4), while preserving the memory of the land of their forefathers at the heart of their hope (Passover *Seder*).

Christians are invited to understand this religious attachment which finds its roots in biblical tradition, without however making their own any particular religious interpretation of this relationship (cf. *Declaration* of the U.S. Conference of Catholic Bishops, November 20, 1975).

The existence of the state of Israel and its political options should be envisaged not in a perspective which is in itself religious, but in their reference to the common principles of international law.

The permanence of Israel (while so many ancient peoples have disappeared without trace) is an historic fact and a sign to be interpreted within God's design. We must in any case rid ourselves of the traditional idea of a people *punished,* preserved as a *living argument* for Christian apologetic. It remains a chosen people, "the pure olive on which were grafted the branches of the wild olive which are the Gentiles" (John Paul II, March 6, 1982, alluding to Rom 11:17–24). We must remember how much the balance of relations between Jews and Christians over two thousand years has been negative. We must remind ourselves how the permanence of Israel is accompanied by a continuous spiritual fecundity, in the rabbinical period, in the Middle Ages and in modern times, taking its start from a patrimony which we long shared, so much so that "the faith and religious life of the Jewish people, as they are professed and practiced still today, can greatly help us to understand better certain aspects of the life of the Church" (John Paul II, March 6, 1982). Catechesis should on the other hand help in understanding the meaning for the Jews of the extermination during the years 1939–1945, and its consequences.

26. Education and catechesis should concern themselves with the problem of racism, still active in different forms of anti-Semitism. The Council presented it thus: "Moreover, (the Church), mindful of her common patrimony with the Jews and motivated by the Gospel's spiritual love and by no political considerations, deplores the hatred, persecutions and displays of anti-Semitism directed against the Jews at any time and from any source" (*Nostra Aetate,* 4). The *Guidelines* comment: "The spiritual bonds and historical links binding the Church to Judaism condemn (as opposed to the very spirit of Christianity) all forms of anti-Semitism and discrimination, which in any case the dignity of the human person alone would suffice to condemn" (*Guidelines,* Preamble).

CONCLUSION

27. Religious teaching, catechesis and preaching should be a preparation not only for objectivity, justice, and tolerance but also for understanding and

dialogue. Our two traditions are so related that they cannot ignore each other. Mutual knowledge must be encouraged at every level. There is evident in particular a painful ignorance of the history and traditions of Judaism, of which only negative aspects and often caricature seem to form part of the stock ideas of many Christians.

That is what these notes aim to remedy. This would mean that the Council text and *"Guidelines and Suggestions"* would be more easily and faithfully put into practice.

Index

STIMULUS BOOKS are developed by Stimulus Foundation, a not-for-profit organization, and are published by Paulist Press. The Foundation wishes to further the publication of scholarly books on Jewish and Christian topics that are of importance to Judaism and Christianity.

Stimulus Foundation was established by an erstwhile refugee from Nazi Germany who intends to contribute with these publications to the improvement of communication between Jews and Christians.

Books for publication in this Series will be selected by a committee of the Foundation, and offers of manuscripts and works in progress should be addressed to:

Stimulus Foundation
785 West End Ave.
New York, N.Y. 10025